SONGS FROM THE MOUNTAIN

Also by Djohariah Toor

The Road By the River

SONGS FROM THE MOUNTAIN

Djohariah Toor

St. Martin's Press

New York

The author would like to thank the following publishers for permission to reprint material from their books:

Reprinted from *Original Blessing,* by Matthew Fox, copyright © 1983, Bear & Co. Inc., P.O. Box 2860, Santa Fe, NM 87504

Reprinted from *Meditations with Meister Eckhart,* edited by Matthew Fox, copyright © 1983, Bear & Co. Inc., P.O. Box 2860, Santa Fe, NM 87504

Reprinted from *Rilke on Love and Other Difficulties,* translations and considerations by John J. L. Mood, by permission of W. W. Norton & Co., Inc., copyright © 1975 by W. W. Norton Co., Inc.

From *The Kabir Book,* by Robert Bly, copyright © 1971, 1977, by Robert Bly. Reprinted by permission of Beacon Press.

Reprinted from *Rumi Daylight,* Threshold Books, RD 4 Box 600, Putney, VT 05346

Editor: Jared Kieling
Design by Junie Lee

Library of Congress Cataloging-in-Publication Data

Toor, Djohariah.
    Songs from the mountain / Djohariah Toor.
        p.   cm.
    ISBN 0-312-11069-3
    1. Spiritual life.   I. Title.
BL624.T667   1994
291.4—dc20   94-2457
                                                  CIP

First Edition: July 1994
10 9 8 7 6 5 4 3 2 1

Contents

Acknowledgments

My gratitude goes out to everyone who has inspired passages, stories, and tales in this writing. The men and women I work with inspire and teach me.

Thanks to my husband, Arthur, whose encouragement keeps opening the doors to life and creativity. Thanks to my daughter Sarah, whose support and humor I constantly felt in our home, especially during the labor stages of the book. I am grateful to my daughter Mariam for her feedback and help editing its rough edges, and to Corinna Stoeffel for wading through the rough draft and offering insights. Thanks to my editor, Jared Kieling, who has shaped the rough gems and who has guided and inspired me to make writing an experience of art.

I want to thank my teachers Marilyn Youngbird and Geneva Topsky Stump for the generous sharing of their knowledge, for their heartfelt prayers in the sweat lodge, for sharing their ways with songs and prods and wise laughter.

Thanks to all my relations who handed me down to life. Thanks to life who handed me down to myself. And to God who gives delight.

Preface

Traditional Native American teachings are based on the laws of nature. We know we are nature. For it is nature that gives us the air we breathe, the water we drink, the food we eat, and the minerals we need in order to be a life. We know that we cannot live without one of these four elements and that nature is the only one that can provide them. Traditional Native American values are not magic, but teach through humanitarian principles and common sense. Our values teach us that mental, physical, and spiritual disease is caused by disharmony within the individual, or by disconnection to the family, community, nature, or the greater universe. When we live in harmony we interrelate with others and nature in a holistic manner. We see ourselves as part of the "Whole."

The stories you will read here are a collection of the author's personal and professional experience. In this writing Djohariah Toor combines her background in Western spirituality and depth psychology with traditional Native American teachings, seeking to bring a balance of emotional and spiritual health to her clients, as well as to herself. Her stories are filled with love and compassion. I know those who read her book will gain insight into their own wellness.

—Marilyn Youngbird

Introduction

Time loosens the secrets
of the Crystal,
Yet who can I tell?
The whisper that said:
"I know you, I am here;
I Am the One within."
—Arthur Toor

Rounding the turn into the next century, many of us on the planet are feeling an identity crisis; but it's an identity crisis that goes beyond the individual. Identity means unity, the essential character of something, and, put simply, disunity is global. Not only is there a disunity among the nations, between religious and ethnic groups, between the earth and technology, and between men and women, but there is a crisis of vast proportions in the human soul.

Songs from the Mountain maps the way back to sacred ground; it explores the directions to personal and spiritual healing, to creativity, and to the divine wilderness inside.

If there's one denominator that consistently comes up in my work as a counselor, it is the dwindling of the resources in our lives that feed the soul. The men and women with whom I have shared the overstuffed pillows in my office have all had one question: *Who am I?* The women I have worked with in women's groups have collectively voiced the same painful questions: *Why do I feel fragmented? How can I live from my truth and not somebody else's?* The retreats and workshops I have experienced and led have been filled with modern-day seekers all asking, *What is soul...and how do I get there?*

My life and work, my children and friends, have generously taught me that people heal and thrive best when they can see themselves at the soul level (even if it's just once in a lifetime). I have worked with people of all ages and ethnic backgrounds, and all of them, with their profound differences, have one thing in common: everyone is looking for an identity he or she has lost. And for a soul that has gone into exile.

What makes it possible to heal psychic pain and to recreate the power and beauty in ourselves is the convergence of our own human path with what my grandmother used to call the "God road." She worked all day long in a small rustic kitchen, moving with a deft grace, and from morning to night she sang over her food. I remember the smell of her kitchen. Sweet wet flour, succulent steamed green beans, rusty pipes, fresh washed cotton, hot black-iron pans, something from her garden in the stew. We looked remarkably alike, my mother tells me, but my grandmother did not live long enough for me to get to know her as a friend. I've come to realize now that what she was doing on those blistering days in that tiny kitchen was cooking up food for the soul. If our work, our life and relationships, our therapy, and our recovery from psychic disunity are going to be successful, they must also be food for the soul.

Healing depends on recovering the place within, where one's longing for wholeness crosses paths with that God road. When we find that crossing, we need to stand in it. We need to awaken the language of the soul, and to speak it every day. We need to be with other people who are alive, who are asking real questions, who are not playing at life (yet who know how to play, how to laugh, how to weep, how to dare, and do not hold back loving). When we start to learn the language of the soul, we'll begin to take more risks, be brutally honest with ourselves, be real with others; we'll take off our persona and throw it into the sea. We'll sing over our food, hum at the office, make waves when life gets cramped, and refuse to give in to the old voices that plunder the power in the heart.

Soul language is generic, nondenominational, all inclusive. No one can teach us that language; it has to come from within. It has to come from self-knowing, hard work, sacrifice, from *kenosis* (humbling oneself, emptying out the past). Soul language is not strictly religious language; rather it's what we speak when we know who we are.

Healing works best when we have friends who will tell us: *This is who you are! Welcome to life, you plum, you beauty, you Rembrandt! What a radiant creature you are!* We also need a container, a safe vessel for the kind of transformation that is going to take us past our wounds so we can hear this and really take it in.

Some years ago, I began, with the help of my clients, to long for a psychology of the sacred. I was trained as a marriage and family therapist, a bodyworker, and a play therapist (a second childhood) and I loved my work. Without exception, every client I saw was my teacher. But the more I worked with men and women, the more I saw that therapy, unless it releases the fiery soul in bondage, can be a dead end. Understanding, in its own limited way, can be a trap; it doesn't guarantee a solution.

As I began to squirm under the yoke of the insight therapy, I also began to recognize that the academic world was dangerous (if not toxic) to creativity. By the time higher education finished with me, the feminine spirit inside had gone bankrupt. I had buried my soul in that agenda. Little by little I began to see how disoriented I was. In my dreams I had to meet a dazed, drunken woman, ill kempt, never dressed right, hair going every which way, and I was always ashamed of her. She was my starving creative, sexual, instinctual, alive-in-the-feelings feminine side. How do you do.

Red flags waving, I got out all my wise women's books, the Jungian women whose writings had been such a salve for me during the darkest days of academia: Esther Harding, Irene de Castillejo, Marion Woodman. I resumed my therapy. The books I had read by the women analysts were powerful and inspiring and they raised my awareness of the fact that the global feminine soul (and the global masculine heart) was in trouble.

I had some wonderful male teachers who challenged me to expose my woundedness: who called me on my tendency to rationalize my feelings and hide my body, and who supported me as good fathers would. What I didn't have were any women mentors or teachers. I began to be hungry for a model and for a container in which I could *experience* the feminine soul. What I needed was a mother, a grand-mother, an old crone who could run to the fields with me and pull me onto her lap and tell me the story of who I was. Many of my clients, like myself, had a mother wound; some had mothers or grand-mothers who were not able to parent them wisely; who were not able to give them a healthy sense of their feminine identity. Likewise, the men I have worked with seldom had the kind of fathering or grandfathering they needed for their own masculine roots. We seemed a generation of people whose households forgot to sing over the food. In our homes, we ate but were seldom fed.

I never met another grandmother figure after my grandma died, but I did meet a Native American woman my own age who had a very mothering presence and who was willing to share the practice of a spirituality very grounded in the earth. Although originally from North Dakota, she had settled in the coastal mountains of northern California, and her home was like a sanctuary. Those of us who sat in her circle (most of whom were not Native American) were given an offering, a way of healing, a way of being that was handed down from an ancient time. I felt privileged to be in that circle because I sensed we were receiving teachings as old as the hills around us. Experiences that took us deep inside.

The breakthrough to the soul that I talk about in this book is a weaving of stories that belong to all of us. The people I have worked with, lived with, touched or been touched by in my life, wander in and out of these pages. Their dreams, struggles, tears, and their resolve to square their shoulders and sing are an offering to all of us who are on a journey, to those of us on a search for new beginnings, deeper meanings, for those of us who long to overthrow the old order of life and enter the sacred side of the Self.

In *Songs from the Mountain,* I hope to offer you a door to your own wilderness. And from the poet Rainer Maria Rilke's *Letters on Love,* this offering:

> I tell you that I have a long way to go before I am—where one begins. . . .
>
> You are so young, so before all beginning, and I want to beg you, as much as I can, to be patient toward all that is unsolved in your heart and try to love the *questions themselves* like locked rooms and like books that are written in a very foreign tongue. Do not now seek the answers, which cannot be given you because you would not be able to live them. And the point is, to live everything. *Live* the questions now. Perhaps you will then gradually, without noticing it, live along some distant day into the answer.
>
> Resolve to be always beginning—to be a beginner![1]

ABOVE
Archetype: Grandfather Sky
Task: Relationship to Spirit
Path: Dialogue/Surrender

North
Task: Courage/Power to Be
Archetype: Warrior
Season: Winter
Path: Endurance/Purification

West
Task: Vision/Self-Knowing
Archetype: Novice
Season: Fall
Path: Introspection/Retreat

SELF

East
Task: Wisdom/Creativity
Archetype: Midwife
Season: Spring
Path: Transformation/Rebirth

South
Task: Love/Compassion
Archetype: Lover
Season: Summer
Path: Forgiveness/Self-Acceptance

BELOW
Archetype: Grandmother Earth
Task: Relationship to Nature/Relationship to Sexual,
Instinctual Nature
Path: Receptivity/Alertness

1. On the Edge of Breakthrough

What is this place lovers speak of
that turns even sorrow to wild joy?

Break out of your thoughts and head for the garden,
leave everything you own at the gate.
Take the red clay path to the meadow and offer
your jewels to the ground. Come lie down
in the wildflowers, and don't feel anything but
these green shoots of loving.
Your body is the shell you penetrate,
your mind is the gate.

Inside rivers run and tumble in green waves
dousing our stony fears. Why are you hiding
in your little house when there are fields outside
as far as the eye can see? Come and walk here
among hyacinths and jasmine, and forget who you have been.
Your pride is the shell you penetrate
your heart is the gate.

Come on Hearts, come again.
For lovers, it is never too late.
—Djohariah Toor

There is a holy ground in the psyche, whether we call it soul, divine wilderness, creative unconscious, or the kingdom within. When we break through to that place, we discover not just healing but an immense creativity. Throughout life we catch glimpses of the power there, that divine fire inside the self; mystics and poets write about it, artists and musicians give shape and sound to it; lovers feel its pulse; children and third-world people live close to it. From time to time I wake up in the morning and I can sense in my bones that I have dreamed that wilderness; or that something in there has dreamed me; that some sacred seed is trying to break through to me.

Clearly all life is intensely mysterious; the psyche and the forces in the human heart are complex, unexplainable. The force of life—its daily demands and tensions, its lifelong pressures; its bitter herbs and elixirs, its light and dark side—is enough to knock some of us for a loop. The people I know who pick themselves up and stay grounded, however, are people who have chosen to crack the shell; who want to see the truth hidden inside. The good news is we have a choice. We can either roll up our sleeves and enter into life as "religiously intentional beings," as author and analyst Sheila Moon puts it, or we can be "pulled along by currents we don't understand."[1] And there goes our life.

While it's true that the psychic, relational, and emotional currents that come against us can get wild, the moment we say yes to break-through work, the unconscious and the winds of heaven cooperate. They conspire together to send us messages, insights, and dreams whose job it is to lovingly shock and awaken us. They bring current conflicts (we'd rather forget about), long-buried memories (we'd rather not deal with), and they crack open the shell. But they also bring us answers, solutions, warnings, road signs; they bring wild creatures, guiding figures, and ancient wisdom.

The breakthrough of these images is a profound gift. The only string attached is that we agree to pay attention to this inner world; to make it a mentor of sorts. That means we turn to the feminine feeling side to guide us, to the senses and the power of intuition. When any of us holds fast to that ariadne thread in the psyche, we tap the creative energy in the unconscious. We literally break through to a deep ground in the psyche; or it breaks through to us. That's where transformation happens.

In the breakthrough process, one suddenly meets the age-old wisdom that has made its home in the back of the psyche, or soul, for centuries. Almost as though by fate, a window is thrown open that lets us see through the outer layers of the personality, until we can see who really resides in this frame we carry around. In the suddenness of breakthrough, we see finally the truth of our self-limiting behaviors. We see the long-festering wounds of childhood, but we also glimpse the wild and life-giving fire in the heart.

Breakthrough sets in motion psychic forces that can be both powerful and humbling; opening doors that, sooner or later, one must agree to walk through. Whether we go into that new territory peacefully, like a novice cradling in wonderment a first vision, or are thrown in by some chaos or wound in our lives, whether we agree or refuse, breakthrough is not always a conscious choice. Most people on the edge of creativity or madness will tell you they did not choose the experience. It chose them. There is nothing to do but surrender to it.

The Man on the Plains

Catching these internal images may happen in many different ways, but generally they appear when we have pulled ourselves momentarily out of the fast lane. They can come in dreams, daydreams, altered states of consciousness, during bodywork, in light trance states, in fantasy or guided imagery. They are profoundly therapeutic if we engage them in some kind of dialogue.

The following image came one afternoon while I was receiving some deep process acupressure. Since this bodyworker was both a therapist and a friend of mine, we had been discussing a recent dream I'd had, in which I had been stuck in a brick building and unable to get out. There was a door, but it was locked from the inside, and I couldn't find the key. Outwardly my life seemed stable and I had been going along in it, feeling content with myself. But the unconscious had been confronting me with a different picture. I'd had a number of disturbing dreams in which I appeared anything but stable. Some years before I had opened the door to the unconscious (through therapy and a study of dreams)—but like anyone with a full load at work, kids to taxi, oral exams to study for, and a hundred commitments, I had postponed my inner work.

Eventually I let all these thoughts go and was just enjoying the sound of the rain outside coming down in windy torrents, as it often does near the coast. I was beginning to relax and drift off when this dreamlike experience appeared, and altered my life.

A dark warrior stands in front of me dressed from the waist down in deerskin leggings that reach down to his moccasins. His skin is bronze and glistens in the sunlight. His face is exquisitely proud, intent; there is a look in his eyes that I cannot turn from. I approach him cautiously, caught in his gaze, waiting for him to speak, but he says nothing. I feel the wind come up; it moves in rushes over the ground until the grasses at our feet begin to dance in rolling waves. Somewhere in the distance the sound of water tumbles in a stream. I cannot take my eyes from him. Slowly he raises his arms outward toward where I stand. In his hands are two eagle feathers, crossed at the center. An intensity passes between us in the silence, and I feel an ache inside. I stand there in the sun in the high plateau land, wanting to understand the numinous crossing of the feathers, yet empty of any conscious thoughts. Aware only of the wind rising and falling, the sound of my heartbeat, aware only of being held utterly by the ancient depth in his dark eyes.

The image had spontaneously appeared, as though a dream were trying to dream itself. I lay there, half of me still on the plains, sensing that pieces of my past and my future had just met. A window in my unconscious had involuntarily flown open, revealing a figure from some ancient time. The rain outside was beginning to let up, and our session was nearly over, but I wanted to linger in that other world. Through moist eyes I gazed out the window into a tall eucalyptus moving in the wind.

Whether this was a vision or not, I wasn't sure, but its effect on me was compelling and I couldn't get the image out of my mind. Later in the day I went home and pulled out a collection of books on Native American legends and stories, books on primitive art and myth, looking for the meaning of the crossed feathers, but found nothing. Although I had little hands-on experience with Native traditions, I had a deep fascination for the world of symbols. Both as a painter and a devotee of dreams, I had learned to trust the symbol as an art form from the unconscious, one that could transmit tremendous psychic energy.

The more I thought about the man on the plains, the more familiar he seemed. Combing through my dream journals, I found him in a previous dream, and his message then had also been a compelling one. In that dream he had taken me to a stream for a cleansing ceremony. He had sung over me and blessed me to go on a journey of some kind. The impact of some dreams can profoundly alter our path in life; but the impact of a loaded agenda can diffuse the power latent in the dream. Fortunately, this figure seemed persistent.

Some weeks later I ran into a friend of mine who had been studying with a Hidatsa-Arikara medicine woman, and who was a student of dreams herself. She was sure this woman would know something about the meaning of my experience. Within a few days the meeting was arranged and I piled into my car to make the drive to her home near the California coast a few hours away, anticipating that something bigger than me was about to happen.

On the Edge

We sat in her living room in a small circle, listening to her teachings, exchanging thoughts, and eventually sharing the sacred pipe in her tradition. Afterward I asked her about my experience, and about the meaning of the crossed feathers. Over the weeks since the appearance of this native in my psyche, I had been pondering what the number four (indicated by the four points of the feathers) might mean. I had some thoughts about the Jungian idea of quaternity, the idea of the fourfold unity, the four parts of the psyche we need to develop for wholeness. In Christian tradition there were the four Evangelists, the four corners of the cross representing the meeting of God and man. There was Lao Tze and the idea of the mandala as an instrument of contemplation, a holy center out of which life originated and continually reformed itself. In Egyptian legend there was Horus with his four sons; there were four posters on my bed and there were four cardinal points in the universe. But what of these feathers and their respective directions, and why had this touched me so profoundly? Why had these dark eyes been so utterly piercing behind the symbol he held toward me?

Sitting in the circle, the Hidatsa woman told me it was true that she knew the meaning of the symbol according to the Native tradition, yet she seemed hesitant to tell me directly. *"Why don't you do some sweats,"* she said, *"some sweat lodges and prayers. In there the Spirit can talk to you and tell you the meaning of your experience."* I sat there, caught up in my own thoughts. For one thing, I don't like heat that much and I hate humidity. I can't stand sitting for any length of time in a sauna. I'm never the last one out of a hot tub. I don't mind the dark, but I don't like the idea that it won't be me that controls the temperature in there. I thought of my busy schedule and the length of time it had taken to reach this woman. In the back of my mind I cooked up another half dozen excuses until a prompt from my unconscious made me speak out. *"All right."* I said, *"I'll do it. When do we start?"*

A date for my first lodge was chosen and I was advised to prepare myself by prayer and a more intentional seeking of the Spirit. I wasn't sure what to expect in the lodge, and she must have sensed the questions forming in the back of my mind. *"When you get in there, there's nothing to do but let go. The Spirit will do the work. Everything you know about prayer will fall away in there. Try not to eat anything until after the lodge."*

She went on talking for a while, telling us the sweat bath was a way to purify our thoughts, to break through denial, a way to lift ourselves up. The heat in there would cleanse us from the wrong turns we might have taken. *"When we pray like that in the sweat, the heat doesn't just wash away the old skin, it's a way to see within ourselves."* I sat on the floor of her house listening intently to her—yet feeling an image form in the back of my mind that wove itself through her teachings. Gradually the carpet under me spread into a soft yellow plain where tall grasses blew in a warm afternoon wind. I could smell the sun baking the earth, musty and fertile; ripe with pollen rising up in the heat of the day. The moment suddenly had no boundaries, and her living room gave way to another landscape that brought me a profound sense of knowing and a longing I couldn't identify. Far in the distance on this yellow land children played and ran, shouting in excitement to one another. Dogs barked and a hawk circled overhead. There were other sounds too: a nearby swollen creek running through a deep crevice in the land, water pouring over rocks and gurgling over smooth boulders, the voices of women laughing and calling to their children. A horse called out, shrill in the distance. I sat at the feet of someone who was going to be a guide to the first part of a long journey, and I felt both fascinated and skeptical.

I drove home later that day in the falling darkness, in and out of a coastal fog that lined the top of the ridge. I had some questions about what I might be getting myself into, but gradually my doubts gave way, and I sang a chant that seemed to come out of nowhere. On the other side of the ridge I dropped below the fog and when I reached the hills over my own valley, I slid toward home under a blanket of bright stars.

The Sweat Lodge

We stood around the fire in the early morning, chatting quietly in between fanning the upright stacks of eucalyptus logs into flame. The fire had already been going for a while and the rocks were beginning to turn a bright crimson around their outer edges. Some were heated through and seemed to pulse with an energy all their own. Overhead in the grove of tall eucalyptus I was told to watch for a family of hawks that often came near whenever there was a lodge. *"They seem to know,"* the Hidatsa woman said.

When the rocks were heated all the way through, she began to pull away the logs and motioned for us to get ready to go into the sweat lodge. *"When you go in, go in clockwise. When you leave the lodge you'll go out in this way. Everything sacred follows the sun."*

Two large hawks circled overhead just as we were preparing to enter the lodge; they dipped low then soared high above the trees, catching the morning currents and calling to one another. I watched them as they dived into the winds, trying to avoid the sudden assault of two or three small but furious starlings whose nest they had been after. The Hidatsa woman, satisfied that the stones were ready, told us, *"Stoop low as you go in, and sit on the ground. It's to remind us to be humble, to let us know we are coming back to Mother Earth."* She went in first and sat down and the four of us followed her, while a fifth woman began to bring in the stones and place them in the earthen pit at our center. A beautiful Pomo woman had come to sweat with us, a basket weaver; she, unlike the rest of us, seemed to know what she was doing in there. Over the first four incoming stones our teacher spoke some prayers in the language of her people, scattering sage on them as a blessing. Smoke from the burning herb filled the lodge and smarted in my eyes and nose, and I slowed my breathing to accommodate the acrid smell. A big bucket of water was brought to make the steam necessary for our cleansing ceremony.

More prayers were said, and a pinch from a long braid of sweet grass was put on the rocks. Sweet grass from the plains swirled over the hot stones in a cloud of pleasant smoke. Finally the lodge was closed and darkness fell over us like a blanket. I shut my eyes and prayed I was going to be able to stand up to this experience. Someone next to me felt frightened when the flap to the door came down. Total darkness, intense heat, the unknown, had taken her to an edge.

The Hidatsa woman told her she had nothing to be afraid of. We were in the womb of *Ina*, in the protective covering of Grandmother Earth.

I had two thoughts when the flap closed. The first was that I wasn't in control here; and the second was that I was in for it. In the dark heat at the beginning of the lodge I knew I was coming to a crossroads inside myself; a penetration of some wall inside that made me too cautious with my life, too inhibited and afraid to be bold with my feelings. When the first several ladles of water were poured over the stones, I felt a searing heat cascade over my body, like a tearing off of my skin. I grabbed for my towel to cover myself; my face and shoulders and arms felt as though they were scorching. I buried my face in my towel and muttered some prayers for help. Droplets of water rolled off me like rain, and in the dark, tiny lights seemed to flash somewhere near the corners of my eyes.

When the flap went up after the first long round of prayers, the summer light poured across the floor and fresh air seeped in through the opening. How precious the sun and the fresh air seemed in its offering at that moment. How often I take these simple gifts for granted. I breathed in as deeply as I could of the cool air, and gave thanks for it. When I looked around me I had to laugh at the five of us, dripping, red skinned, muddy, small fragments of the ground stuck to us in odd places, completely undone and halfway into an altered state. We knew from nothing.

When the flap went down for the next prayer round I knew I wasn't going in this time with my second thoughts. Again the choking ash rose up as the newly added stones burst into steam, and again the almost unbearable heat drove me inward. In the lodge a song began, high-pitched and ancient, a chant that both pierced and re-assured me. In that song I was aware that I sat inside this womb in safety. This Grandmother, whose elements were of earth and soil, water and steam, stones and fire, was my refuge, not my enemy. My fears had to do with something else. This time I let myself fall farther down; I let go of my handholds and plunged headlong into the dark tunnel inside.

During the fourth and final round, and well after the searing away of my conscious thoughts, an inner voice clearly said, *Can you really walk what you talk? Why are you afraid to live your passion?* In my mind's eye, or in the heat of the sweat, I imagined I saw my man on the plains again. His gaze was still profoundly compelling. We stood on the top of a long bluff and in my shaking and sweating, I stepped outside my body and gave myself to his gaze. *Can you live from your heart and not be afraid to be who you are? Can you create out of your flesh rather than your intellect? Live what you know! There are no obstacles to this journey!*

I sat back against the wall of the lodge a little stunned by the intensity of the words I had just heard. I could taste the salt from the pores of my skin and from the corners of my eyes, and it hurt to breathe. I might have thought the dark and the heat were playing tricks on me. But something deep in my unconscious knew better.

The journey to the self is hard work, not so much because of its periodic intensity, but because it demands superhuman honesty and a lot of attention. For the most part, it's a lifetime project, which is why most people don't do it; which is why I had been taking a little break. But the unconscious had spoken in the sweat and that was that. Something in the darkness, some inner voice told me I had possibly only played like a dilettante with inner work. Some voice in the steam that hissed from the water on the stones said my knowledge was a dead thing unless I was willing to really walk it. Although I had the small consolation that at least I had already done some work on myself, I also knew there was still a woman inside who was afraid to experience either her own full power or the wild cry of the Spirit inside. There was one who had frequently chased after the wisdom of others, but had rarely believed in her own. While it's true I had insights, it was also clear my insights weren't going to save me. I could feel my feelings on some days but I also felt my ambivalence about them; I could speak my heart, but my words were often tentative and there was no power rising behind my breath. I felt life with intensity but I did not own my passions consistently. I sat profoundly shaken, rolling with droplets of salty water, covered with at least one layer of mud and earth, perfumed with the smell of sage and sweat. In the black heat inside the lodge I couldn't help but imagine that Somebody had my number.

Two Paths Up the Mountain

> Every human person is . . . born from the intimate depths
> of the divine nature, and from divine wilderness . . .
> —Meister Eckhart[2]

Over the years most of us have experienced the emotional dilemma of being in the soup. The pain of crisis, the unsettling feeling of conflict, the surfacing of old feelings, the dilemma of feeling a little crazy and still having to go to work, the bursting through of repressed childhood memories; these are the initiations that begin the process of healing. This first level of healing work generally deals with conflict resolution, relationship problems, working through the past where some of our earliest impressions were formed; it often means getting into unconscious waters with somebody who knows something about the currents.

There is often an element of danger and task in the initiation process; the key to this work lies in lancing our wounds, facing our worst fears and our best-kept secrets, then making conscious choices for transformation. Typically an experience of initiation spins us right into the pain of the past, headlong into the denial we've lived, then to the truth we've ignored, until an insight opens itself to us. We emerge from the experience with a newer, more potent sense of ourselves.

A man I know who had been part of a men's weekend came away from that initiation with some profound changes under his belt. *"I never thought I could feel that much, cry and rage that much, bond with other men like that. It was an incredible experience to be that close to others, to myself. It was the first time I really felt the force behind the Spirit like that."* There is a tremendous power in the initiation process, and particularly in group work, because the container for change is a supportive one. The collective energy there is often a safe place for opening our deepest wounds; for seeing the inner figures that both disempower and empower us.

The second level of work is always an encounter with the divine ground in the psyche. Breakthrough is a means of exploring what Western mystics call the divine wilderness. Although the routes to that place are varied, one gets there not by insight, but by a surrender to the world of the senses; via imagination, intuition, dreams, body-work, by a descent to Spirit. I don't mean this to sound magical or otherworldly; moving into divine wilderness is not magic, but an encounter with the collective unconscious; with the power that resides there. Sometimes we experience breakthrough because we have engineered it in some way; because we've worked hard and sweated through years of trials and we've run life's gamut; because we've been faithful about scrambling through our dreams, untangling relationships, about working our recovery. At other times the Great Hand takes us directly into that wilderness without a whole lot of preparation.

Zen Buddhist teacher Thich Nhat Hanh tells a simple story that illustrates the essence of the breakthrough process. When a young child, for instance, has a certain joyful experience, he smiles or laughs and feels happy. Maybe life comes along, however, and mistreats that child, and the seed of laughter and joy is covered over, maybe for thirty years or more. But in a moment of spontaneous awareness of the soul inside, that seed can take on life and become rooted. When that seed takes root, the soul has awakened, no matter what one has suffered. That is the breakthrough moment.

The deeper healing work we do leads us to the creative side of the psyche. When we begin to move into that territory we discover the fertile potential buried beneath our personal blueprint. Eckhart describes breakthrough as a reentering of the divine within ourselves. *"In this breakthrough, I discover that God and I are one."*[3] It is crucial, once the window is open, to work hard to keep our breakthrough a reality; and to continue to bring the images, dreams, and symbols in the unconscious to life. With the help of the Spirit inside, possibly an analyst or an honest friend or holy person, we are free to ask the big questions. We are empowered—once we glimpse our own beauty— to do the work we need to do in order to manifest the potent seed we left behind in our youth.

Sketches of the Original Self

The new meaning of soul is creativity and mysticism.
—Otto Rank[4]

I sit often with my clients, listening to their stories; they recount with me the dramas of loss, abandonment, broken dreams; the outlandish escapades most people launch themselves into to avoid pain. We sit together and brace ourselves for what is to come. For some of us, the conflicts that childhood brought somehow miraculously crystallized into challenge; the hardships and tough hombres we faced sometimes served to strengthen us, to put a wind in our sails. For others the abuse and hurt went too deep and there were no reserves, no challenges; nothing to be had from what we suffered except the grim task of survival. Some of us got pulled from the divine wilderness so utterly and so long ago we have all but forgotten it. Yet there is a well in the unconscious that, deep as it is, still runs with fresh water. The trick is to find that well.

A man in the midst of a big upheaval in his life once said: *"When I was a boy there wasn't anything I wouldn't take on. Everything was a challenge, every event was an adventure. I wasn't afraid of anything. I remember climbing huge boulders, wandering in the mountains, fording rivers; I had hind's feet in the wilderness and a spirit that took anything on. Sometimes I wonder now where that wild boy has gone."* In childhood we were to some degree still in touch with our original self, the terra firma in our unconscious that gave us a sense of bearing. Yet when the split happened between us and the persona we developed, we were left with the only child that could survive that environment. The other one eventually went into hiding.

The original self is, indeed, like a seed in the psyche, a microcosm of power and magic in the deep architecture of the cells. Children often possess a vital language most adults have long since parted company with. It is a language called the wild, and in it there is an uncompromising passion for aliveness, for the things most of us no longer ask of life. Unfortunately, one of the problems we face when confronted with the task of growing up is that the wilderness in the core self must eventually be sacrificed to convention. By the time most of us reach adolescence, the original self has gone into exile. This loss of the wild soul permeates everything: personal power, self-esteem, relationships, work and professional life, creativity, relationship to Spirit.

One of my friends as a child used to wander down by a creek below her house. *"I sat down there by the water and I saw life happening in the swirling waters. I heard voices on the wind or inside that told me things. When the world outside was nuts, I had these life-giving waters I stuck my feet in, played in, bathed in. I was only six or seven, but I always felt loved and protected there. That was my church."* Another woman said, "*As a child I had a fiery imagination. I told stories, painted pictures, wrote poems, danced on the furniture, howled like a wolf when the moon was full. In the summers I lived up in the crotch of an old weeping willow and I had wonderful councils up there. The tree spirits came and spoke to me and told me I was fine the way I was, no matter what my parents said.*" The problem was, however, these women had forgotten the creek and the willow tree. Both were creative women doing demanding work in a corporate world that neither one of them really identified with. A nemesis to any creative fire, the corporate agenda had brought ulcers to one, and nightmares and periodic depression to the other.

By mid-life many of us have wandered a long way from home. Gradually we have lost contact with the wisdom figures and fairies of childhood. Reasoned out of our instincts, talked out of our wildness, distracted from the direct intensity of our passions, most of us have forgotten the divine wilderness we began from.

One woman recently commented: "*I began to realize that my mother liked me best when I was a nice girl. In time I managed to become that girl. My father liked me when I was capable, strong, and bright. I became that girl too. My teachers liked me when I could perform and do well. My Sunday school teacher mostly liked my religious side, my savvy about holy things. I walked trying to imagine myself a saint. My friends wanted somebody venturous that would do the things they didn't dare to do. I became very daring.*" I could relate to this story. It's a universal tale of what happens to us as children when life pulls us out of the tree; we become adaptive rather than creative.

One woman said, "*Sometimes I think I have glimpses of my deep self, my wild woman, the one who is honest and real. But the bottom line is I don't give her much room to breathe. I want to tell her I love her tears and rage, her playfulness. I want her to be assertive and powerful and take risks and throw caution to the wind. But when she starts to embarrass me I pretend we've never met. At work the other day I felt like I wanted to confront my boss about something; I wanted to stand up for myself. But I lost it, I just couldn't get the words out.*" Her original child had started out on the planet with a fearless intensity, but the environment came along and talked her out of the adventure.

The lament I hear most often from clients, friends, and from passersby on the street who have resorted to talking to themselves, is a sense of loss: loss of the core self, of the creative spark in the original divine child. People who live secondary lives are people who have forgotten how to honor themselves, how to imagine they are deserving, empowered, capable, fiery creatures. Indeed, so much of the way we talk about and regard ourselves seems to extinguish that fire. We are lost in a terrible dichotomy between worlds: one bathed in the brilliance of our potential, the other overcast by a gloom that seems to obscure the way utterly. We are players in that Faustian drama where the forces of light and dark must have their way with us, where, *"The radiance of Paradise alternates with deep, dreadful night."*[5]

In the process of breakthrough, one has an opportunity to reclaim the fertile germs in the unconscious. Although sometimes buried and seemingly lost to us, they are still viable. They are like the Hopi seeds that, once stored and hidden in deep caves in small earthen vessels, can be brought to light again, and flourish.

Breakthrough to the Divine Wilderness

One of my colleagues told me that he had a powerful visual image once during a meditation in which he had suddenly recalled a part of his childhood he had forgotten about. He remembered that as a child he had lain on the coast of Maine during storms, pressed into the sanctuary of a high outcrop of rocks. That had been his power place. *"I was safe there in those storms. Thunder and lightning roared all around me and the waves of the sea came crashing up the cliffs. I watched the shapes in the clouds; some were wild horses rolling over me. 'All is well,' they said. There was wonder and grace and power there over the sea and I knew it, storm and all."* The return of this childhood image had been particularly powerful and life-giving to him because it came at a time he had been facing some big changes in his life and had been feeling anxious and unsteady.

In breakthrough, there is a special dynamic at work that involves the spontaneous emergence of the Spirit of life. Spirit can and often does transcend the personality. Jung called this a process of touching the deep feminine streams in the unconscious; he saw it as a descent to the *"realm of the Mothers."*[6] When we get down that far, we surpass our limitations and get to the germ of our potential. Once the images begin to come from this place, the breakthrough of one's inner man and woman is under way.

A man I worked with experienced a powerful breakthrough in the course of just a few sessions of work. He said that he had been feeling a painful conflict at work, and in relationship to his parents. He said he felt as if he couldn't stand up to people, that he felt easily intimidated and out of control, and he was anxious and unable to sleep. In some imagery work, he experienced a sudden illumination. In the spontaneity of that image, he saw an uncle he had been close to as a child. When he remembered the old man who had been his boyhood friend, a profound shift came over him and he began to weep. Then another image formed. I asked him what was happening, and he told me that the old man had taken him on his shoulders and had begun to carry him around. *"I can feel his body under mine. We're going down a long beach where we used to go in Maine. He's laughing and running with me on his shoulders. Just like he used to."* Suddenly he sat up straight and said, *"He's telling me, 'This whole sea knows who you are! I know who you are!'"* Then he heard the old man say: *"Look here, you forgot the strength you had as a boy. You're afraid because you forgot to believe in yourself. But I never forgot."* The whole sea echoed the old man's words.

The whole thing had seemingly happened in his mind's eye; he had recalled a loving figure from his childhood; together they had run to the sea inside where the truth about the boy's strength and his capacity to know himself had been rekindled. The power of the image restored his faith in himself. He left with an inner presence that supported and encouraged him. He also stood up to his boss, moved out of his home, and got a life of his own.

The work that uncovers these important archetypal figures does not necessarily require months, or years of therapy. It does require accessing some part of the original self—the inner potential that life never gave us a chance to develop. Healing, of course, always means we continue to penetrate the crust over the personality, cutting away the unhealthy side of an old self-image. But until we have a glimpse of the beauty and power of the self, we don't have the whole picture.

A woman I had been seeing for some months was troubled by a problem in her self-esteem. In a current relationship, although her partner was often abusive to her, she repeatedly found herself going back to see if she could make things work. In time we began to make our way through some of the tapestry of her childhood, and at some point she recalled an early-childhood experience of incest.

In working through the trauma of this memory I once asked her if she could make a picture of the time she was molested by her uncle. Gradually, as she recalled what had happened to her, she began to feel not so much anger or rage as guilt, an overwhelming sense of sadness about the loss of her innocence. I asked her if we could experiment with another image. She nodded. I suggested that she imagine herself at her present age, looking at the incident as though she were observing from a far corner in the room. I then asked her if she could imagine seeing beyond the actual abuse; if she could see inside the essence of the little girl on the bed. She said she could imagine this. I asked her what she saw. *"There's a light inside her."* We sat in grateful silence for a while. I thought of the twelfth-century Rhineland mystic Hildegarde of Bingen, who said once, *"Since my childhood, I have always seen a light in my soul, but not with the outer eyes . . . the light I perceive is brighter than the cloud which bears the sun."*[7]

After a while I asked her to envision the picture in her mind's eye again; to imagine that even though her uncle was inappropriately touching her body, that deep inside there was a child who was not touched at all. Inside was something ancient and holy that could never be touched. As she looked at the scene before her eyes, her face became peaceful and soft and a tiny smile formed around the corners of her lips. I asked her if she could picture the soul inside free of any shame or judgment. After considering this new possibility, she began to feel the reality that there *is* a life inside of her, independent of what had happened in the past. For years she had unconsciously carried a silent but terrible curse over her identity; and though she didn't know it consciously, all her relationships were determined by this impression. Finally she said, *"I've never felt like this before. I actually feel separate from that experience. It happened, but who I am goes deeper than that. I'm beginning to feel this child inside me as innocent. I've never thought of myself this way before."*

By the grace of the Spirit the use of the imagery became an experience of the sacred. She was able to heal the wounds in her self-esteem by getting a real glimpse of herself. Something holy had said to her . . . *This happened to you, but it's not who you are.* Not long afterward, she was able to stand up to the abuse in her relationship and eventually to leave it. This is typical of the alchemy of breakthrough.

A woman who had been dealing with some issues in her self-esteem told me once that she had dreamed often of a white snow goose. Exploring what the dream might mean, I asked her why the white bird might be an important symbol; what it meant for her personally. She told me that the bird had a great wing span, a great strength; that it could rise far above the ground and soar almost effortlessly. Her face changed as she spoke; light seemed to fill her eyes, and a radiance replaced her pensive expression. I asked her if she could be the snow goose. We stood together and I moved my arms in flight like the bird that soared majestically in her dreams. As she began to do the same, she was suddenly ecstatic, embraced by a freedom more powerful than that of her physical movement. It was as though she really were this great bird. Then just as suddenly, she stopped, pressed her arms inward toward her sides, and froze.

I asked her what was happening. *"I feel scared. I can feel myself holding on. I do this to myself when I'm about to experience something new or powerful. I'm afraid of my freedom, what it might bring."* I motioned to her, asking if we could try the flight again, this time going with her fear, even flying into it. When she nodded yes, I took her arms and gently formed them once more into the great wings. I asked her to breathe and imagine herself this snow goose. We took off and flew together and suddenly there was no roof to that house. She burst into tears and laughed and cried, and did not stop her flight this time. The symbol of that snow goose was a figure of empowerment and freedom that didn't agree with the ways she held herself in.

So often the growth we achieve is short-lived because the mind is fraught with saboteurs: inner figures that convince us we should be afraid, that we should honor caution above risk-taking, that what we are attempting to do is stupid, or self-defeating. These voices make up a whole panel of judges who serve as jailers and executioners, if we let them. Once we silence the internal censors, the process of breakthrough is often more keenly felt when we can give free rein to the imagination, and when we allow the body to take that initial image—and express it.

Feeding Breakthrough

The more I listen to dreams, confront the demons of memory and conditioning, the more I see that an *essential self* is always trying to surface. Any significant inner work one does involves breaking through to the inner man and woman (and the child in there) who lives from the wilderness in the soul. But we have to feed that essential self, once we see it. We have to pay attention to it and we have to mind it, look after it, talk to it, or that child with the fire in the soul will not thrive.

At some point it is essential to ask ourselves what happened to the inner child who once held such fiery promise; to ask the whereabouts of the fearless boy who had hind's feet; to look for the girl who once talked to the fairies, or sang barefoot in the creek. The ancient wisdom figures in the psyche, the grandfathers and grandmothers, the people who will run with us by the sea, my friend on the plains—these are all figures we would do well to chase after, to sit on some rock by the river and talk to.

Following up on breakthrough is difficult for many of us because typically, after a powerful psychic experience, we have to go back home, or back to work; or possibly back to some conflict we've put on the back burner; the illumination we have returned with can fade. But the wisdom figures in the psyche (or those whom we know in the real) will tell us to care for and protect the new seeds that we've gathered. Anyone who has had an experience of breakthrough needs to take time out to be alone; to reflect, to wander off on long walks, to go fishing or to begin to take play seriously; to do whatever it takes to give sacred time to what is trying to surface.

In order to nurture the breakthrough experience, we have to give shape to the unconscious messages that have begun to come our way. There are a number of ways to do this. Some people can access this realm through dreams, active imagination, bodywork, breathwork, art, some through meditation, or therapy; there are many routes to the inner man and woman. Yet any psychotherapy worth its salt— if it's going to be lasting and productive, not just relief-oriented— must offer to help us *birth the images* in the unconscious. Since many therapies are geared toward insight, behavioral change, alleviating symptoms, creating new goals—in other words, toward the first level of the healing process—it is sometimes difficult to find someone who will take us, without apologies, into the wilderness inside. A friend of mine expressed it in this way: *"I've done my basic recovery work and I've been clean and sober for fifteen years. Now I need to recover from being in recovery. I want a program that comes from the inside out."*

Another person said: *"I've been in therapy two years and I'm beginning to feel like I need more than just healing. I need something for my soul."* Therapy needs to be like a mountain we climb, that when we finally reach the top, we can see for miles. But it isn't the topographical map that takes us to the summit of a great mountain, it is our love for adventure—and the Holy Wind that leads us there.

To go there, we have to create a language more suited to the right brain, to trust our mystical nature and be willing to follow it. Meister Eckhart (who often inspired Jung) knew that the language of the mind (reason and intellect) would eventually trick the best of us. Jung commented once that to have an intellectual "grasp" of something was no guarantee we were going to get it; we might have a *concept* of the thing, but concepts are not enough. People I see often understand their problems (and the solutions) perfectly. But to change takes more than understanding or mental acumen. To Jung, the *unknown* language of symbols was the magic work. But in order to be able to know the language of symbols, one had to bypass that "cheat" in the intellect.[8]

If any of us is going to put flesh and bones on the images from the unconscious, we have to feel and sense what they mean; we have to capture and express them in some way. Hildegarde of Bingen, in her *Book of Divine Works,* has a number of remarkable drawings and paintings that give shape to the images that came to her in dreams and visions. We don't have to be mystics or artists to work with symbols. But we do have to put our known language aside for a while, and we have to experiment with something new.

The practice of letting go of the mind—taught by Eastern and Western mystics for centuries, actually helps incubate the powerful forces in the unconscious. Jung comments: *"We must be able to let things happen in the psyche. For us, this is actually an art of which few people know anything. Consciousness is forever interfering, helping, correcting, negating, and never leaving the simple growth of the psychic processes in peace."*[9]

In the descent to the *realm of the Mothers,* one learns, indeed, to let things happen, to proceed as though there were some bigger choreography afoot. One simply sits with the unconscious like a gatekeeper, allowing moods, feelings, dreams, images, the sensory world, to have a voice. The inner figures that have begun to pass through that gate will eventually have a word with us.

2. Dreams and Sacred Ground

When the old people sing over crimson stones
and steam shoots out its breath song,
when the robe of dark earth covers me,
I feel immense joy in my four bodies.
They say there is a spirit path in the lodge
a place where that other world
sits in its robe and hears our heart's lament.
"Don't sit on that line," they say.
"It's holy. You're no spirit yet, so don't
sit on that place." We laugh in
that fiery womb. We pray for our relations,
for the people in our lives that don't
know love. These four endurances, they
deliver us from ourselves.
They wash the landscape in the soul
where the Spirit sends a voice.
I am a child in that searing, sitting inside
fragile bones—praying to feel some
solace in the Great Heart.
—Djohariah Toor

In the months that followed the first sweat lodge, I remained uncertain
of the meaning of the crossed eagle feathers, but one thing was clear:
this wild man in deerskin with his dark skin glistening in the sun
came from a wilderness within that I had forfeited over the years. I
guessed the shape of the symbol he had shown me to be a sort of
mandala, a circle with four equal sides. In myth, the circle is an
ancient symbol for birth and growth and death, for cycles, seasons,
holy goings on. I knew it to be a potent medicine in the psyche, often
closely linked to the feminine in both men and women; a symbol of
protection, completion, and wholeness. I had for years recorded these
circular shapes in dreams, often sensing some mystery was connected
to the circle.

As I drove again toward the lodge one morning, I suddenly recalled an important dream I had had some years before, in which I had seen an enormous full moon over the altar of a monastery. *In the monastery I was greeted by a pale young monk and taken to a room outside a large interior chapel. The young monk explained to the sexton there that he was escorting me into the chapel. The sexton made it clear that no women were allowed, and that therefore I could not enter. However, when the sexton looked up and saw me, he said, "Oh it's you." And he let me pass. We walked through the doors of an old chapel, and to the left of the altar there were three sarcophagi containing the bodies of three dead men. As I passed by, one of them awakened and took my hand. I then sat down with the three priests and began a conversation. They thought I was a poor peasant girl and assumed I could comprehend nothing of what they were saying. It was then that I saw the moon over the altar had begun to move and to grow very large. The image of that huge iridescent moon was so numinous, and the power of it so startling, I awakened.* The moon itself had been the color and texture of mother-of-pearl, and at one point it seemed so immense and radiant in its rising that it overshadowed the three priests I had been sitting with, completely dwarfing our conversation. I felt awed that it had moved toward us from behind the altar; that in its rising it had become so huge and iridescent that I had been startled awake. I knew back then that this was an epic dream, probably the first big dream I can remember. It was during that time that I had first begun my work and study of feminine consciousness. I had only the vaguest idea what the dream meant at the time.

On the road that wound down the coastal side of the mountains toward the sweat, I pondered the dream anew. I was certain that the cyclic feminine time (represented by the moon) must be connected to the mandala shape of the eagle feathers. It was clear that the symbol of the circle wanted attention. I felt grateful my unconscious hadn't given up on me after so many years. I was also aware how persistently it sends us messages—fantasies, dreams and waking dreams, visions, intuitions, sudden insights, or real life situations—that demand we acknowledge the deeper streams of knowing inside; as though to signal us it's time to deal with something we have overlooked and pretended not to notice.

It was another warm day and the sun poured into the grove of eucalyptus where the lodge was. I stood by the fire fanning the flames with the Hidatsa woman, feeling glad to be back, wanting the heat, the darkness, the healing breath of the steam pouring over me. The hawks came again, circling, calling to one another or maybe to us, moving in close, then spiraling upward into high clouds, their red tails catching the backlight of the sun. We began to enter the lodge, and this time I went in not with resignation, but with excitement.

We sat down, and before the pipe was lit we were told that the low ceiling in the lodge had a twofold purpose. First, it keeps the heat in, and second, it makes one bend low, close to the earth in an act of reverence toward the Creator. I was struck by the immense difference I felt stooping to enter this earthy womb—made from willows, blankets, tarps, decorated with eucalyptus leaves—and my memory of entering cathedrals like Notre Dame, or St. John the Divine, with their elegant stained glass and splendid high ceilings, their great marbles, frescoes, and tiles. In Native ceremony, the ground is ultimately the way to God; it must be touched first. The lodge itself, when the flap is closed, is not only hot, the darkness in there almost invariably pulls one out of the intellect and into the feeling world. In there are no distractions, nothing to see, nothing to "elevate" one at all. There was no way to go *but* inward. The Scripture "Be still and know that I am God" came alive in there.

Sweats to the Indians are a prayer time; a time for cleansing, reckoning, listening. Although my prayers in those early sweats were mainly monosyllabic, my unconscious seemed fertile with images. The moment that flap went down and the lodge filled up with hot steam, I went way down deep. As I sat there in the lodge, in between prayers and ladles of water and searing heat, a more recent dream came to mind: *I had been sitting in an old Gothic church, listening to a sermon spoken entirely in German. Not only did the language make no sense to me, but there was also an unspoken rule in the church that women could not participate there except as spectators. An adolescent girl next to me was having trouble breathing. Gradually it became clear to me that these people weren't speaking my language and that the air in the place was far too stuffy. We got up to leave but instead of going out the front door, we were shown a back staircase that led to a ground floor below. As we wound down the stairs I began to sense something pleasant and familiar. A dark Hindu woman dressed in a sari stood on one of the landings, offering me a fragrant bouquet of spices. As I passed her I took my first deep breath, relishing the aroma of her cotton gown, the garland she held,*

*the sweet musk scent in her hair. The long stairwell led down to an outdoor
market filled with rich green produce, sweet and pungent aromas, sounds
of life, children, sitar music, anklet bells.*

I was beginning to understand something. The child who couldn't
breathe in the church or understand the German pastor was similar
to the peasant girl in the monastery, whom the three priests were
certain couldn't speak *their* language. I had the unpleasant thought
that the priests and the pastor in the two dreams might represent an
inflated masculine (my intellectual side). They were all condescending
to the feminine, and talked over her head. The subtle dichotomy was
that one side of me talked the *language* of feminine consciousness. I
spoke and lectured about and analyzed others' dreams. I had done
years of personal work myself and had filled at least thirty journals
with what I was certain were luminous insights. Half of me paid
respect (lip service anyway) to the yin of life. The other half, however,
went on with my agendas, with an intellectual program that lacked
the painful *kenosis* (emptying) required of inner work.

And there I was in the dream, on a hard bench in a church with
high ceilings trying to decipher a foreign language that made little
sense to me. Some part of my psyche, according to this dream, was
still sitting in a pew in a stuffy seventeenth-century German church
that silenced women. I began to see I had cheated myself—or that
my intellect had cheated me. These dreams (and others like them)
were telling me that I had little or no ground in which the feminine
could thrive. In my work there was accomplishment, but no creative
fire. In my relationships there was satisfaction, but not much soul. In
my church I wasn't feeling as if I "spoke the language." It dawned
on me that the circle that had been trying to break through to me
meant wholeness and feminine cyclic time—and that I had been living
outside it.

I needed to find a sacred space for my soul. My life was too scattered,
I was too busy, overcommitted, and I talked too much. I had a perfect
understanding of my problems, but I had analyzed myself enough.
Something bigger and more powerful than the wind of my ego was
beginning to blow inside. I needed to find a way to engage something
holier than the intellect (the high German church) that kept going
over my head. I needed to breathe bouquets of spices, not the dank
air of an old Gothic (and probably Victorian) church.

In inner work, there is always a trickster. In any pursuit of the unconscious, there are always blind spots. The more we know, the more danger there is of falling victim to our hubris (that stuff in the ego that says, "Now that you know a thing or two, you can sit back and relax"). Over and over I hear people say that intellectually they know what their problems are, but emotionally there are synapses that don't meet. Most of us tend to climb the ladder of insight and stop there. But the feminine way is down the ladder, down the stairs to the basement of the church, down to the dark woman with the spices.

On the drive home from the lodge, the shadows from the tall eucalyptus and fir along the road gave rise to a fantasy. The wild man with the feathers came striding into the church, scowled at the German preacher, took the hand of the child who couldn't breathe, and carried her out of there. The sound of wild drumming flooded the old organ in the church as the two of us made our dramatic exodus. The man with the blue braids said: *Get this child free! Take her where she can breathe! Let her play and run and feel joy. Let her be, and don't ask her to think too much. Find the stairs to the woman in the sari who waits to give you sweet spice. Take off your shoes, and go on down to the earth in your bones.*

As the year went on I continued to study with the Hidatsa woman, wandered away from the busyness of my life, and continued to boil like an owl in the sweat lodge. I began to read less and write in my journal more, gathering up more time for quiet pondering. I listened intently for more bold words from the figures that lived and spoke from the dark initiation I had begun.

Maybe You'll Get Lost

I made it a point the following year to keep company with Native American and third-world people who knew about earthiness and sacred ground. If they were old and silver-headed, all the better. One old Athabascan grandmother I visited the following year in the interior of Alaska invited me one morning to hike down to the river with her. She and her tribe had just won back their fishing rights on the river, and had spent several days together with people from another village building a big fish wheel. She was proud of that wheel. The big sockeye that would lodge themselves in the basket at the center of the wheel would be a major part of her diet.

After a cup of black coffee, she suggested we go for a run down to the river. With two wonderfully raised eyebrows, she said, *"Let's go take a walk down to that river and see if there's any big ones. Might be some bear on that trail though. Only thing is, I got no gun. We'll go see Jimmy, he's got a good gun. You know how to shoot?"* I told her I did. We arrived at Jimmy's down the road; he was outside chopping wood. He soon disappeared inside his house to find the shotgun we had asked for, and when he returned he showed me how to load it with rifled slugs. Then, with a grin, he advised me not to use the safety catch, in case I had to fire in a hurry.

I had shot clay skeet with my father as a kid, but I never imagined I might have to shoot a grizzly bear. We walked down that trail about three miles that morning, a couple of her grandchildren trailing us. The whole time she joked and laughed or fell silent, walking with ease and beauty, now and then humming little trail songs to herself. The whole time I had my mind on one thing; which side of the narrow, brushy trail the grizzly might come charging out of. On the way down she told of bear incidents that had happened in or around the village over the years. She had a little smile on her face as she spoke.

Later that night I took a sweat bath with her and a few of her grandchildren. She had made a broom of alder branches for the sweat. We dipped it in a bucket of warm water and doused ourselves all over, then cooked ourselves for a good long while before stepping out into the chilly Alaskan night. Nobody in there spoke much, and thoughts of the day rolled steadily upward. This old grandmother had walked like a child in the wilderness, laughing, joking, profoundly silent, contemplating each step, unflinching at the thought of grizzly, unperturbed at the swarms of mosquitoes, mindful of the fish she might find. I had walked willingly, bravely even. But underneath I had these big bear concerns. Under my stoic appearance I cursed the mosquitoes, the little whitesocks that left such fierce welts on my skin. I resented the drizzle. And I wasn't at home in bear country.

That night I had a dream that awakened me sometime before dawn. *I dreamed of a huge black she bear who had been looking in through my cabin window. When I saw her I was afraid, thinking she might try to break in. Then I heard a shot ring out and suddenly her huge form crumpled. I ran outside just as a small cub had ambled up to her. The mother bear lay there bleeding, a huge hole in her belly. The cub and I stood wide-eyed, in shock, grief-stricken.* I turned on the light and wrote in my journal, feeling sad, puzzled, upset about the presence of such an omen.

Later that day I thought again of my waking dream the year before, and its challenge to live my life without so much compromise; without scattering my creativity (or the feminine I longed to know) to the wind. Like my man on the plains, this Athabascan grandmother was a model of wholeness. She lived a simplicity I longed for. She lived, it seemed, in cyclic time, without any help from the German church; true to the wisdom inside herself. Down by the river she had lain on her belly in the green grass and withdrawn into herself, not talking much; just playing with the soft grass and tiny red berries with hands that knew all too well the earth, her elements and seasons. I talked about the *realm of the Mothers,* but she was living it.

In the breakthrough process, powerful images are released to consciousness. These things are *wakan,* or sacred.[1] But unless we go after the numen (the spirit) in these images, the gates to consciousness shut before us. Then we start giving in to our fears again, to the pressures and distractions that pull us off the track; we start thinking there are bears in the woods that want to eat us. We turn around nervously and imagine some catastrophe follows us from behind. We are subject, then, to what the Tibetan Buddhists call the "hungry ghosts," negative and frightening fantasies that want to come and carry us away. It is only human nature that most of us on any growth quest find ourselves stranded in the middle of these two worlds. Power and creativity on one side, and goblins on the other.

The Enclosing Circle and the Dream

Earth and Heaven are in us.
—Ghandi[2]

If any of us is going to change, it's not because we have understood our problems intellectually, but because we have rolled up our sleeves and gone into the unconscious; into the *realm of the Mothers* where we can heal and do the work of transformation. Whenever any of us brings the images from that realm to life, we "enflesh" the images and symbols in dreams. Then we can talk to the ghosts in there, and likewise to the heroic and enlightened characters that have been trying to get our attention. Getting to these creative energies in the unconscious is a lifetime work. The good news, however, is that the key here is time, not brilliance.

Anyone living outside the circle (and that's most of us) is living in some kind of stress. Being fragmented is epidemic in the West. In order to heal the psychic divisions in our lives, we need sacred time. First of all we begin to make an "enclosing circle" around ourselves where we can sit with the messages that will start to come our way. The circle that encloses us while we do this work restores us. When we slow down and take time to reflect, to listen and go within, the scattered sides of the personality can gradually reunite.[3] The "hungry ghosts" settle down.

Aside from time, we need to bring the symbols in our dreams to life, to roust out the archetypes that bring healing and creativity. People often say they pay no attention to their dreams because they are incomprehensible, tedious, or frightening, or because scrambling through those hieroglyphics down there takes too much time. I would know this kind of avoidance. Yet dreams keep the doors to our breakthrough experience open. They give us direct access to the most potent side of ourselves.

Before leaving Alaska that summer, I found myself a tree near the Tanana River, parked myself under it, and looked hard at the dream motifs in my journal. The more I sat with the bear dream, the more I saw that I had rigged the shooting myself. This bear was my wild side, my hugeness for life, my ability to hibernate and shut out the world; she was my connection to the primitive self. She was peering in to ask something—shouldn't I be listening to my instincts, minding them, hibernating, foraging in the inner world, taking time?

I had not only shut her out of my life, I had gravely wounded her. Somehow there was a gaping hole in my solar plexus (the Greeks say the solar plexus is the sun in the body). Undoubtedly my life energy had been so violated by my caretaking agenda that I had all but killed off the creative springs inside.

I listened to the river run, to the insects buzzing around, to little swarms of knats and tiny biting creatures. A moose and her calf came walking down the creek bed, foraging on the bottom. I leaned into the tree, sad, pondering how I kept blasting the sun in my body. The dream of the wounded bear had been a warning that I needed to protect and honor the creative fire inside; and in no uncertain terms to hibernate without sabotaging myself.

The feminine, after all, doesn't dwell in the head; she is flesh and passion and relationship. She knows what she knows by her experience, by risking to feel, by following the unknown path of her instincts. Feminine awareness is grounded in the senses, and she lives from her solar plexus.

Whether men or women, most of us have been programmed out of our bear nature; conditioned to mistrust our senses. Most people I work with are caught in agendas, work, and relationships that betray the solar plexus. No matter how much we know, how brilliant we are, how much we understand about ourselves—life is just an intellectual exercise until we heal and integrate the sacred side of the instincts we have abandoned.

I agreed at last to build a fire under myself. I listened more intently to the dreams of clients and friends, and with renewed passion I mapped the dream motifs in my journal that had accumulated over the years.

Enlightening Nightmares

In the way of synchronicity, many of my clients also began bringing in dreams, images, and stories that reflected this loss of the wild. One motif that appeared often involved animals, wild and domesticated. Some were lost or out of their element; some were caught in traps, kept in cages; some were wounded, but most were in some sort of trouble. Animals in dreams often portray the split many of us experience between the natural body with its sensate (and sensual) nature, and the rational (or religious) mind-set that negates or condemns the body. Archetypally, animals symbolize power, passion, independence, companionship, spirit, and at times, guidance or divine assistance (as in the Greek legends of dolphins guiding the souls of the dead to safety).[4]

One woman dreamed of a huge lion perched in a tree. It was sunset on the Serengeti. When she walked near it, the lion slid from the tree and attacked her. As she rolled on the ground fighting this creature, it suddenly changed into her house cat. It simply got up, brushed itself off, licked itself clean, and sat looking at her. *"I felt this cat was something inside I was neglecting. A wildness, a kind of independence, an ability to be alone, a fierce kind of aloneness really. I want this kind of independence in my life, but I'm still tied to what everyone else wants. I'm terrified that I won't know what to do with my independence once I get it. That I won't be able to trust myself, that I'll attack myself when I'm not looking. But look here, it's only a little house cat."* Cats are feral creatures, independent; they come and go as they please; they don't mind saying no from time to time; they stretch out lazily in the sun and have no guilt about it. They cannot ever be completely tamed.

Another woman dreamed of a field of horses running *"They were so beautiful when they ran, with their tails stretched out, their manes in the wind. Then I noticed they had got cornered in a small corral, and they couldn't get out. The owner of the horses, a big cowboy, told me to feed them, but all I had was spinach. Horses don't eat spinach, I thought to myself. They need wild oats and grains and fields of grass. This man is trying to trick them, so they won't want out of the corral. I woke up wondering how on earth I got myself into such a tight place in this relationship I'm in. My horses are all fenced up, and I think they'll starve in there. I've got to fire this cowboy."*

A man I'd been working with on his issues of masculine power dreamed of a wild wolf. *"I was lying asleep, or maybe I was an old miner in the hills. Maybe I was wounded and had been left to die. This wolf comes and begins to attack me. He's eating me alive and I can't move. He tears out my insides, and I can't wake up, but I can feel him eating me. Then I become the wolf, and I run and run and feel the power of the man inside me. It is as though we are running together. I feel the strength and power of the wolf, and then we are one."* The dreamer here understood that the wild instinct within him (unless he could run with it, express it, integrate it somehow) would eat him.

A woman I know dreams she is swimming in a river and suddenly a huge mother whale is diving in and out of the water nearby. *"It's a huge killer whale, black and white and shining like the sun and the moon all at once. The light on her body was immense. She made huge waves. She was absolutely beautiful. But I thought, this is dangerous. I knew she wouldn't hurt me intentionally, but the waves she was making in the river could overwhelm me. I got out of the water and stood on the bank of the river and watched her. Suddenly I felt incredibly sad that she was somehow totally out of the sea, and that she could breech here and die. I got frightened and ran to look for help."* This woman knew her own inner whale was in trouble. She knew she had gotten out of her element (too much work, too many commitments) and that she needed to make waves (although she was afraid to, for fear of reprisal, loss of job, loss of approval). She also knew that in the environment she was in at work, unless she changed something—indeed, she could breech.

A man dreamed of a wounded animal. *"I had been hiking in the woods when I came across a black bear which had been attacked by another bear. I knelt down by its side, feeling torn and hurting for it. I took mud and herbs and gently spread it over the wound in its stomach. I awakened with the thought that something in myself was wounded too, something had been torn into."* In working the dream, he sensed his own emotions were raw; that perhaps he had taken in possibly too much pain from others; from the condition of suffering in the world. *"In my work I can get too attached to things and people, to outcomes. I think the message of the dream is about detachment and letting go."*

Other dreams that caught my attention were the dreams of Mother Nature in revolt. All manner of natural disasters blew through my office: hurricanes, tornadoes, hailstorms. Rain and snow storms assaulted some dreamers; rivers and seas flooded their banks, sweeping away everything that wasn't nailed down; avalanches and landslides pitched other dreamers into one cataclysm after another. Volcanoes and earthquakes erupted with tremendous force. One woman dreamed: *"I'd been walking along a city street and had just come into my office building, when suddenly the ground began to heave. It shook the building like a rag. Things began falling, crashing all around me. Outside I could hear whole buildings collapsing, there was chaos and pandemonium everywhere. Suddenly the floor gave way and I was pitching downward, spinning into space. I woke up screaming and really terrified."*

Another woman who had a number of repetitive dreams of hurricanes and cataclysms said once: *"What was puzzling to me is that these dreams seemed so opposite my conscious thoughts. My outer life seemed fine, yet these were dreams about chaos, nature going wild. When I really got honest, I had to confess that I had a kind of split inside that was about to erupt. My whole life I'd been going from one commitment, one responsibility, to another. But these little programs and successes in the world had finally begun to take their toll. I pushed and drove myself. I never stopped except at red lights. My body and my psyche were fatigued, and Mother Nature was irate."*

Clearly these dreams of upheaval are the consequence of a life lived in discord. We may not know that, but somebody inside knows it. Mother Nature, when continually programmed by deadlines, stuck in traffic, starved on Slim-Fast, stuffed with fast food, squeezed into high rises and high heels—when she gets pushed into lifestyles that have nothing to do with the sacred—she just gets upset. When there is an inner child who is impish, fiery, creative, wild, and for convention's sake we leave her behind—nature within us goes berserk.

Dreaming the Abandoned Child

Over the years people have recounted to me a number of dreams related to children, adolescents, infants, and babies. Most of the youngsters have had a hard time of it, winding up lost, neglected, orphaned, mistreated, or in danger of some kind. The theme of losing or abandoning the child emerged consistently, and I paid close attention. The child in myth is our innocence, our trust in life, the eternal seed of the soul, the divine child. It is the self struggling toward autonomy, the fragile shoot of the plant.

A woman dreamed she had given birth to a tiny infant, and just as suddenly as she birthed it and cut the cord, she wrapped it up and put it on an ice floe. *"I don't know why I did that, it seemed so strange. But on second thought, I think I do this to myself; I put myself on ice. I won't let myself feel my feelings, let alone say them."*

Another woman dreamed of birthing a baby and then losing it repeatedly. In these vignettes she would be holding the baby, caring for it. But then as she became involved with her chores and projects, she would set the infant aside, leave it in the crib. When she returned to look for the baby, it would be lost or stolen. She would panic and begin to search everywhere, realizing that she had completely neglected it. This lost child is a common motif and turns up often. *"I used to dream I'd go shopping, taking my baby along in a carriage. Then I'd get interested in something at the store and turn away for a few moments. When I looked, my carriage would be gone. I'd rush around the store crying for my baby, searching frantically."*

One dreamer took her infant to church and when she got tired of holding it, she propped it up on the pew (where it continually slid down or rolled over). *"I sat the baby down and then went off to visit with others in the church. But whenever I left, this baby fell over. Finally I got very angry and I grabbed it and said, 'Can't you sit up on your own? Grow up!' "* She had been putting enormous pressure on herself to conform to the big demands she felt in her life. She needed to be self-contained, in control, always available, always presentable, and on top of that, holy. She had no room for herself in such a psyche.

Oftentimes individuals report themes in which the baby or child is in some kind of danger; there is a repeated threat of invasion, kidnapping, violence, or natural disasters of one sort or another. *"I was walking with my baby down the seacoast, when suddenly a huge wave came crashing around us, engulfing both of us. We were swept out to sea and I lost the baby in the waves. I was frantic and swam around calling and searching. As the storm subsided I could see a tiny distant figure on the shore. I swam toward it, and as I approached the shore I saw that it was my baby, drowned. I grabbed it up into my arms and began to give it mouth-to-mouth resuscitation. It was completely blue. I kept breathing into its tiny mouth and praying and rocking it and aching inside, and finally it opened its little eyes. When I woke up I thought, my God, what am I doing to myself?!"*

A man told me of a nightmare he'd had in which his youngest daughter had been killed. *"She was lying on the floor very sick, like she was about to die. She looked up at me and said, 'I love you, Daddy.' Then I put my hands on her chest, and I pushed the life out of her body. I woke up in tears, totally undone. I didn't even want to go to work."* The dreamer began to see that it wasn't really his daughter he killed but his own feminine side. That dream had a powerful effect upon him and as we discussed it, he decided it was time to pay close attention to recovering his inner woman.

Many of these dreams are symptomatic of self-betrayal. The common denominator of these hurt or abandoned children is that some vital part of ourselves is missing and needs to be reclaimed. Another dreamer told me: *"I had this little girl who would come to me. Her dress was tattered, her face dirty, her knees and elbows always skinned, sometimes bleeding. Her little eyes were dark, and in there was a hurt, sometimes a faraway look. When I talked to her, she stared at me vacantly. It used to make me really sad. Then one day I knew that child was me. I'd been abused as a child, and although I've come a long way in my recovery, there's still a side of me that's beaten up and uncared for. There are still ways I abandon myself. Sometimes I deny what I'm feeling, what I know. I talk around what I want to say. I don't listen to my own gut feelings."*

These dreams of self-abandonment, nightmares that they are, address the problem of living in ways that have nothing to do with the "enclosing circle" and the life inside of us. No matter who we are or what we have accomplished in life, all of us have forfeited something. Whether it's our ability to feel, to love, to be vulnerable and accessible, to feel pain, to feel power or pleasure, to feel the Spirit pushing through, all of us have something that wants back in the circle.

Birthing Dreams from the Realm of the Mothers

In the birth you will discover all blessing. Neglect the birth, and you neglect all blessing.
—Meister Eckhart[5]

Jung observed once that at the core of the alchemist's life work is the idea that there is a "mysterious centre" in man, a "celestial substance" that has always existed.[6] He saw the psychological implication of that substance to mean that in the unconscious there are potent seeds of creativity and a vast consciousness waiting to awaken. He saw this "mysterious centre" to be like a womb, a uterus in the psyche.

When one has worked with the unconscious for a while, dreams will commonly shift. Birthing dreams, for instance, are often symbolic of a redemption motif beginning to take shape; a gradual shift from abandonment to emergence. What has been lost or fragmented cycles around and waits for a chance to regenerate in the psyche.

One of the women I know, working steadily over the years through deep wounds of abuse as a child from both her parents, dreamed: *"I was about six months pregnant and had gone to the doctor for a checkup. He said I had a uterine infection and that I couldn't carry the baby any longer. He told me if it was born prematurely it would die—but it would die at full term too because of the infection. He said he would deliver the baby for me, but that it would die. I was devastated so I went to my bodyworker, M., at her little house on the beach. She told me she would take care of everything. She gave me herbs to induce labor. Then I went into labor and delivered the baby. He was small but she wrapped him up real good. She told me to keep him warm and feed him and he'd be okay. She gave me herbs for the infection. Then I told her I was going to New York and she said, 'No, you're not strong enough; stay here and I'll take care of you, and when you and the baby are strong enough, you can begin that journey.'"* We talked about the immense work that she had done over the years, her struggle to heal the mother wound (her father abused her, her mother looked on, probably in a dissociative state, and never protected her). Her need to bypass the male doctor (reason, intellect, power, focus on action) and instead consult the female body-worker (who knew just what to do, including when to wait) was a way in which she needed to honor her feminine wisdom.

Had she employed her masculine side to assist the birth, the baby would have died. Such an effort would have been premature. The feminine in the dream, symbolized by herbs with natural healing properties, a house by the sea (the eternal germinative mother ocean), a nurturing midwife, and the advice to wait a while before the journey— was what saved the infant inside her. In reflecting on the dream, she said: *"In my life I'm at a resting point. I'm just letting myself be surrounded by nurturing women who can love me, who can help me, people I can depend on. I've done a lot of conscious work, but now I just need to rest and heal a deep mother wound."*

Another dreamer said, *"I dreamed I gave birth to a tiny infant, very fragile and beautiful. It was so delicate I had to wrap it up and care for it very carefully. I went back to it frequently and picked it up and held it, rocked it, nursed it, until it grew. I knew that unless I did this, that it would not flourish."* This woman (a survivor of incest) had worked at her own healing for some time before having this dream. But now the dream had come, signaling her that she was ready for a turning, a shift into deeper, more fertile waters. *"After the dream I knew I had to take more time out, to really make a commitment to myself to cancel out whole days just for myself; for the paintings that wanted to come."*

A year or so after my visit to Alaska, I had a birthing dream myself.

As I pondered it, I realized it had a certain universal tone to it; it seemed to exemplify the split many of us feel between ourselves and the divine wilderness inside. But it also has overtones of rebirth.

In the dream I was giving birth to a baby. After a while the labor stopped and, as dreams go, that was that. I got up, walked outside the hospital, and followed a path deep into the interior of a tropical forest. I saw a small circular hut with a thatched roof and a simple opening, and I walked into it. I squatted by the fire in the center of the room and began to feel my labor again, this time with much more intensity. The baby's head was pressing down hard on the walls that line the birth canal, and in my groaning and pushing, slowly the infant emerged. Just at the same time I was giving birth, the dark earth next to me opened and the baby emerged from the ground upward. A tall man picked up the infant, swaddled it, and handed it to me, smiling. I felt an intense joy as I woke up.

The breakthrough process is always about emergence. Pondering the metaphor of birth is essential, no matter what our sex is, or whether we have ever conceived.

In the dream, it was clear why my labor had stopped. I couldn't give birth in such a sterile antiseptic setting as the hospital. The ground where the baby broke through was dirt, humus; it was the rich compost of Mother Earth that yielded this baby. The tropical forest seemed to symbolize some sort of wilderness: wet, green, moist, verdant, lush; just right for birth. The shape of the primitive hut was a circle, like the feather mandala, the shape of the womb, the opening of the cervix, like the abalone shell moon in the monastery, the sweat lodge, the salmon berries I filled my pockets with on the trail down to the fish wheel. Round and full and bursting with life.

The shapes related to the circle, although in large part feminine symbols, also relate to men. The creative fields in the unconscious, the *realm of the Mothers,* informs a genuinely neutral ground where healing images can emerge. The symbol of a baby or young child is, after all, a universal one; the child contains the seed, the mystic center imbued with innocence and trust, with a primitive instinct not only for survival but for adventure. To see life through the eyes of that child is transformative.

A man I was working with once told me that he had been very depressed. We talked about what he might be doing (or not doing) that might be causing depression. At one level, his life was successful; at another, it was so full of work, students, others, that he had abandoned himself. In the previous months he had been focusing on losing weight and taking care of his physical body, and had, in fact, lost about 100 pounds. His body felt much better, but something in his heart began to feel too exposed, too vulnerable. It was as though the flesh over the wounds of his own childhood had worn too thin. After a while we lapsed into some prayer and visualization. Then he had an image of a small child sitting inside his heart and solar plexus. The spontaneity of that picture surprised him. But he sat with it for a while, and finally he said: *"That's me I see in there. I haven't really taken care of myself. I haven't given myself the help and attention I've given others. I've put that boy on hold. I can see he's wanting a lot more from me. A whole lot more."* The portrait of the boy within him stirred some remorse in this man; but at the same time, the boy he had been denying could begin to materialize.

Emotionally and spiritually, the idea of a womb in the psyche belongs to all of us. Yet some of us run a whole lifetime from this rendezvous.

The Ground Wants a Word with Us

The mandala given to me by the man on the plains, as I continued to feel its potency in ritual, imagination, dreams, and inner work, seemed a summons to touch the earth within myself; to spring loose the more germinative seeds in there. I knew my intellect, my insights, and the men in black robes in the church had taken me about as far as they could. I was acutely aware that the mother bear (my feminine instinct) was wounded and needed a healing place. And that I never *had* dealt with the dead men in the sarcophagi in the nave of the church. For all I knew they were still in there. I became more and more aware of the presence of the "hungry ghosts" that followed me, making sure I compromised myself and didn't get too wild.

In those days, I continued to show up for the sweats whenever I could. I went because they took me to an edge in myself that I wanted to stand on. And I went because I loved praying on the earth, giving myself to her elements. I had a lot of revelations in that heat, but mostly the sweat lodge was a reminder that my appointment with God was a descent inside. I took my dreams in there and just asked the heat and the dark and the Grandmother to incubate them with me until I found some direction.

During one particularly scorching sweat it occurred to me that this ground we were sitting on was truly sacred. There we were in total darkness, praying, sweating, weeping, wincing, laughing sometimes, profoundly humbled. We sat in there cooking ourselves like the old alchemists, straining out lead from gold. On one occasion my shorts came out of the sweat with a good-sized scorch mark. Yet I felt a joy I hadn't felt in a long time; a resolve to live my life from the ground up, rather than the other way around. I longed for this kind of earthy circle in my life, in my prayers, work, and my relationships, for this sacred ground where there was no veil between myself and the Spirit.

In time Native traditions and ritual, as I came to experience them, became a way to work with my clients that involved more potency. I began to venture outside my office, to make sure that from time to time we could meet as a group in some natural setting where Mother Nature could soothe and speak to us. I moved my workshops from the city to the country, where wind, water, mountains, animals, storms, and wild beauty could invade the senses. I gave myself permission to experiment with poetry, with gourds, rattles, drums, chant, and song. I burned cedar, sage, and sweet grass and let go of my self-consciousness about the world of the Spirit I had seemed so cautious about sharing. I prayed I could get out of the stuffy church in the back of my mind and call forth in others the gift of sweet spices that the dark woman in the sari had held on the stairs to the basement in the church.

Native ways began to teach me that life, and those of us in the middle of it, were in a hoop; that amid all our struggles, conflicts, and incompletions, we are in a sacred process of unfolding. We are *not* our past nor the split most of us grew up with in our thinking. The power in the metaphor of emergence means we can transcend our blocks and recreate our lives, if we hang on to sacred space.

All of us need an "enclosing circle"—a hut in the forest or a cave in the woods where somebody calls our name and gives us a chance to regroup. I had begun to see that the infant breaking through in so many dreams was a collective child whose creativity wanted to come to birth. It felt clear that healing the fragmented feminine, whether in men or women, first meant an appointment with the earth; the feelings, the senses, and the soul—rather than the high rafters of the intellect. Enlightenment seemed to want to come from the ground up.

3. Time on the Mountain: The Vision Fast

On the mountain there are songs on the wind
big gale or soft breeze, there are stories out there.
In the daytime rustling of leaves in warm sun,
in the sweeping howling gale, the biting frost wind,
the secret life in the earth has songs.
In the nighttime sounding of voices in dark air
secrets are told, old knowledge comes,
words of encouragement, ancient songs spinning
our name on the stars, rousing us in the long
needles of ancient pine and juniper. Soft echoes
of songs from times long past. Hearts,
when you walk on the mountain, its ridges and trails,
when you lie in flowering meadows,
just listen how the wind calls your name.
Be silent! the gates of the soul open here.
—Djohariah Toor

Sacred Winds

Because solitude often opens the doors to the unconscious, it is a valuable friend in breakthrough work. Retreats, a wilderness trek, or a vision fast can all be containers for change. When the opportunity to do a *Hanbleciya,* or vision quest, came up the following year, I signed on. A group of about twenty women began to meet regularly with our Hidatsa teacher in order to ready ourselves for the *Hanbleciya,* and to learn about her traditions, many of which were closely akin to those of the Lakota (to whom she was also related).

In the long preparation for the vision fast, I began to understand that the crossed feathers in my waking dream symbolized what Native Americans call the four directions (the Hoop and Four Winds). In Lakota teachings, the earth is said to be a circle with "a great, sacred hoop as its boundary."[1] The circle, according to Native traditions, is holy because it's the most basic shape of nature; it stands for wholeness, order, and living one's life in a good way. The hoop is the shape of life itself. There is an old Lakota teaching that says that when a person cuts through something living, he always finds a circle. The old people say that when we are in that hoop, we have life. We don't go to the Sacred Rim until the time of death. Likewise, a broken hoop is symbolic of brokenness and disharmony; it is a life in trouble.

The sacred four directions, like the cross, form a mandala divided into four quarters (a circle intersected by a horizontal and a vertical line). To the Lakota, the center of the earth is not a geometric location, but wherever one stands to pray.[2] The center of the hoop is a *crossroads* where the four winds meet, and where our path merges with the Holy. In Islamic mysticism that center is called the *Kabir,* the sacred point of union between heaven and earth. At a psychological level, that ground is the meeting place for all the different sides of our nature; the "enclosing circle" where all the wandering and split-off sides of the personality can come home and reconnect. The circle is the mythic shape of the self.

Straight from the heat of the lodge we began to receive teachings about these *wakan* powers, the four (primary) directions. Some Native Americans call them the "four old men," protecting spirits who walk with us into life.[3] They sit in a vast circle: West, North, East and South, and like the Christian concept of the trinity, they serve the Above. A Chippewa friend of mine called these helping powers the "children" of the Creator. The Hidatsa woman sometimes referred to the spirits in those directions as "Grandfathers."

In the Sweat Lodge Ceremony we always honored the directions. According to Ed McGaa, Oglala Sioux lawyer and author, the four directions come into the lodge where we pray, and "carry the life blood out of the lodge to the four quarters of our planet."[4] Our "life blood" is our sweat, our tears, and our prayers as they join with the prayers and the sweat of others in the lodge. Being in the *inipi,* or sweat bath, was a communion between us and the Creator, and the altar was always the earth and her elements. It often struck me that what we were doing in there was coming home to those elements; earth, air, water, fire—they were our offering.

From the West, we learned, comes the power of introspection and reflection; from the North, courage and purification; from the East, wisdom and rebirth; from the South, love and compassion. I began to sense that these directions, if one could consciously walk them, were a kind of medicine walk for the psyche. Here was the dream mandala shaping itself up.

In some ceremonies, the sacred pipe was often smoked and passed around the circle. Before the tobacco was lit, the Creator was always honored first, and the "children of the Creator" were honored next. Once the pipe was lit, the prayers began the circle West, North, East, and South. Our prayers were always said in a "sunwise" fashion— that is, following the natural rhythm of the sun, the same way we entered (and exited) the sweat lodge, or any sacred ceremony. Part of a holy order of things. Petitions were said to the helping spirit, the "Grandfather," in each direction. At times these four directions were also associated with an animal spirit, or messenger. The animals that were the spirit helpers in the directions were the Bear (West); the Buffalo (North); the Eagle (East); and the "four-leggeds," the Deer (South).

Each of the powers of the four directions is also symbolized by a color, but the colors (as well as the animals) ascribed to the directions vary among the tribes; the significance of one color or animal over another can depend on where one was raised, who one's parents were, the ceremony being conducted, or the particular persuasion of the medicine teacher. The blending of the tribes over the years adds to the differences one finds today.

In some of those early sweats it often seemed to me that sitting in the dark heat was like having a dream. The world of symbols often came mercurially to life. Under that dark blanket the conscious mind gradually gives way to the unconscious, to the chthonic and mysterious underworld of our conscious thoughts. In the total darkness, and often in a deep trance state, I often felt very near the archetypal energies that are the root of myth and story, the very fabric of religious process. The sweat was, like a retreat, a place where I could thin the veil between my busy mind and the rich images, thoughts, and feelings that wanted to come to life.

The West, characterized by the color black among many of the Plains tribes, represents a retreat into solitude, into the dark inside. It is the place of introspection. One Native American teacher said once, *"These Four Winds, they are a path for us. Each has a power from the Creator, a meaning for our life. Each has a spirit that helps us. When we pray in that way we ask for that spirit to help us to see inside ourselves, our thoughts, all that we do. When we face the West we ask for the power to examine ourselves, to see inside."* In the sweat lodge when I addressed myself to the old man spirit in the West, I asked for honesty and clear vision. I asked to understand my dreams, the feelings I still held in and the woman within I was only vaguely familiar with. Sometimes I contemplated the bear, who symbolized the kind of hibernation and solitude my life lacked. The bear is a solitary creature, at home with herself, and able to thrive in the coldest weather by knowing how and when to take refuge.

To the Hidatsa woman, the spirit of the North brings the ability to stand firm in the midst of trials. *"When we pray in that way we pray for courage. But we don't just ask to face the hard things in our life. We ask for courage to be ourselves, to say what is true, to be who we are. We need strength to do this."* The spirit animal in the North is the buffalo. The color of the North is white for the Lakota, but our teacher often spoke of the color red, symbolizing strength, boldness, and passion. The North also stands for purification, and in that direction we were reminded of the "power to stand" that the buffalo have when they have to endure the cold North wind. I have only seen buffalo from a distance, but one old man from the Plains once told me, *"These Buffalo, they have a strong spirit. Once they decide to move, they move. If there are fences in the way, it doesn't matter. The Buffalo moves through them just like they are nothing. When they stand, they stand and nothing can move them. The snows, the storm that comes down from the North, the cold, they can withstand anything. I have seen them and I know of this Spirit."*

When one faces the East, one asks for the blessing of dawn and new birth; for the light that brings wisdom and good vision. Because the sun comes from the East, it symbolizes new beginnings, a chance to start over every day. This direction reminds us to let go of the past, to release everything that might limit our way of seeing. The East governs our creative power, healing, and insight into the spiritual world. The spirit animal in this direction is the eagle. The Hidatsa woman told us, *"The Eagle Spirit is our Grandfather. He carries our prayers to the Creator. He is sacred because he is the closest of all the creatures to God."* The color she associated with the East was yellow, the color of the rising sun. In many mythologies yellow represents solar power, denoting goodness, intellect, intuition, renewal, the coming light. The Lakota honor the color red for this direction, also associated with sunrise. In myth, red is also a solar color, but depicts the full sun: fire, ardor, energy, and generativity.

To the South one turns to the heart. *"In the South we ask for a good heart, for all the ways of compassion, kindness, trust, love; we pray that we can always be humble, and remember to care for one another in a good way like that."* According to the Hidatsa tradition, the animal spirit in that direction is the deer, representing the four-leggeds, the gentle creatures that correspond to the nature of the heart. She often spoke of how important it was to watch the animals, to notice how alert they were. She told us we should practice that kind of alertness, both toward ourselves and others. The color she talked about for the South was white, describing gentleness, purity of heart, and transparence.

After the four cardinal directions, the pipe was filled again with more tobacco and pointed toward Father Sky, to the Spirit of life that listens to our prayers and receives our smoke offerings. My teacher prayed beautifully and simply and always to the point: *"Tunkashila, we are only here to pray for health and help. All our life begins and ends with you, Grandpa and Grandma. We are your children, your little ones, and we need your help so that we can always walk in a good way."*

Mother Earth, the land and all its gifts and creatures was honored next. *"When we touch the ground, we give thanks to our Mother Earth for all her blessings, for her beautiful land, her waters, and all that she brings us. We remember that we belong to the earth, and we are a part of all things; even the little creepy crawlies, they are our brothers and sisters."* The earth was to be our mother and our teacher. She was the place where we could center and renew ourselves.

Our teacher called God Father, Mother, Grandpa, Grandma; her prayers were always about relationship to the Creator. Although many Native Americans are patriarchal not unlike the early church fathers, our Hidatsa teacher was from a matriarchal background; to her God didn't have a gender. Likewise some of the old people I later met (on a reservation in northern Montana) were profoundly simple in their theology. They were, like the best of the Western mystics, creation-centered; God was in everything. In their prayers there was never any rhetoric; there were no sermons, no high rafters, no duality between flesh and spirit. God was everywhere.

Both my Hidatsa teacher and a Seneca/Iroquois woman I met the following year from the East Coast taught that there were actually seven directions. The Seneca woman once said, *"Sometimes we say there is a seventh direction too. Inside here, in the heart. This is where our paths cross with the Spirit. Here in the heart is where the Holy Spirit speaks to us. In here we hold everything that we know. In other words you and I are the seventh direction."*

I was intrigued by the directions not just because of the eagle feathers my friend had given me on the plains, or the studies of Native ways I had begun; but also because the Hidatsa woman, with her humor, her wisdom, and her simple quiet ways of knowing, sounded like an ancient Jungian analyst reflecting on the collective unconscious. I was struck by the similarity between the paradigm of the directions and Jung's concept of the archetypes; latent energies in the unconscious that can prompt healing—when we access ways to draw them out.

At a psychological level, the West represents the power of introspection. It initiates our journey into the inner world. Often the first stage in our journey to wholeness is an initiation; it takes us inside ourselves. Once introspection is under way, we begin to open the wounds that block healthy consciousness. We confront our own darkness and focus on what needs healing. In the West I often imaged the archetype of the monk or novice; the one who leads us into a retreat inside. The novice summons us into the unconscious; to see the things within us that are both terrifying and enlightening. The mystics of all ages have made such a rite of passage into the self.

The North, because it represents power and courage, is the warrior archetype, the one who steadies us in the midst of the strong winds that blow over the soul. This archetypal figure, like the solar hero, ensures us both a combat power (when we need it) and the strength to know our weaknesses. He or she symbolizes the task of standing strong through the process of purification and the cleansing of our past. The power of the warrior represents the courage it takes to be ourselves.

The East is about wisdom and giving birth. In this direction we meditate on the daybreak star and pray for understanding. In the East we try to "rise above" our complexes, we ask for clear vision so we can know our life purpose. The figure that emerges from that direction in the psyche is the age-old wise man or woman who sees beyond the material world to the inner realm of Spirit. As I meditated on the rising sun, on renewal, it seemed to me the archetypal energy we can draw on here is the midwife, one who mediates the light of consciousness to us. Our task in this direction is to midwife creativity.

The South, representing the things of the heart, is the lover arche-type; the inner figure that prevails over our feeling world and our relationships. The inner lover sees to it that we confront and move through our fears and rejections, to genuine love and compassion. The key to this archetype is our ability to feel the nature of loving from the inside out; to feel genuine self-respect and self-acceptance as a foundation for loving others. When love is in balance, it is a powerful nurturing and life-giving force.

The more I learned about the directions, the more they seemed a model for healing. The directions not only spoke to me of a helping power, they came alive for me as I meditated on them. Over time, the archetypal meanings of each of them sprang to life. Before I could relate in any meaningful way to these inner figures, however, I had to submit to a number of hard teachings. The directions were calling to me, and it was time to experience and to listen, not just talk.

Crying for a Dream

The Lakota say the fast means "crying for a dream."[5] Over the next year, our Hidatsa teacher began to prepare us for our first vision quest. Asking for a vision often means one goes off to a remote setting to fast, to pray, to empty oneself completely, and to wait on the winds of heaven. Fasting often helps clear the mind; it puts one in a kind of "zero" state, an emptiness that is pregnant. Fasting feeds the soul because it invites the Spirit to magnify and fill us. It offers us a chance to open the unconscious, to greet the images there, both frightening and empowering. It challenges us to sit with things we have too long scattered to the wind. One way or the other, it is always a swift severing of the things we have grown attached to, and a sure way to take one's defenses down.

My initial thought about doing a vision quest was a welcoming one; a time for solitude, prayer, rest. Yet over the weeks I also began to entertain a long list of second thoughts about fasting in the wil-derness. Unnerving images of cold, rain, mosquitoes, bear, and de-hydration crowded their way into the back of my mind. Being hungry was not the issue here.

When fear and doubt surfaced over the next few months, and they did, I reflected on the man on the plains, primitive, compelling, his dark hair almost blue in the sun. He would know something about the earth and her wisdom. At times I could almost smell the pungent ground we stood on baking in the hot sun, the scent of sage nearby rising on invisible waves of a midday heat, a leathery smell mixed with sweat and cedar. This image steadied me.

Gradually I began to realize that the inner figure I had met on the plains was an arthetype for wholeness; he embodied the wild—sensuality, earthiness, wisdom, power. Instinctively I knew he was coming to show me the healthy side of the masculine, to integrate the warrior and the lover I had split off. Whether he was an animus figure or a god or a spirit from beyond, I wasn't certain, but I had wild dreams about him. We rode his dark horses across the plains, ran through fields of sun-colored wheat, stood on the mountain together and faced dark storms, and we listened to the voices in the thunder. We stared at one another without speaking. I doubted the strength of his presence at times, and I was tempted to dismiss these fantasies, until I understood that we were healing the deep wound that had kept me from trusting the wedding of the deep masculine (the warrior) and the deep feminine (the lover).

What's more, these directions to which the inner warrior had been pointing had to be lived, not just intellectually studied or understood. Reason (that hubris in the intellect that has a tail like a peacock) had to bow before experience.

The Hanbleciya

This first vision quest, Lakota-style, high in the Rockies of Colorado, was a radical departure from my own comfortable spiritual practice. On the mountain I met fear, cold, isolation, hunger, boredom, and at times a joy so deep it ached. I also met some flaws in myself. Being alone in the wilds is like being in labor. It exposes the places in the heart where the wounds of trust, abandonment, and our worst fears lie. It also allows something sacred to emerge.

The day we arrived at the camp site in the southern Colorado Rockies, some ten thousand feet in altitude, it was raining. The land chosen for the *Hanbleciya* was a generous level meadow perched on the side of a large mountain. From the road above the camp we could already see the tent sites, the big sweat lodge, the groves of aspen shivering in the late morning shower. The friend who had driven my traveling partner, Mary Ann, and me up from Durango had brought along her little dog, an ancient dusty cocker spaniel. When we pulled up to the site, the three of us and the spaniel tumbled out, stretched, began to explore the camp and to greet the other questers. Mary Ann and I busied ourselves unloading our gear while our friend from Durango took her dog for a walk. The rain had released a warm shine to the grasses in the meadow, and the air smelled sweet with musk and green earth.

Mary Ann and I went about the work of choosing a tent site and had begun to clear away the pinecones and sharp rocks, leveling the ground that would be our camp for the next several days. We worked silently, out of reverence for each other; perhaps too out of a sense of anticipation of what lay ahead. All manner of thoughts would surface during that day, some welcome and some not, and quiet seemed the best way to greet them.

Later that morning a very nervous cocker spaniel and my friend arrived back at camp. The spaniel's hair was slightly on end and my friend was breathless and flushed with anger. *"I was just told no dogs are allowed here on the site. They say they bring bad luck, bad spirits. They told me if I left this dog in camp, they'd kill it."* We all stood there wide-eyed for a moment, then collected ourselves. In that case, we decided, the dog had to go. My friend from Durango picked up her old dog, loaded it into the van, and patiently began the long drive back home. Watching the dust the old van kicked up on the road, Mary Ann and I looked at each other not knowing whether to laugh or start hitchhiking.

I had been scheduled to go out on the mountain that same afternoon with the first group of questers. But because the airline had lost my luggage, and because we had arrived late, everything suddenly seemed a bit rushed. Inevitably came another list of second thoughts. In the Lakota tradition, one's first vision quest is generally only one night out, and I finally reasoned I should just trust my fate and go for the mountain. I had been eating lightly for some days already, and had begun to fast the morning we had driven up, so at some level, at least, I felt ready.

I finished unpacking, put a few things together with a sleeping bag, and went off with the group to assemble the traditional cloth "robes" (prayer flags that honor the six directions) that would mark our fasting spot. Each prayer robe was a large square of cloth representing the color of the traditional directions for the Hidatsa: black for the West, red for the North, yellow for the East, white for the South, blue for the Creator, and green for the Earth.

Each piece of cloth was carefully spread on the ground. Blessed tobacco was placed in one corner, closed off with string and a young eagle's feather, and tied to a long stick. Each of us took these sticks to the spot we had chosen for the night and busied ourselves digging six holes in the hard ground, one for each direction. The colored robes, carefully staked to the ground, would be our guardians for the long night.

There were other prayer ties going out on the vision quest with us. Months before our teacher had told us to begin the long task of making our tobacco ties—405 small squares of all six colors, tied at one-inch intervals on a long cotton string, each representing an aspect of the Spirit. Each square of cloth contained a small plug of pure tobacco which was to represent something or someone we wanted to pray for. Tying the tobacco cloths was always to be done in a sacred manner. *"When you think or pray tying these bundles, everything you do should have your attention. Remember, your thoughts are your prayers; so be careful what you take to the mountain. Try to be alert when you pray in that manner. Be alert when you walk, when you are sitting still, when you are talking. Try to be alert so that you will know when the Spirit is talking to you."*

By about four in the afternoon, the first group of us was ready. We met in the sweat lodge for our prayer blessing and a ceremony with the Sacred Pipe. To the Plains people, the pipe marks a time of communion. Tobacco is considered sacred because it is the smoke that sends our prayers to the Creator. In many traditions women are not allowed to use the pipe in any public ceremony, but since my teacher's ancestors were matriarchal, we had all learned how to use it. To "receive" our pipe was symbolic of receiving the blessing of the medicine teacher. During the quest one sits with his or her pipe, holds it all night long in a sacred manner, waiting for the Spirit. Some of us had been readied to have a Sacred Pipe at the time of the vision quest, and others had not. (This was a decision based on each person's ability and commitment to be a pipe carrier, and on the teacher's discretion).

Those of us who had no pipe received a sage bundle wrapped in a strip of red wool; this would be our "pipe" during the night.

Dressed in my buckskin shirt, a skirt (the traditional woman's garment for the quest), a pair of cowboy boots (not a good idea), a warm jacket, a wool hat, and clutching my sleeping bag and prayer ties, I started off with the first group. We met our helper in the camp, who would carry our bundle of ties and accompany us to our fasting spot.

One by one we located ourselves on the hillside above the long meadow near the camp. A helper accompanied each of us so that we could be "sealed" in for the *Hanbleciya*. As I entered my spot and sat down facing the west, my companion began to unravel the long bundle of colored prayer ties she had carried for me. I could hear her praying softly, carefully circling around and around my site, until the ties were hung. The colors of the tiny bundles wrapped reverently around me stood out in the rays of the setting sun. Vibrant, fluttering, caught up in the wind, all my prayers, all the moments of frustration, consolation, tears, all the intercessions that went into the work, hung around me like a tattered and splendid cloak. As one can feel ready and totally unprepared at the same time, so I was.

After my teacher sealed me in she prayed, asking the Creator Spirit for a good night for me. As she turned to leave, I experienced a profound sense of excitement. It had been almost two years since my dream, and I felt grateful to be here at last. I was aware of my tiredness too, of the long list of things I had managed to do before leaving. I thought of my clients, my family, all the people whose names went into the prayer ties. Gradually these slowly began to drift to the back of my mind. Big tears streamed down my face as I settled in for the setting of the sun and the open window I felt coming in the night sky.

I was aware of a swirling pattern of light the sun made through the trees as it began to fall behind the mountains. Spirals of brilliant light seemed to dance through the aspen, something I didn't recall ever noticing at sunset. I wondered at the beauty before me, sad that I had so seldom seen the full splendor of the sun's descent. I let the last rays soak into my body. Somewhere in the distance a pack of coyotes sang.

As night began to roll over me, I noticed that the silhouette of the trees directly in front, to the West, seemed to form into a man: a tall

Navajo dressed in the traditional way, a band across his forehead. His presence felt familiar. This Navajo fellow and I were going to have a conversation about why I should trust my own unconscious. The way he stood rooted before me, a powerful warrior guardian in the night, seemed no coincidence. Sometimes one senses that such figures have been there all along. Over the years they patiently protect and counsel us, uplift us as our parents should have, bless and hold us like guardians. We spoke late into the night, he and I, until the stars came out and he had convinced me that my darkness was a potent place. He told me that there was nothing to fear; it was what remained in the darkness that I should fear. I thought of the Gnostic gospel of St. Thomas in which Jesus is known to have said: *"If you bring forth what is in you, what is in you will save you. If you do not bring forth what is in you, what is in you may destroy you."*

A cold wind blew up the canyon most of the night, and I sat there rocking in my sleeping bag to keep warm, slipping down the embankment from time to time on the slick pine needles. I suppose it was a bad omen, but in one gripping slide, I knocked over the stick with the blue flag on it, the color given to the Creator. In trying to dig it back into its hole in the darkness, I snapped it in half. I sat holding my broken stake, wondering what it might mean. It bothered me to think that somehow my relationship to the blue robe, to God, might be broken in some way.

In the long night on the hillside, I noticed that the ground underneath me had become as hard as granite; I was aware that my backside felt frozen into the ground, and might stay that way permanently. I got up to go to the bathroom, and exited through my "door" to the south, attempting to find a suitable outdoor toilet in the pitch dark. Fumbling around without light, I fell over a rock into a tangle of underbrush, startling some elk grazing nearby and myself. Some distance away I could hear an owl hooting; a sentinel that must all along have been overlooking the small handful of us that night. Aside from her haunting cry, everything had grown silent. The trees with their continually changing shapes brought me more visual revelations, until a full moon gradually rose up, obscuring the silhouettes. Once or twice I fell asleep sitting up, startling myself by falling over.

When my helper came in the morning, I was both relieved and disappointed to see her. My vigil was over and I could soon break my fast with hot coffee, but I felt incomplete: the big revelation I hoped for hadn't yet happened. I had just lost my tolerance for the cold ground when I spotted her standing quietly behind me. We walked in silence back to camp.

The Return

The small group of us was led back into the lodge and given water to drink, blankets to warm us up, smiles of welcome from the women who had not yet gone out. One by one we sat in a circle and eventually began to speak about our night out on the mountain. In some traditions, the sharing of one's experience is an important part of the quest.

One of the women said that she had chosen what she thought was a good spot near a big tree, and only later discovered she had staked her flags near a huge anthill; right away she had to reconcile spending the next twenty-four hours with a pile of red ants. She realized that making this sort of hasty choice was something she did often. Another woman shared that she had become afraid, cold, really miserable until about three in the morning, when the wind gradually stopped. Just as she was beginning to warm up, collect her thoughts, settle into some reflection, a cougar had screamed loud nearby. *"I knew I couldn't leave my place, but every hair stood up on the back of my neck and for the first time in my life I felt utterly vulnerable. The only thing to do was to throw myself on God's mercy and sit it out. Then everything got very peaceful and still, and for the rest of the night, off and on, I cried tears of joy."*

Another woman spoke of her communion with a huge elk that was feeding nearby. *"I thought at first I might frighten him by my presence in his grazing field. Then I thought he might attack me. Then I dropped all that and made friends with him, just offering my prayers and knowing I was safe. I saw many shooting stars. The brilliance in the heavens was incredible. God was so beautiful in the dark."* As each woman spoke, she received some good counsel—a nod of affirmation from our teacher.

When it came my turn to speak, I told about the Navajo man, the warrior in the silhouette of the trees who seemed to call me to more honesty, who called me deeper inside. I spoke about a great figure to the North whose presence in the foliage of the trees seemed to have a voice too, telling me not to fear saying my feelings. I mentioned that I had chosen to sit on a slope, and that all night long I had found myself sliding down the mountain, until I had broken my stick with the blue robe. I apologetically, jokingly, recounted how I had chosen my spot in something of a hurry, wanting to be sure I didn't hold up the next person (since there had been only one trowel for all of us).

My teacher looked up at me, her smile vanished, and with an edge in her voice she told me that I had been sliding down the mountain for a long time. As my mouth was dropping open, she added: *"It's because you don't have any trust."* I tried to defend why I had hurriedly chosen my spot on slippery ground, but she was convinced otherwise; breaking the stick with the blue robe was a sign that there was a problem between my Creator and me. I don't know what a pin drop sounds like in a sweat lodge, but the quiet in there was painful. When the circle finally finished its sharing, I left the lodge feeling disappointed and somewhat humiliated, but looking forward, at least, to the hot coffee I could smell brewing on the camp's stove.

Sitting down by the creek later that day I decided that this unpleasant turn of events was not coincidence. I hadn't agreed with all that she implied, and I objected to being rebuked after a night in the cold, but I knew there was a reason this was coming up. Everything that happens on a vision quest is part of the process, and I stretched to take in the hard lesson. For one thing, the experience of humiliation felt like a huge test for me. As a child I had been familiar with its sting, with the paralysis I felt when shamed. That part of my past needed healing. I knew I needed to stand up to the rebuke and not shrink inside. I had to hear it, take it in, own what was mine, detach from the feeling of wanting to find approval, to make things right; or from the need to be favored by authority figures.

My poor choice of a spot was a teaching. I hadn't honored myself in my hastiness. Sitting down by the creek that afternoon, I knew I needed to allow her words in. Falling off the mountain, falling out of the tree, living outside the circle; they were all exits from the ground I most wanted to be in. All of them were symptoms of a life lived too quickly, with not enough inner quiet, and ultimately not enough trust.

Walking the Winds

Not long after my studies with the Hidatsa medicine woman had begun, I began to understand that the symbol of the enclosing circle was a message to stay within the framework of the germinative feminine, and to stay close to the world of Spirit. It was further not just a message to study the directions intellectually, but to try to meditate on them in some way, to feed the archetypal energies there, and to actively use them in my life. I had an appointment with each of the archetypal figures in those six directions, and they were going to teach me something. West, North, East, South, Grandfather Sky (the Creator), Grandmother Earth, all of these directions would be my teacher.

Although the meanings assigned to the respective directions differ from tribe to tribe, Native American traditionals *will* agree that the directions are sacred; they are the vital energies from the Creator that support our walk through life. The powers in the four directions that govern introspection, courage and purification, wisdom and rebirth, love and compassion are mirrored within each of us. As such they reflect a collective model for wholeness that has a mythic structure centuries old.

To Jung, the archetypal images that come from the unconscious (and from stories, myth, art, literature, and religious experience) are innate patterns of energy within the psyche, or soul. When consciously invoked, they can constellate wholeness. They literally guide the individuation process. Jung saw the psyche itself as divided into four parts, which he called the four functions. Each of those four functions has its own character that can guide the personality. There's an enlightening book that explains how these four functions work in the male psyche: *King, Warrior, Magician, Lover* by Robert Moore and Douglas Gillette. In the current mythopoetic men's movement there is a lot of attention paid to these four functions. They are, like the "old men" that hold up the four corners of the world, inner figures that we can bring to life.

Although there are strong parallels between these basic four healing archetypes and the concept of the four directions, I don't propose to equate them. To do so might be possible, but I want to approach this through the feminine creative side, which has fewer linear agendas. The parallels I do draw in this writing are more or less intuitive ones, and reflect a more experiential approach to the work. My hope is to offer the following chapters as an invitation to explore these Sacred Winds and arrive at one's own conclusions.

People who have marked out time to work on themselves or to get a clearer picture of the Spirit have often found that the agenda they have started out with is not the one they need to follow at all. Any new experience, any journey we make to the *realm of the Mothers,* often demands we let go of our expectations and just follow the lead from within.

In my own meditations, for instance, I have found myself drawn to honoring Mother Earth as the fifth direction, and turning to the Creator as the next, or final direction in my prayers. I have chosen that sequence for these next chapters as well. The important thing to remember is that the directions are not a formula for the linear mind, but simply an invitation to walk inward and to pause and reflect on whatever direction each of us is intuitively drawn to. In this way hopefully each of us can keep to the safe path of a beginner.

Not everyone has to make a trip to the wilderness, or undergo a vision fast or a sweat lodge, in order to make such a journey. The work itself is deeply personal, nonprogrammatic, and can be done in one's own backyard. The important thing is to enter the ground inside ourselves with a willingness to experiment, to release what we already know, to hunger for what we don't know. The important thing is to empty ourselves, to open our hearts and minds to the winds, so we can hear their wisdom.

4. The West and Sees Within

In that first year after my vision quest I began to understand that the paradigm of the directions, as they took on flesh and bones, was a way to explore the wilderness in the soul. Throughout the year, my thoughts went frequently back to my first night on the hill, and back to an image that had had a profound effect on me. I had been watching the setting sun fall gently into a distant indigo lap of the Rockies, spilling wild colors in its descent through a ring of clouds that hung on the western horizon. Gradually the sky had turned a bright crimson and the clouds took the shape of a red horse with a small rider on its back. The shape of the clouds remained somehow constant for nearly twenty minutes, and I could not take my eyes away from the image. My thoughts suddenly carried me back to a time in childhood I hadn't remembered for years. When I was eleven my parents silently divorced, my mother inconspicuously remarried, and no one in the family had ever discussed it past the announcement phase. I remembered that during that time I began making friends with a huge dappled gray horse at a stable not far from our house. I took him out alone and rode hard, pitching the sharp edges of my grief into fantasy adventures in which I was always in a cosmic drama of one sort or another. I sat on his great back in those days and in the wind that swept past our dance, I forgot my sadness.

As the sky that first night on the mountain began to change I heard an inner voice, subtle yet unmistakably clear: "All throughout your life I have held you, carried you, never left your side. When you sit tonight on this mountain, open your heart to the night and let it carry you where it will. When you leave this mountain, don't be aloof from the child you see in the clouds, for that child is you. Give in to her needs. Give in to her sadness. Give in to her exuberance. Carry her as I have carried you." I pulled my jacket up around my ears and wondered how I could be so intelligent and so stupid a creature all at once. I had made such endless demands on this child, neglecting her at times, demanding that she fit my agendas, that she conform to what I imagined others wanted to see in her. What would it take, I wondered, to plunge even more deeply down inside; to pierce the subtlest of my defenses; to confront my ego and all its games and intellectual strongholds; to walk with more certainty into what some mystics have called the dark night of the soul?

Each time I faced West that following year I asked for the resolve to enter the dark house inside like a novice, with an open mind and few judgments about what I might find there. I asked again for the patience it took to spiral down inside. I prayed I could stand up to the gutsier inventories inner work demands. I had become familiar with many of the characters in my dreams—the sirens, judges, thieves, and urchins—and I was looking for ways to make room for them in my life. Like most people I had known, however, I could see and name my faults and weaknesses, but I had trouble seeing and naming my strengths. I had trouble imagining that some radiant creature lived in there on that vast plain. I'd had glimpses of her fiery soul and her passionate heart, but she was elusive. This psychic dilemma is shared by many of us on a healing path. Few people in our past have accurately mirrored the truth inside the soul; few have really ever looked deeply enough within our eyes to validate the original self; few have ever called forth the wild radiance inside or the God of Original Blessing. In the West one must reckon with self-abandonment, but at the same time search out the beauty still cloaked inside the inner child.

The West is the first direction one turns to in the Lakota Hidatsa tradition. The Hidatsa woman used to say that facing the West, the place of the setting sun, was about learning to honestly face inside oneself, to navigate the dark in one's heart. Jung's work with the unconscious began on the Western shores of the psyche—in the pitch dark of the unknown side of the mind. John of the Cross and Theresa of Avila spoke frequently of the journey into the soul as a foray into night, into the hidden fragments of one's past. Mystics of every tradition tell us that one must not fear the dark, but make friends with it. It is the fertile darkness that incubates the light. The psychic blueprint here is that one cannot meet the Big Holy without first opening the door to the self and walking through it.

The West and the Novice

In the lodges my Hidatsa teacher often spoke of the West as the power called *"sees within."* She joked with us often about how we non-Indians seemed to make our life centered in the head, whereas the Great Spirit often chose the heart as a dwelling place. *"Sees within"* was a way to keep the doors to the inner world open; a way to confront the coverings over the personality that keep life permanently on hold.

To many of the Plains tribes, the helping spirit that sits in the West is the Bear. To contemporary Lakota teacher Wallace Black Elk, the Grandfathers that sit in the West are called Thunder Beings, the keepers of thunder and lightning.[1] In myth the dark that follows the setting sun represents the forces of night, and the inner world of dreams and self-knowing. The color of the West is typically black.

The season represented by the West is autumn, marking a pause after the long daylight of summer, a time to slow down, pull in, and introspect.[2] In the fall I start to think about laying up wood for the fire; I pull out last year's undone projects that are best done on long winter nights. It's a time of sorting through things, of processing summer dreams. I become a little like the bear in the fall season. When I have seen them in the woods or along some of the streams my husband and I have fished in the wilder parts of British Columbia, they are private creatures. Unless they are mating or cubbing they seldom like much company. Their solitary wanderings are instinctively motivated, and they know where the best caves are.

Each of the directions, with its companion archetype, as I walked and prayed it, appeared as though to help me chart the unconscious. As they more or less took shape in my imagination, each of these figures seemed an important psychic function I needed to know more intimately. In the West the novice drew me to explore a more primitive side of myself; feelings, instincts, the sensory world underneath the intellect, the body, dreams; this was all her territory. The novice figure in each of us (as any good bear would) disdains our books, our linear mind, our worldly knowledge; she calls us to an appointment with the unseen. A good rule of thumb here is openness, honesty, and a willingness to let go of old knowledge (what we think we know). The novice is an adventurer into inner vision.

The Visions of Black Elk

The sacred directions I will refer to in this and the following chapters are related to a prophetic vision a young Indian boy experienced in the mid-1800s (before the battle of Little Big Horn). I want to recount part of that story here, since our look at the directions will partially parallel the vision. I came upon *Black Elk Speaks* some years ago, while a student of clinical psychology. The small text offered itself to me as a salve during a time I needed a renewal in my spirit.

Oglala Sioux medicine man Black Elk, while still a young boy of nine, had a profound vision in which he spoke with the Ones the Indians call the Grandfathers, the keepers of the sacred directions. During a grave illness, in which he was thought to be near death, he was taken out of his body and brought to the spirit world. There the boy saw a great tipi, the door of which was a bright rainbow. Peering through the entrance, he saw six old men sitting in a row inside. The oldest of them spoke gently to the boy and told him not to be afraid and to come inside. *"So I went in and stood before the six, and they looked older than men can ever be—old like the hills, like stars."*

When Black Elk looked more closely at the six old men, he saw that they were the Ones the people called the "Powers of the World." The oldest of them spoke again and said: *"Your Grandfathers all over the world are having a council, and they have called you here to teach you."* When the young boy looked first to the Power of the West he saw a wooden cup filled with water, and in the water he could see the sky reflected. From the voices of the Grandfathers in his vision, the sacred spirits from the West, Black Elk heard them say: *"Take this [the cup]. It is the power to make live, and it is yours."*[3]

If I look at this vision with a beginner's eye (how else does one look at visions?) it seems the West is an invitation to hold the cup of the self, to look deeply at what's reflected there. The water in that cup is the water of life. When we take up that cup, the journey begins.

More than any of the other directions, the symbol of the West in the psyche is about delving into whatever the past has shaped in us that's painful and disruptive. The work we face in this direction is about lifting the lid on the defenses we normally carry around and talking the truth to ourselves. The point of *"sees within"* is to encounter the feeling world we've abandoned; to experience tears, rage, sorrow, fear, and to give ourselves to the task of letting go.

Facing into the West begins with the hard work of inventory and the honest making of amends that people in Alcoholics Anonymous and analysis do; but even more than that, it's addressing the issue of abandonment and failure at a more personal level. That means getting to the root of our primary loss and opening that wound. Most of us in time can see our wounds. But the problem is, we try our best not to feel them.

All of us at one time or another have experienced psychic hurts; somebody in our past hasn't loved us enough, affirmed or encouraged us; someone may have abused or deeply betrayed us. For most people the first line of defense we learn teaches us to adapt, ignore, or cover these pieces over. Gradually we press them out of conscious awareness and "move on." The West is an honest appointment with the pain underneath our denial.

Any breakthrough experience can be an occasion for personal awakening, but there is a trick to staying awake. The role of the novice shows us how to work with a beginner's mind; as though we were seeing and feeling everything for the first time. The novice accepts the task of showing us how to be honest with ourselves so our initiation won't be short-lived. In each of us there is this "power to make live." Somewhere inside, no matter what the past has been, is always the possibility for choosing life without the dead weight of the past.

Inner Vision and the Black Light

In the sweat lodge when the door is covered and the ceremony has begun, the naked eye sees nothing because all the openings are sealed. But with the inner eye one can sense a light, a knowing from one's spirit, that comes from this seemingly total darkness. Contemporary Lakota teacher and medicine man Wallace Black Elk talks about what he calls the "black light," a phenomenon one sometimes encounters in the sweat lodge ceremony.[4] When we enter into the work of introspection, and our eyes grow accustomed to the dark, we see into our hidden nature, into the past that we have forgotten or covered over. We feel our way into pain and hidden conflict, but eventually we encounter light. Yet the first task is to allow the dark side of the unconscious to release its secrets.

I worked with a woman who had a frightening dream that kept repeating itself. In the dream a large shadowy figure appeared in the doorway of an old childhood house. The figure grabbed her and pressed its huge form over her until she couldn't breathe. She screamed and struggled but no one heard her. Each time the dream repeated itself the impact of it intensified. As she told the dream her hands rubbed her lower stomach and hips. I noticed this and asked her to be aware of her hands, and what they might be doing. She closed her eyes and continued the circular rubbing movement. Suddenly she began grabbing frantically at her sides, as though a child might do, trying to pull up her underwear. Her whole body then collapsed onto the floor and she began crying out in the sudden memory of being sexually assaulted by a friend of her older brother. As the memory flooded fully into consciousness, she lay in my arms and sobbed. As dark and frightening as this experience had been for her, she had encountered the truth that would begin to heal her divisions.

Many people are anxious about uncovering the pain of the past, but memory can be toxic to the body and the psyche if we don't allow it a way out. To open secrets, especially the more painful ones we may not even remember, takes gutsiness and resolve, but the work always opens vital insights (light) to consciousness.

One woman told me that after she had been in therapy about a year she had suddenly become very depressed. She had been trying to deal with emotional and physical abuse from an alcoholic father and had, at first, done fairly well in her recovery process. Then this black cloud descended over her and she felt paralyzed. *"I stayed stuck in this awful cloud for about a month. I couldn't do anything. It felt like my life was over, that the betrayal I felt would never go away. There were days I felt such rage I thought I was going nuts. Then one day I got in my car and headed to a river that was near our old family cabin. I went down to the water and picked up these huge stones and threw them, one after the other, into the water. I smashed them on the bank*

*and I screamed and yelled and cried until I just fell down in a heap. I
had so much inside that no amount of understanding was going to help.
I just had to get it out."*

In the West not only do we uncover trauma or feelings we have
long repressed, but we also disrobe old messages, negative impressions
that keep our "power to make live" trapped. Memory, when fragments
of it split off into the unconscious, gradually forms into a "voice" that
governs us from below. Moods, airs, vague feelings, or attitudes we
suddenly experience (that seem to come from nowhere) can sabotage
us before we know what is going on.

Many people tell me that the moment they begin to peer inside,
they notice something they hadn't seen before. Namely, that different
days bring different moods, feelings, thoughts, attitudes, and behaviors; as though a random life lived its life inside of us. These "moods"
are often remnants of past impressions; things from the past we've
stored away and long forgotten. When we see within, we start to experience how these old impressions govern our thoughts and feelings.

In therapy or group work, as people begin to see themselves mirrored in the cup, the list of characters that emerge from the unconscious is impressive. There are the voices that have encouraged us
(thanks to the people who have affirmed and loved us); there are
voices and impressions that discourage and confuse us. Many of these
negative voices feel it their duty to judge, condemn, criticize, deny,
inflate or deflate us; left unchecked they can pirate away our best
goals and intentions. These negative voices are adaptive elements of
our personality that have formed from defenses, insecurity, from the
bum steers we often get in childhood.

Contemplative Thomas Merton once said, "Every one of us is
shadowed by an illusory person."[5] That person is a private (but
wounded) self that wants to convince us to live outside the circle of
God's love. In most of us there exists a voice that comes from this
false place. It is a product of our failures (or the generational failures
before us). One woman said once, *"There's a petty tyrant inside me I'm
beginning to notice. He jerks me around, tells me I'm wrong, that I can't
do it right, that it's not okay to make mistakes. He seduces me into feeling
like I've got to live my life constantly on guard. The Christ in my spirit
tells me I'm lovable like I am, but the tyrant inside can't wait to bring
me down."*

Other negative voices in the unconscious tend not to deflate, but to inflate us. I know people who think what they do is just about perfect, who have no trouble asserting themselves, who can justify and excuse themselves (or blame others) at the drop of a hat. Othello-like inflations tend to overdefend the ego, masking dangerous blind spots. (I work with some people who imagine that if there's a problem in their life, that it's someone else's fault). Along the same lines, addictive behaviors often need an inflated inner voice that protects one from feeling too much conscience. People in any sort of recovery work often say they fell headlong into their own brand of addiction because they lied to themselves about what they were doing. Uncovering these blind spots, and working to release them, is the task one faces in the West.

Denial, the opposite of "sees within," can infect an emotional wound and keep it in the dark indefinitely. Adult children, for instance, who have been abused in some way often cover that wound out of shame. Over time, the rage underneath the betrayal they experienced as a child builds an enormous pressure in the unconscious. Sometimes the conflict stays hidden at the conscious level; but unconsciously, what has been squeezed into a back corner in the mind suddenly acts out. If we don't lance this wound, we remain the victim of that abuse (and continue to allow others to abuse us), or we become a perpetrator at some level. A man who suffered at the hands of a dominating and controlling mother marries a woman who, after the romance wears thin, turns out to be just like his mother. He is victimized twice. A woman I know, once emotionally and sexually abused by her parents, and in overt denial about how that had affected her, eventually turned and emotionally abused her two children.

Few individuals caught in denial notice the red flags before the pressure builds up to dangerous levels. Without the ability to see within our own darkness, what we fear and hate the most is suddenly liable to show up on our own doorstep. Fortunately it will also surface in the "black light," given the right container for healing. When one agrees to this kind of inventory, the potentially destructive energies of the dark side can be transformed.

Once any of us confronts the dark inside, most of us also see that a tremendous potential for growth exists there. The key to this work is a willingness to suspend our judgments about what we'll find, a willingness to let go of our fears long enough to see how they limit and disempower us. Once past the lancing of our oldest wounds, we discover there are gems inside, hidden potentials in the darkness.

The West and "Going Behind the Blanket"

The West symbolizes the season of fall, and represents one's need to slow down, rest, and reflect. Author Evelyn Eaton tells a story about the Indian custom of "going behind the blanket." Once while looking for a friend on a reservation she was visiting in Owens Valley, California, she accidentally aproached the wrong house. She knocked at the door and stood on the porch and waited. Just inside the screen door she saw an old woman cross the room and sit down in her rocker. Choosing not to acknowledge her guest, she then covered herself with a large blanket. The old woman sat there slowly rocking, wrapped up in her quilt, until her unwanted guest went away.[6]

Going behind the blanket, a key to introspection, is a way to bolt the door to the outer world for a time, and to enter a more conscious silence. *"No flies come into a closed mouth,"* as the Indian expression goes.[7]

To face the West means we initiate a dialogue with ourselves. It marks a time we set aside daily, in order to find a more inward rhythm. Without an internal sense of ourselves, the original self has no ground to stand on, no way to express its needs. To some degree, all of us get foiled here. If caretaking others, pursuing noble causes, making a living, staying fit, being productive, or chasing after outcomes keeps us away from an honest dialogue with ourselves (and it will), then we need to retreat. When we stay in this obsessive, addictive, half-crazed state, when we value production more than the art of living, our goose is being cooked. This is no new news to mystics and children; convention has duped us. For a sip of the elixir of security and productivity, we betray ourselves. In the Western world most of us avoid healthy solitude, but introspection needs a time and place to germinate. Kabir has the idea when he says:

> *Suppose you scrub your ethical skin until it shines,*
> *but inside there is no music,*
> *then what?*[8]

When we wake one day to find how far outside the circle we've gone, and can finally admit it (which takes some doing), it's often wise to get help from someone who is in the circle, or at least who has some bridges to it. The task in the West can seem overwhelming, but our role here is really one of a student. Any process of initiation needs a teacher or guide; someone who can read us the roadsigns in heavy fog.

Shadow and Radiance

In *The Road By the River* I described the unconscious as a coin with a dark side and light side. On the light side of the coin is something like our potential self, our full-blown radiance. There's grace and power, creative fire and genius. In that place are artists, poets, musicians, and ordinary people who have learned how to risk being fully present to life. German mystic Hildegarde of Bingen addresses this side when she says:

> *Good People,*
> *most royal greening verdancy,*
> *rooted in the sun,*
> *you shine with radiant light.*[9]

One doesn't have to be a mystic to know about radiance. One simply has to have slept under the stars enough; or possibly to have believed in the magic of one's childhood long enough. Science and most mystics say that there is life buried in the dark house of our cells. We have resources within that are restorative, creative, waiting to germinate.

The other side of the unconscious, which we've previously touched on, contains a darkness that eclipses our radiance. When our childhood path has been unsure, difficult, or hurtful in some way; when others have dealt wounds to us, we sooner or later erect building blocks in the personality that help us survive and adapt to our world. It is these building blocks, however, that eventually form a thick wall around our feeling life. The shadow, that character in the psyche that acts out whatever events we have repressed and whatever energies our parents didn't like, gets its start whenever we begin to deny our feeling world.

A colleague of mine once said, *"When I was a kid, I had no childhood. We had to be perfect; good grades in school, quiet in the house, no making waves. My mother was a good woman but she breathed religion and perfectionism down our necks. Where was shadow going to live in that house? I only met him on Saturday nights. From that point on, I got into plenty of trouble—drugs, sexual acting out, wild parties. I was fairly split down the middle, with these two irreconcilable people inside."*

This hidden corner of the psyche has to carry an enormous load over time, especially if we don't acknowledge these hurts and, moreover, try to cover our pain with accomplishments—which most of us do. A young man said once, *"My childhood was wonderful for a while. Then a rift happened. It started with kindergarten, with parents who said, 'Don't make noise, learn the rules, do well, don't disappoint us.' Pretty soon it wasn't safe to be myself; to have real feelings, temper, tears, needs. My feelings disappeared, went into hiding. I ate to cover my hurts. I buried myself in my room with books. I became obsessed with the world of cum laude. Until now I never realized how much I sacrificed of myself to keep up these pretends."*

By the time most of us have experienced the first few initiations of childhood, not only have we rejected our feeling world (and thus created shadow), but there is also a cloak around our brilliance, our capacity for aliveness. Addictive processes often have this sort of early-childhood beginning. We are hungry for love and affirmation, and when it is denied, we fill ourselves by the striving of the mind, and the intake of foods or substances that become a substitute for affection. When the heart is starved in childhood, we will find ways to fill it as adults.

A woman said of her adolescence: *"In my late teens and early twenties I experienced a certain moodiness. Sometimes an anxiousness or melancholy settled over me which I could never explain at the time. I thought I was doing what I should be doing in my life, and outwardly everything appeared to be in order, but sooner or later this melancholy would show up. Had I not had my potter's wheel to spin these moods out with, I am certain I would have been in deep trouble. Obviously, as I look back on it now, I was melancholy because I repressed so much of my instinctual world. In my family behavior got rewards, not feelings. I finally realized that growing up I should have mourned and raged at the terrible losses I felt in my childhood; my father, my spontaneity, the rakish girl who loved lightning* and summer storms, who never wanted to come in out of the rain; the one whose passion was so full. My inner child was a mix of unexpressed sadness, rage, a fiery love for life, and yet I kept her in for years. She was cloaked under pink organdy."

Most of us lock up our power and aliveness this way. One woman said to me recently, "I want to do this inner work but I'm scared. Something in me says it's right, but I'm scared of what I'll find there. I'm scared someone will really see me. Maybe what they see, they won't like. What if my wildness comes railing out and hurts somebody or gets me into trouble, what then? I long to know her, but she terrifies me. I'm afraid of this much passion."

Although they seem like opposites, however, radiance and shadow are mutually interdependent; they share adjoining rooms in the psyche. Radiance, our capacity to love and feel, is released when shadow is confronted. One of the reasons these two energies get tangled up in the first place is that when we are children—and we are too wild or exuberant or too hurt or disillusioned—the energies of our radiance have no place to go; the unused potential within is locked up and gradually slips off into some corner in the unconscious. Personal power, love, sensuality, our capacity to feel, is energy that, when denied and unused, eventually falls into the wrong place, eventually manifesting as a symptom of one kind or another.

Almost every person I have worked with over the years has something in the heart that has been neglected, overlooked, forgotten, covered over, both negative and positive. But the power of the heart, when it is kept dormant, is never growth-productive. When we are not allowed to love and rage and feel freely as children, to express our innate wild, a crippling results, and these feeling states become reversed. When love is wounded, we can feel hatred, rejection, abandonment, and mistrust, and can carry a fear of intimacy that goes back to the original wound.

A woman in a workshop said once of herself: "I feel such self-doubt. I feel like I'm not good enough, not pretty enough, not smart enough, that I'll never have a life. I just feel so critical of myself. It's not even a rational thing, because I know better. I know I'm capable and talented, I know I can love. But emotionally, I don't believe myself." If in childhood the container of the heart was closed because of criticism, abuse, invalidation, then the covering over the heart blocks the feeling world.

When we look within, we often have to go to the root of where the heart got put on hold. The original wound has to be released to consciousness.

This woman, in subsequent work, began to feel as though she had been sexually abused by her father. As more and more memory fragments became conscious, it was clear that she had been. The women in the family hushed the secret until the work of repression in the child's mind was complete; but the heart of the child had known it over the years, and it tore her level of trust in herself. Her shadow and her brilliance were both imprisoned. This abandonment that she had experienced as a young child was something she had carried half her life.

Abandonment has its roots in the past, but we continue to levy it against ourselves in the present. A woman I knew once said she was afraid of letting her real feelings out because her husband couldn't cope with conflict. She later admitted that it was she who wouldn't allow her real feelings to emerge. *"I always wanted to get out of the house and work, to pursue a career, yet he never wanted me to. He always said he'd rather have me home, even after the children were grown. I felt angry and frustrated about this for years, but never asserted myself or confronted him. I just kept it all in and tried being inconspicuous with my own interests. Then one day I noticed I had developed some painful cysts in my breast. I was suddenly struck by the fact that at some level these cysts were my unspoken feelings, my rage and hurt and tears unsaid. I knew from then on that I needed to let myself out. I needed to stand up to him with my feelings, no matter how they came out. I knew for a fact these cysts could turn into a malignant bitterness if I didn't."*

A young man recently came to see me because he had had what he thought was a heart attack. Taken to the hospital with symptoms of numbness in his body, pain down his left arm, rapid heartbeat, and loss of breath, he was surprised to hear his heart was fine; it was his stress level that wasn't. As we worked it became clear that although he was very successful at work, although he had the appearance he was his own man, there was somebody inside being oppressed. On the outside there was this performer, a there-for-you kind of person. On the inside was a wild Irishman who wanted a lot more passion out of life. For fear of rocking the boat, however, he kept his inner fire stifled. Shadow got stifled too; speaking his true feelings, having a different opinion, behaving rakishly, dancing on the bartop, saying "no" with some conviction, all these things got stuffed into the recesses of his mind. Yet when the fire can't come out, when our self-control or self-consciousness is too constraining, it erupts as a full-blown anxiety attack. This was the shadow as a trickster, coming up in a physical way to complain he'd been under raps for too long.

Among other things, divorcing shadow can cause depression, panic attacks, melancholy, addictive processes, and somatic symptoms. Yet the trickster in the shadow doesn't just put a hold on sadness, anger, hurts, and needs; it also adamantly withholds our joy.

The Story of Raven and the Seaweed Coat

In Tsimshian legends among the people of the Pacific North Coast there are stories of what happens when a person and their shadow become separate. In the book *Raven's Children,* Raven is portrayed as a god, a Creator figure whose job it was to create life and look after it. Over the course of time, however, Raven took on the nature of a trickster, thinking only of the pleasure of food and the good life. One day he met a figure called Shadow and they decided to travel together.

In the story, Raven and Shadow were paddling along the shores of the ocean and Raven suddenly felt very hungry. When he saw some people on the beach drying fish near their village, all he could think of was a way to finagle some food. Realizing he probably didn't look like someone who could impress the villagers, Raven grabbed up some shiny seaweeds and mosses, some fancy strands of small mussel shells, and draped them as impressively as he could over his plain appearance. Then he told Shadow to go ahead of him. So as to impress the villagers, he was to tell them "an important *chief*" was about to come—a great person they should naturally invite in. Raven hid behind a bush while Shadow went down to deliver the message.

"Shadow walked along the beach, and when the people there turned and looked at him, he called out: 'An important thief is stalking by your village, my people, invite him in!' All the people ran into their houses. Everything was quiet."[10]

The story goes that in spite of what Raven commanded Shadow to say, Shadow always said the opposite. Yet no matter what trickery found its way up Raven's sleeve, Shadow got the blame. Eventually Shadow got tired of being held accountable for everything Raven did, and the two parted company.

The story asks how we mortals might keep from alienating, and not underestimating, the power of shadow. We need shadow to remind us when we're not being honest with ourselves. There are times I drape myself in seaweed and moss pretending to be a wondrous thing in the eyes of others. I stand tall in my inflations, and I forget shadow and I are related at all. The only thing that saves me, when I want to disown my shadow, is to turn instead, and face her head-on. The truth is shadow is one of those inner characters that is an enigma; on one hand she's an embarrassment; on the other, she's a valuable friend I need to listen to.

When we agree to release anger, pain, grief, or the hurts in the past, we automatically begin to transform the destructive side of the shadow we have been hiding. But most people are suspicious of what they cannot predict or control. Rather than allowing the release of the shadow energy, people often judge themselves, feel shamed, anticipate rejection, get paralyzed, and, like Raven, go around in a wrap of seaweed.

One of the major obstacles to breakthrough is the problem of external referencing. When we are very young we don't learn how to respond to life without depending on and finding approval from others. The first thing that happens is that we often got lost in other people's expectations. Willingly or unwillingly we got tangled in their complexes, fears, hopes, and dreams, in the best and worst of their conventions. In order to appease and impress the people around us, the contents of our shadow side had to become the enemy, to be driven out of consciousness.

Clearly the conditioning we experienced as children, namely that of having to placate, survive, or get along with others, means we had to both give up our original self and, like all good children, become responsible for the people in our environment.

The complication here is that our self-image begins to live somewhere outside the circle. When any of us relinquishes our ability to think, feel, and respond from our own inner point of reference, then our self-esteem is vested in others and what they think; and what we *think* they might think. Being responsible for others amounts to self-sacrifice; it also means shadow energy will begin its repressive journey and the heart will go into indefinite hiding. We cripple the "power to make live" because we have betrayed out own identity.

Dreams will often illustrate the conflict between the old identity, the new one trying to surface, and the shadow we'd like to disown. *"I am traveling by train somewhere. I get on and sit down and for the while the ride is beautiful, the landscape we move through is spectacular. It is like the fields and mountains I knew as a child. The train stops and I start to get off, but my purse is gone. I have lost it, or someone's stolen it. I am frantic because I can't get off without it. It's got all my credit cards, my wallet, my address book, but I can't find it anywhere. A dark gypsy woman enters the train and looks angrily my way. She sits down next to me and stares hard into my eyes. I feel my heart beating wildly. I sense she will attack me. I want to get up and run from her but I am paralyzed."* The dreamer here is moving through the old identity (the landscape reminiscent of childhood) and is attempting to come to a new one. When she comes to the new place, she's suddenly without means (the security of her old identification, symbolized by everything in the purse). The gypsy enters angry and threatening and the dreamer is terrified. Apparently the old identity has had little tolerance for the gypsy (the wild side, colorful, spontaneous, free, creative, a bit of a renegade). Naturally the gypsy, furious at having been stuffed away and denied in the name of convention, wants to throttle the nice woman on the train.

The way through external referencing is no easy route. It helps to observe how we get caught in it; to note how the world outside controls where our point of reference is. During a weekend retreat on personal growth I asked the group to do a certain exercise as a sort of warm-up. In the first part, I suggested that the participants walk around the room and greet one another, say their name, do whatever they do to introduce themselves. In the second exercise I asked the group to try another kind of greeting, one that might be a surprise to the other person. I asked them to greet one another in a very unconventional way, do something outrageous, socially unacceptable; something they'd never do in the White House. The whole group faltered, the smiles of greeting vanished, the handshakes and how-do-you-dos hung in midair. No one knew what to do to be outrageous; and no one wanted to be socially unacceptable. A silence crept over the room until finally I walked over to a tall, dignified-looking scientist, pulled off his sock and stuck it in his pocket, then turned to someone else and stuck my head under her skirt. Gradually some life came back into the room.

If we are externally referencing most of the time, as most of us are, we're in touch with somebody else's feelings (as we imagine them to be) and not our own. This is self-abandonment. A self-consciousness then sets in that acts like Rasputin. When we subsequently strive for *self* approval, we are a target for an internal judge that will cause us no end of trouble. Looking for self-approval always implies that there's an inner critic inside whose sole function is to target our slightest mistakes and imperfections. But how can the divine wildness emerge when there's a critic standing at the gate between the conscious and unconscious mind? In the West, one learns to identify and confront the internal voices that intimidate and disempower us.

It's enlightening to ask ourselves what of our vitality and radiance has been tied up in shadow. Most importantly, how do we reclaim the energy that the dark side of the unconscious holds? To the novice exploring the unconscious—whether the territory is the shadow, the pain of past abuse, repressed anger or sorrow, blind spots in a relationship, or a big ego that suddenly crashes—the dark is never the enemy; shame is the enemy. The darkness is fertile. If we can trust destiny, keep our sense of humor, and embrace the thing, the shadow has its light side.

A young boy had a dream once that poignantly sums up what it means for us to begin embracing the dark. He told this dream to his grandmother while they were on their way to a conference. *"There was a dragon in this room I was in. He was jumping up and down on a big trampoline. The dragon had no eyes, no ears, no feet, no hands, and no heart. I knew I had to jump down its mouth and I was scared. I had to jump down and I did, but I came out its tail."*

Later on during the train ride with his grandmother, he said, after telling her the dream: *"I think the dragon did have a heart."* His grandmother, a psychotherapist, told the dream at the conference, a workshop expressing the power of dreams and inner work. In a sense, if we are going to cleanse the wounds that have hurt us, we have to face the dark of the dragon's mouth until we are ready to slide out the tail.

I felt very touched by the poignancy in this boy's dream. When any of us faces the dragon with the huge mouth, we confront our worst fears: we walk into our hurts, our abuses, the wounds of the past. We walk into and face the ghosts in our family tree; we confront the unclean spirits in our own face-saving defenses; we take on the demons of self-doubt and self-judgment. We slide through the worst and we come out the tail. Then we open the heart.

Going into the darkness inside is a passage we have to make if we're going to cultivate our feeling world. Shadow is powerful not just because it holds pain and repressed memories from times past and wants release, but also because it guards the gates to our inner brilliance.

Dialogue from the Dark

Whenever one agrees to confront the past, and to throw open the window to the dark side, the shadow that lives in there loses its negative charge. Suddenly new energy is free to move, discharge, reprogram itself into something productive.

If we know something of the language of symbols and dreams, then all the better. The characters in the personal unconscious, once we relieve them of their need to be defensive, can actually help mediate the inner world to us. The images and symbols in the creative side of the unconscious, once released to awareness, can be healing and illuminative. When these more positive symbols are made conscious, sacred ground is nearby.

This is how dialogue works. When I acknowledge the images and symbols that come to me, a bridge is strung between the different characters in my unconscious; between the conscious and unconscious mind. Those characters who cause me the most grief and pain are characters like Raven and Shadow (who have stopped talking to one another). For instance, if I have a certain inner figure that tells me I am capable, strong, intelligent, and another that convinces me I am stupid, incoherent, and unworthy, my performance is going to be altered. If my inner child is all set to get into some delightful mischief but the judge shows up, and scares me half to death, demanding in a loud voice that I control myself, then those two sides are going to have an argument. Chances are, the bigger one will win.

In opening up dialogue, the best thing to do is to resort to talking to oneself; noting with some acuity the different characters that show up in the back of the mind throughout the day. To amplify the dialogue with self—it helps to dramatize the thoughts, feelings, moods, tempers, and fantasies, and the characters that come along with them. That means we give fear and sorrow and anger and ambivalence, and so on, a voice. When we find a way to do this consciously, these things won't be sneaking up on us from behind.

In therapy or group work, there are always people who are willing to take one of these roles and play it out for us. This kind of mirroring flushes conflict out into the open where we can see and deal with it. In some groups people work with shadow by acting it out in a role-play. Likewise the judge, Nurse Jane, Don Juan, or Mae West (different parts of the persona that slip into our relationships) can be acted out in healthy ways. Giving voice to the wild side, the poet, the bag lady, or the imp (the side of us that wants more play and creativity and less restraint) is always a good exercise.

Many of the people I work with keep a journal, and in terms of honesty and dialogue, it's the place where we can retreat and talk honestly with ourselves. I sometimes ask people who have survived a dysfunctional parent to begin to "talk" to that person (at first by entering that process into the journal) and later to dialogue by role-play or a letter. When the subject comes up whether to send the letter, to make (or not make) the call, we dialogue with the opposing voices, the fear behind resistance, or with the side of us that feels suddenly threatened.

In my workshops I will often include clay and paints as a way of getting to dialogue. Making clay mandalas about one's life journey or one's dreams—or to give "voice" to the unheard (or opposing) sides of the self, is always a good way to see within.

Bodywork is also a very potent way to access the unconscious. Some kind of therapeutic touch frequently bypasses the strong defenses we normally carry. Professional bodywork will often bring to the surface conflicts, feelings, old traumas contained in the cell structure itself. Long repressed memories stubbornly out of the reach of verbal therapy will often yield to touch (though only when a person is ready). I often recommend some kind of "process" bodywork, in which one is free to feel and talk through the emotions, the images and thoughts that come up through deep touch.

To work with the rich symbols in the sand tray is another way to dramatize the unconscious; specifically one asks the symbol to be part of the dialogue. The following examples of group work illustrate the versatility of sand tray, voice dialogue, and Gestalt to get the symbol to talk. In one group, we imagined the unconscious to be a stage in which we would discover and act out three major players. All of these players would play out a conflict of some kind.

I asked the group to imagine the tension between the shadow we sit on, the persona we like to show others, and the pressure of our radiance trying to break through. We all sat for a bit and reflected on what our own dialogue between these three might look like.

One of the women in the group said, *"During my bodywork recently I had a lot of intense pain in this left hip. What I got in touch with is that I have to bring my beauty and power alive.* (That side was her radiance.) *If I don't, I'll die.* (There was the sympton talking, her shadow energy all bottled up and enraged.) *I am literally buried under my caretaking and drivenness.* (That's her persona talking—the side she tries constantly to perfect.) *And there's no room for me in here at all."* Being a health-care professional herself she knew about psychosomatic processes. She was clear that unless she stopped sitting on herself, on her power and passion, as well as her joy, that her body would somatize her emotional withholding.

I asked each of the women in the group to choose a handful of play figures from the sandtray to dramatize this conflict. The woman with the pain in her hip chose five figures, a carved saint, an Aztec figure, a huge dragon, an angel, and an Eskimo carved from obsidian. *"These two are my parents, the saintly one is my mother, and this carving is my father.* (The carving was a clay replica of an Aztec flute that had the shape of huge male genitals.) *I chose this Aztec for my father because I believe he molested me. He had sexual feelings for me, and my mother never noticed, never intervened. These two dragons are my rage toward my parents for abusing and never validating me, never seeing me."* To the side of these figures she placed the Eskimo figure and a tiny angel, her persona figures. *"The Eskimo sits in a supplicant position; he's got a placid smile on his face, because he never noticed anything."* Somewhere in the center of her tray she placed a wild-looking woman with a crystal ball.

Pointing to the carved saint and the phallic figure, she said, *"These two created the angel and the Eskimo, the always smiling side of me, the pleaser. They created the little girl who always does well at everything. They also created these dragons. But that's not who I am at all."* Motioning to the sorceress, she said, *"I want to be this woman, the one with power and beauty and aliveness."*

After a while she picked up another sandtray figure, a dancing couple. Pointing to the embracing couple in the dance, she said, *"I've put these parts in my black bag: romance, tenderness, intimacy, sensuousness, sexuality. I've also stuffed this sorceress: my earthiness, my intuitive side, my inner gypsy. I go about being nice and my shadow comes out as judgment, silent condemnation, criticism behind someone's back."*

Eventually she moved the figure of the sorceress onto a Navajo rug we had been using as an altar. Suddenly the tiny crystal ball the figure held aloft lit up with a bright red light, a reflection from the glow of a heater behind it. She looked at the crystal now filled with a warm glow and said, *"That's exactly the kind of fire I want within."* The symbol of the wild woman was her sexuality, her feeling world, and, ultimately, it was also her wisdom. After a while I asked her to begin to feel the fire in the crystal she was reclaiming, as a fire at the base of her spine. As we went on she experienced a vibration in the heart center that gradually spread throughout her whole being. As she began to reclaim the body she had rejected, she sat rocking back and forth, feeling a gentle current of warmth in her senses, and in her sexual center. Tears came, and a song which she spontaneously sang, a celebration of what she felt was a holy fire rekindling itself. A peace began to fall over her. In this sacred "play" with symbols, the dialogue that came from it, and the deepening sensate awareness she felt, she began to recover the body she had abandoned.

In another group working with sandtray figures, a woman chose a mother and child figure, and an angel, as her two major personas. She described herself on the outside as nurturing, good, caring, responsible, there for others. *"One figure I stash is a little girl, spontaneous, and alive, but afraid to come out. She's buried somewhere underneath the angel. Sometimes I feel I want to scream, to laugh wildly, to cry, but I don't. I've stuffed my anger, my sadness, also my creativity, my spontaneity. I have a magic wand somewhere inside, but I've stuffed that too."*

Another figure she described as buried in shadow was an Indian woman with a lance, a wild woman she feels excited about discovering but fears at the same time. As a child, she told us, she longed for her mother's love and approval and tried to earn it by being good, but she never got mother's affection. *"My mom was very dysfunctional, a drinker, abusive, explosive, but sometimes okay. Dad was kind, empathic, there for me emotionally more than Mother ever was—although he traveled a lot."* She had had no sense of a nurturing mother at all; as a child she felt no support to risk her true feelings, to trust herself with those feelings. Fingering the small toys in front of her, she says, *"The little angel is being so good and perfect. But she's lonely in there all by herself. Outwardly she says, 'I can do it,' but inside she feels inadequate, weak."*

Like so many others, she had been a good caretaker, she had accomplished and managed a lot, she stood out like an angel. But on the inside she withheld feelings of abandonment, fears of rejection, a gut-level mistrust of intimacy and vulnerability. The dilemma of the split is that many of us reject and abandon ourselves because we don't risk touching this rakish inner child; we don't call forth the wild woman with the lance. On the outside we have become the world mother, while on the inside our own inner child is starved and ready to scream.

These insights (and the feelings they bring up) are hard to accept. No one wants to be enlightened the hard way. The good news is that once we get used to the dark, once we see what we've been missing, a shift occurs. Ultimately this gift of "sees within," backward blessing that it is, forces us to feel our way into the very territory that most frightens us. The power of the unconscious self-image can destroy us (if we don't dig it up), yet what we find down there in the dark gradually begins to transform us.

Dialogue with Solitude

The season of the West is traditionally fall, a natural time for more inwardness. The old Paiute woman's custom of "going behind the blanket" symbolizes more than a retreat from unwelcome guests; it becomes a retreat into inner quiet. A blanket or robe symbolizes the wall of protection between us and the world outside that becomes so necessary for personal and spiritual growth. Without this kind of practice, the mind stays too busy, the thoughts too distracting, our habits too addictive.

Among other animals that are used to solitude, bears innately know the seasons, what task each one calls forth; they know where to forage or hunt for food, they innately know the times and rituals for migration, mating, hibernating, refueling. When we practice some degree of internal hibernation, we begin to know how to be on the planet with more stillness and reverence. The contemplative in the West gently but persistently grabs us by the back of our belt until we slow down and find a more natural rhythm, one that doesn't continually betray the feminine.

A colleague of mine recently went on a "medicine walk" to prepare her for a four-day vision fast. The walk is aimed at changing our pace a little before the actual fast, and it's usually done a week or so beforehand. One slows down, breathes, starts to silence the internal time clocks, the chattering in the mind, to still the programs most of us normally operate with. The "medicine walk" is a time to practice silence and to listen for inner guidance. A professional and a busy woman most of the time, she reported to me that she had always had trouble really listening to Spirit. She had gone on a long trek alone by a tidal lake and had picked out a huge boulder to perch on. *"All of a sudden I found myself totally quiet inside. I sat down, took off my watch, wrote for a bit, then just stretched out. I felt an incredible presence around me; even the air was silent. It felt wonderful. Once in a while my old 'what if' voice would interrupt the silence, but instead of my usual response to this program, something amazing happened; I discovered I had another voice that spoke like a little Buddha inside. The 'what if' voice would say:*
'What if it rains?'
'It doesn't matter.'
'What if the tide comes in around my rock and I have to swim back?'
'It doesn't matter.'
'What if I get lost?'
'It doesn't matter.'
It was wild. I actually felt a profound sense of inner peace." The experience for her had been a revelation; an opening to a world she hadn't been free to access before. This sort of internal dialogue is where the voice of our radiance clearly begins to speak.

Experiences like this are profound teachings, reminders that silence can be a holy event. Once on a sabbatical in Montana I went to a memorial feast for an old man who had been an important leader and medicine man. No one spoke at the feast except the two men praying over the food the women had cooked in honor of the deceased. A colorful row of silent older women with apple faces sat on the ground to my left; a few of their grandchildren tucked under their aprons or nestled up under their old breasts. No one talked except to give instructions about how the foods would be served. After the food was served by the men, small pockets of brief, sometimes humorous, conversation rose up among the people present. No one spoke to me, so I sat quiet, sampling the chokecherries, the new pungent taste of tripe stew, pemmican, the sweets piled on top of my huge plate of food. When the feast was ended I helped the women clean up and eventually got introduced to some of the people. Still no one spoke to me.

Some of the family wandered off to the giveaways at the powwow near our own tent. One or two women sat down in the shade and I sat down too. One of them offered me a smoke. I smoked and felt grateful for her gesture. About an hour later a conversation began between us. In the hours since the feast had begun and ended, time seemed to have suspended itself in the warm Montana afternoon. I had been painfully aware of myself, my own churning struggle with the silence, my second thoughts about how these people might be feeling about me. I had come with a long list of questions I wanted to ask about their traditions and beliefs, but their natural ease with silence stilled me.

I knew that I needed this rest from my own thoughts, from the busyness in my mind. Gradually I began to welcome the silence; to accept being there; to experience my thoughts and feelings without speaking them. A profound quiet soon fell over me, and time with its endless measurements stopped for a while. I distinctly heard sounds around me with a new intensity; the cries of children mimicking the tall beauty of the dancers in the arena, the wind that came in warm gusts and rustled the leaves and the sides of the canvas tent. The singers and drummers down below us were not just singing at their annual summer powwow: they became the voices of warriors, men chanting and chasing the buffalo, young men courting, voices from some past century calling on the gifts of the directions, imploring the wisdom of the Grandfathers. I wouldn't have heard them had I been talking. This kind of silence, slow in coming at first, has gradually taught me more awareness of my connection to the things and people around me.

A friend of mine, just days before her second vision fast on the desert side of the Sierras, took what her trainers called a "night walk." During the year before she had taken that walk in a rather peaceful way. There had been no apprehension, no fear, everything had gone well. But on this second year out, she had a different experience. She had been going along a dark road in the desert and had seen some men, presumably drinking and partying out there in the sagebrush. Unsure of whether she had been seen by them, she kept walking. But all sorts of fears began to follow her down that road. *"All of a sudden I had fantasies of these men coming after me; then I saw all these evil spirits running around. I really prayed for protection. Then I distinctly felt a presence walking behind me. I asked, 'Who are you?' Then a voice said, 'It's just me.' I knew I was being protected and I wasn't afraid after that. But I knew that my first year out, I hadn't had these kinds of fears, because I just sat on them. I controlled fear when it came up, rather than allowing myself to have it. There's a strong masculine side I have that won't let me show any weakness."* She became aware that this strong animus figure in her sometimes took over, paralyzing her feminine side. Animus figures do that.

"I felt this figure was often trying to take over my life, and I wanted to confront it. I wanted to shout at it, to shout 'No!' to tell it to get out and stop controlling me. But I couldn't shout at all. All I could do was to tell it to go away, that I'd had enough of its criticisms. Then I felt really disappointed I couldn't yell out loud; it felt like I had to, to get this thing out of my system. But I couldn't yell and I was sure I'd failed. As the night went on and it came time for me to go back to base camp, some little birds started flying alongside me. They seemed to stay right with me for a long time, so I asked them if they had a word for me. 'Even a small voice is heard' is what they said." By the time she finished her night walk, she had walked with her fear and her critic; she had met them both out there partying in the sagebrush, and she had come back feeling peace.

Those of us beginning the work of introspection must eventually stand face to face with ourselves, our past hurts, and hidden conflicts. In the West we level with our worst fears, with shame, old family secrets, denial; we stand in the dark side of our own shadow and learn to see how we often project it onto others. Gradually we learn to trust the "black light," to converse with the characters in the unconscious that mirror the oldest wounds. Eventually, amid this darkness, we begin to see well enough to touch the fire of the Spirit inside. And lastly, when it's time to move away from introspection, we take off that dark robe and fold it, lay it aside, and walk toward the next part of the circle.

5. The North and the Way of Courage

When I had turned to face the North that first year on the mountain, the sky had turned from its earlier fiery red to a deep, pulsing black. By midnight the darkness had become an elegant backdrop for a burst of bright stars. A cold wind blew from the North and I covered myself with my sleeping bag. I had to laugh at myself, still dressed in cowboy boots, a wool hat pulled down to eye level.

I pushed the thought of being cold out of my mind, telling myself I shouldn't be so attached to warmth. The moon gradually came out, flat against the sky, casting long shadows through the aspen and illuminating a grove of trees.

A large branch snapped close by, and the hair on the back of my neck rose straight up. I imagined, for a fleeting moment, that I might look like a stuffed cabbage leaf to a passing bear. The wind kept up its gusty behavior, sometimes welling up and blowing leaves, or sounding in waves through the long-needled pines. I looked up in the direction of its noisy rustling in the trees, and a shape silhouetted against the moonlight stood out. It wasn't a bear; it was the figure of a big man with a shield and a buckler of stars. The outline of his shape was so distinct I was caught off guard, transfixed. In the sudden stillness an inner voice spoke, "In your life, don't be afraid of anything." I felt a numinous presence hovering in the spaces between me and the figure of the warrior. Any thoughts of bear or the cold night vanished. I realized the huge figure in the trees could be one of two things: a figment of my imagination, or a guest from the spirit world. At the time I hadn't known about the helping spirit the Lakota call *Waziya*; the one who makes the people grow "straight and tall like a pine tree."[1] I only knew that from the direction of the North a powerful figure had sprung up and was engaging me.

I knew that my fear was not of ordinary things. I took on dares in childhood like some people take on guilt. I once swam across a cold river during a high spring runoff, with my brave friends cheering me on. In my twenties I climbed Mount Whitney with my husband and a seven-month-old son on my back, just in time for the first snowstorm of the season. In my thirties I learned assertiveness and how to speak in front of large crowds without fainting. In my forties I survived a mid-life crisis, and began to ask for help when I needed it (a difficult task for cowgirls). But there were other fears harder to acknowledge. In the arena of relationships, I still withheld saying my feelings when they brought conflict or raised eyebrows. I lacked courage to speak the bold words in my soul. The stillness that descended on the mountain as the wind died down seemed to amplify the moonlit shape of the man in the trees. I felt certain his presence was calling me to own the courage that was still in exile. I wrote this in my journal that night: *These stars that you see, these are your brothers, your sisters, your relations, the ones who have gone on before you. They have made mistakes, been hungry, hurt others, fallen short, they have had self-doubts, but they have triumphed too. All these ways of learning are not easy. Have the courage to be patient with yourself so that your mistakes teach you, so that they don't shame you. Have courage to stand in the midst of your hurts and disappointments. When you doubt yourself, you doubt us. But all along we are here to help you, to spread a light on your path, to remind you where you came from. So when you doubt, come outside and look up. Look up and remember who you are. We are the light in your darkness.*

North and the Warrior

Facing North opens to the power and wisdom of the warrior. There is a belief among the Lakota that a great figure stands in the North, called *Waziya*. This spirit both tests us and watches over us. He brings us trials that will strengthen and purify us.

In the primitive instinctual body, warrior energy is "fight or flight"; in the body of the psyche, that energy is courage, integrity, endurance, might. In the body of the soul, courage means to "take heart." The Hidatsa woman was most interested in that kind of courage.

The animal that presides over the North is the Buffalo nation. On the rare occasions when I have seen buffalo, I am always awed. I once saw a large herd in the fall in the interior of Alaska near Delta Junction. I was freezing and complaining about it, anxious to get to a wood stove, have a cup of steaming coffee and thaw out my feet. And there they were; standing unperturbed in the cold wind, like great dark boulders, withstanding even the storm that moved in on the valley. I still carry that picture in my thoughts.

Native Americans speak often of what they call medicine. Although medicine often refers to healing herbs or substances, in Native tradition it also means personal and spiritual power. At the psychological level, there are two kinds of courage. Early on in life most of us need the strength to grow and to face the world (and the people in it) head-on; we need to be able to carve a place for ourselves where we can feel safe, secure, and know that we belong. Or we need to protect ourselves from the unpredictable events and people in our environment that we can't control. The masculine generativity of the warrior is know-how energy that tells us where our backbone is: how to succeed, how to stand up to conflict and not shrink. That sort of energy fuels the strength we need to face a crisis or some psychic or relational undoing, and not fall completely apart. Working this direction means we explore our resources of power and healthy assertiveness.

Then somewhere in mid-life, the courage that we have previously identified with the ego has to shift and go inward; to an inner strength. The kind of courage the Hidatsa woman stressed was the strength it takes to be ourselves, to say who we really are, what we feel. People who are working to free themselves from the past, from its negative imprints, are often working to feel and express the life inside. But being real means allowing vulnerability: giving permission to oneself to occupy the deepest wound and to consciously stand in the tension one feels in that place, without giving up.

The season of the North also symbolizes winter—when growth goes underground, when hard rains come and snow spreads its purifying blanket over the land. In Black Elk's vision of the directions that I spoke of earlier, he also saw a white cleansing wing (a symbol of purification and endurance). In that same vision the Grandfather from the North spoke to the boy: *"Take courage, younger brother, on earth a nation you shall make live, for yours shall be the power of the white giant's wing, the cleansing wing.... They are appearing, may you behold!"*[2] The symbol of the cleansing wing speaks to me about walking through pain with an open mind; facing fear and discouragement; breaking through the defenses in the ego, stripping sometimes down to the bone. Whereas in the West one opens to an awareness of the wounds of the past, in the North the task is to stand firm in the cleansing currents until we transform the wound.

Facing into the Winds

One of my friends, a mountain man, said once, *"I'm not Indian, but I face the North all the time in my thoughts. When I sleep outdoors at night, I'm always gazing North. The farther you go up there, the smaller the trees get; everything is gradually reduced in the cold. I think it reminds me of that territory inside that's barren and hard, like the cold winter; it's hard to be out in it, but it's pure."*

I have worked often with people who have met big winds in the psyche. Like the great buffalo, they have had to just stand and take the cleansing; to *"cleanse the terrible darkness in the mind,"* as St. Augustine put it. Once uncovered through introspection and "sees within," all the wounds of childhood—incest, abuse, ritual abuse, loss, abandonment, betrayal—need to be purified. Once they are released to consciousness, we have to walk through them steadfastly, patiently, enduring the cleansing process as best we can. We have to feel this kind of intensity before we can move *through* it. There is no place to go when this happens but inward, where one longs for the light in the midst of the dead of winter.

Author Elizabeth O'Conner, in trying to cope with a severe arthritis that all but crippled her for more than twenty months, found that in the beginning of her illness she felt acutely discouraged, afraid, and isolated. As she fought to stand up to her illness, she found it brought her more in touch with life. *"The disease which raged in my limbs and stole my energy also made me open to anything that might make me well, an attitude that is one of the primary gifts of pain. It unlocks our closed world."*

One of my clients told me that although she felt her healing process deepening in good ways, she also felt painfully aware of how anger and darkness had worked in her life. She told me that there were times during her drinking years that she had no hope and had only been filled with self-hatred. *"I was in a total eclipse in those days,"* she said. *"I was so ashamed and in such denial I never let in the Spirit at all. My parents were atheists. They were alcoholics too. There was a cloud over all of us."* Healing means owning and walking through the shame of things we have either done or failed to do, as this woman was doing.

Metaphorically, as the light (of the conscious mind) decreases and we reflect on the power of the North, winter can be an advent of sorts; a time of waiting and deep inner searching. It may be the time to listen for the deeper meaning of the cleansing or the trial we may be having to face. We begin to explore what Meister Eckhart called *"magnificent vulnerability."*[3] This is the energy of the inner warrior. If we can stand in our weakness, without denial or the padding of our defenses, then we understand this medicine.

The Talking Stick

In many Native traditions, whenever a circle of elders met for a talk or a counsel, it was often customary to begin with a "talking stick," a carved stick or small branch on which was hung a cluster of deer hooves. After an opening prayer, the talking stick was passed around the circle. Before each person spoke the stick was shaken, signifying that the group would listen to that person's words in silence, honoring each person's right to speak. Our Hidatsa teacher sometimes began our circles with this ritual.

Native Americans say that speaking with power and conviction, with truth and humility, is medicine. But only a few people I have ever worked with were ever "given the talking stick" as children. Most people I know have trouble speaking or acting from the truth within themselves, because few of us have developed the healthy side of the warrior archetype. Clear, clean assertiveness and communications skills were seldom modeled for many of us. To be outspoken, to express that primitive assertiveness that children sometimes do, was often behavior that drew a humiliating blow. Most of our families disdained and feared honest self-expression.

Most people in recovery from emotionally abusive or emotionally repressed families have to fight hard to express themselves and even to feel they have something worth saying. In some families, talking was only done by the people in power, and some of us never saw a talking stick except the one over our heads.

The choice to speak for ourselves is abandoned when we don't feel self-love. A woman I know stayed for years in a violently abusive relationship with an alcoholic husband. *"I hoped he'd stop drinking, that one day he would remember how much he had loved me in the beginning. I prayed all the time he would remember, but he never did. It wasn't until I saw my son beaten unconscious one day that I finally got the nerve to stand up to him. When I finally got help, I knew I had to leave. I knew I had to find my voice."* The tragedy is that some people spend years without a voice.

In a small Indian village in Alaska I visited once, I was disheartened and angry to learn that most of the young girls there had experienced some kind of incest or sexual abuse. Worse, many of them had passively resigned themselves to it. Among an ever-increasing proportion of clients (both men and women) who have experienced physical and sexual abuse, I find this same passive resignation.

Finding power in the voice is difficult if, as children, the parents that should have been listening to us didn't. I hear stories frequently from adult children of alcoholics and from incest survivors that the mother or father they should have been able to confide in was absent, preoccupied, or disbelieving. One woman told me that on the way to a neighborhood park one day she was attacked and sexually abused by a gang of older boys. When she came home dazed and crying, with mud all over her clothes, her mother yelled at her for getting dirty. She was sent to her room. *"Of all the people I needed to talk to at the time, it was my mother. But she totally abandoned me when I needed her the most."* When there are these terrible invasions to our personhood, our power to speak is lost, sometimes for years. The natural instinct to protect oneself, to express outrage, to speak, to act, to confront, is overwhelmed by this wound.

Even in families where there is no overt abuse, saying the truth about what one is feeling or seeing is seldom encouraged. Some families make it an unwritten rule that it isn't okay to have thoughts, feelings, or needs that don't serve the needs of the family. When the first rule of thumb in a family is to look normal and to serve the powers that be, self-expression is seen as selfish; any attempt at individuation is seen as disloyal.

When any of us loses the ability to claim the talking stick for ourselves, we invariably learn to pick it up and use it to manage others around us. It works like this: *I'm not going to talk about me; I'm going to tell you about you. I'm going to tell you how to live your life my way.* But this kind of control (through managing others) is destructive. People don't thrive in that kind of environment because the people in power are telling us how to be, how to think and feel, and there is no growing power in that. In homes where no one models how to "take heart," the courage to be ourselves is lost.

A woman who had trouble finding her voice in the arena of relationships told me of a frightening repetitive dream. *"I'm sitting in my house as a kid. My mother and dad are there by the fireplace. We're all watching T.V. Suddenly the fire goes out, and a huge cellophane wrap descends over the living room and covers my face and I can't breathe. I wake up terrified."* The fire going out in the living room illustrates what happens in families where people speak *for* one another, rather than from speaking truthfully from the "fire" in the heart.

People frequently tell me they have similar dreams of being silenced, cut off, controlled, guarded, or chased by someone with a hypodermic needle (the ultimate silencer). Yet it isn't the "outside" world that inhibits us anymore. It's our own fear of speaking and being humiliated or rejected that keeps us silent.

Men and women who grew up in cellophane environments have trouble being decisive; they give their power of speech away by being too polite, too self-edited, or by letting someone else speak for them. Or they suppress honest talk about their own feelings and needs, and talk about others. A colleague said, *"It's one thing to get involved speaking for the rights of others, the minority groups I work with, abused women and kids; it's one thing to be assertive and outspoken and feel like I've put my two cents into the fray. It's a much more difficult thing to feel my own deepest feelings and to speak from that place."*

The power of talking, saying what we mean and who we are, saying what we feel and stand for, is essential to healing. But the tragedy of our modern age is that honest talking (the kind our ancestors used to do around a fire pit) has become increasingly rare. The power to speak is not only silenced by our past and the people in it, but also by a loss of our own personal center. People who gather around the television or prioritize work agendas above self-expression forget how to talk to one another. This is a common problem among most families I see today. When that happens the cellophane descends and the fire (the courage to speak) goes out, and we are out of touch with ourselves; we get lost in an abstract world where, without the power to speak and tell our own story, we are rootless. The talking stick for me was a reminder that I have a right to be my own storyteller.

Trickster Warrior

Not long after learning the prayers to the four directions, I noticed that my meditations on the North were always fairly intense. In one of the early sweat lodges my teacher addressed herself to me: *"You are very strong, and you have much courage for life, but at the same time you have this fear around you. There is an old man spirit in here that says, 'You have nothing to be afraid of. You have nothing to fear.'"* She didn't know me well enough to have observed this hidden side of me; but in the sweat she had seen a little cloud around me, notwithstanding the dark we were sitting in. That was back in the days when I seemed caught often in that frozen state between gutsiness and fear. One side of me agreed I had a lot to say and should just say it; the other side held my mouth in a brace.

Courage to face fear (and to speak) can be elusive, particularly for the Raven character in all of us. Raven, after all, would just as soon avoid the truth if it meant any sort of confrontation or emotional work; if it meant someone might see his shadow, his inflation, or the puffed up ego under the seaweed. Raven would much rather spend the winter in Miami than face the cleansing wind in the North.

Warrior energy is about "taking heart" in life. It's about challenging our fears and inflations; it's the strength one needs to cut through defenses. The trouble is, many of us have *needed* to protect ourselves in the past. Thus a major obstacle to ongoing breakthrough work is often a person's strength, or what they perceive as their strength. Anyone who has grown up in a patriarchal culture anywhere is prone to concealing vulnerability. Cultural whitewashing of the feminine feeling world gets us into this sort of trouble. The kids I used to teach in an inner-city school loved being tough. They grew up needing to be. But underneath their banter and jive and street talk, under all the threats and intimidating stares, lived abandoned kids. Kids who grew up having to fight for themselves, take care of themselves, speak for themselves, because nobody else did. Sometimes one needs this toughness to navigate life with. But the fighting energy here that has been bent to this task will often turn around and work against us later by being overvigilant; we simply won't be able to feel or express vulnerability.

A woman whose husband had died some time ago of cancer told a group of us at a workshop that she had never really given herself permission to grieve. *"I've never fully let go. I've had to be strong. I know I've been protecting my children from my grief. I don't want them to worry about me; I don't want them to know what I'm suffering. So I just don't let it out. Instead I take care of them, of their needs. In fact, right now I'm feeling that I'm taking too much time away from the group with my own problems."* And after a pause: *"But at the same time, I know that even saying this, I'm trying to take care of you, and not me."* The group encouraged her to take all the time she needed. It was a new experience for her to have her own need without rescuing everyone else.

The trickster, always pretending to act in our best interest, tells us we are strong only if we appear to be strong. Like any good combat trainer he or she convinces us that our life is only as safe as our defense system. He says, Don't need! Don't feel! Don't rage! Don't live too much! She loves power struggles, covert manipulations, behavioral trade agreements, lots of compromise, lifeless relationships, status quo niceness, long cold wars.

False courage is often the result of emotional bankruptcy. A woman I know who would normally take on any obstacle, cause, or challenge said recently she felt herself playing a role she was tired of. *"When I was young my older brother and sister used to terrorize me. They were big and I was small and they did everything they could to humiliate and scare me into playing by their rules. But their games and tricks were cruel, and worse yet, no one ever came to my rescue. I think I've always felt a tremendous need to prove myself. I won't let my guard down with anybody because it doesn't feel safe. But now I'm the one who's playing games."*

Pride and anger, games of hiding and deceit, lack of confidence to be wrong or just human—all is familiar territory to the child who has had to struggle to justify her existence. The false warrior inside wants to protect us from our worst nightmare; but the wall that defends us is fear and withholding, and there's no authentic power in that kind of defense.

I knew a wonderful cop once, a huge, rowdy, big-hearted man who had all kinds of courage on the job. His work was demanding, dangerous, and taxing to the spirit, but he did it skillfully and stayed strong in the most trying moments. The challenge that frightened him the most was the nerve to go into his emotional pain, to penetrate his defenses and feel his father's abandonment of him. Just before letting go finally, and coming heroically into tears and rage, he said, *"I'm afraid if I really let go, I won't stop. I'll just come unglued."* The group with whom he was doing this work unanimously gave him permission to come unglued. When he did, the other men there wept too. Risking coming unglued themselves, they loosened their own defenses and sobbed in one another's arms.

This work touched me deeply because I had some of this man in me. As he struggled to let go of his wall of strength, his self-sufficiency, his control, I saw how I held on to my own defenses. Being vulnerable, showing pain, asking for the reassurance of someone else's touch, this is where my own glue got him. After the men in the group finished holding him, I embraced him too, feeling in the depth of his huge chest a pain not unfamiliar to me. My father wasn't there for me either; I was a loner, I didn't risk intimacy or ask for help. It was a good day for both of us.

Finding the Power in the Voice

Finding our voice is the first step in regaining the power to tell our story. This archetypal energy isn't one that we can touch by reflection or can accomplish alone in an introspective way; it has to be actively practiced with others. When any of us finds out how the false side of the warrior blocks our ability to self-express, we can turn that energy around and put it to work for us.

People in group and workshop settings often come with a range of feelings that take a tremendous effort to express. In the beginning of the opening circle, when participants say something about who they are or why they have come, some hearts thunder like Niagara Falls. Breath gets constricted and no one is anxious to go first. People say they don't have anything in particular to work on, but they're sure someone else does. Groups can be intimidating at times, but they are one of the best ways to unseat the false warrior and see instead our authentic inner strength.

A key to recovering the power in the voice is learning how to read one's body, its signals, signs, and symptoms. Jung felt that the body itself had its own story to tell, and that it could teach us a good deal about ourselves. During the time I was learning to occupy my own body more consciously, I began to ask it questions; namely, why my heart was racing or my throat was tight, or my shoulders ached; or why my foot used to tap and fly in circles when I was mad or unsure of myself. As I began to listen to these body symptoms I soon learned that what sabotaged my power to speak was a rivalry between my feeling world and the vigilant censors in my thoughts.

The false warrior, for instance, tells us we should keep a stiff upper lip. The inner man or woman is tired of that regime and wants to talk. Consequently the body gets a knot in the solar plexus. The trickster warns us never to leave our feelings unguarded. The inner woman strains under that yoke and suddenly has a yearning to say something real. So the body feels a constriction in the throat. The inner man wants to rage but the outer man won't. The body gets a headache. In a safe setting—whether in a relationship or a group— we can explore this conflict. Our task is simply to follow the symptom and pay attention to what the body is doing.

A woman in a training group I was leading began by saying that she had an ache in her heart that felt like a "sack of potatoes." She was afraid to speak, and yet afraid not to speak—she had struggled with this fear all her life. We talked to the sack of potatoes, the weighted-down feeling that she experienced whenever she wanted to say something real about herself. The sack of potatoes turned out to have the face of her grandmother, a mean little Irish woman who had the countenance of the grim reaper and who never said an affirming word to anybody. This "sack of potatoes" had given her the message as a child that she was stupid and that she had nothing to say.

Another woman tried to speak in the group but complained of having "butterflies" in her stomach. When she talked to that symptom, it never became anyone's face, but it did become an old message she had gotten as a child about needing to be silent. Yet underneath the

fluttering sensation was also a profound sense of exhilaration, a genuine excitement that she clearly had something to say. On the other
side of this woman's shyness was a desire to come out, to let her voice
be "carried on the wind." In a creative piece of imagery work she
did, she let these butterflies fly into the room. They buzzed around
the heads and shoulders of the people there, spun around the room
in flashing colors and took a little piece of her beauty to each of the
participants in the group. As she was having this image she said:
"Inside is power and intelligence and creativity, and it wants out!"

The power to speak is often hidden in the most subtle body language. The problem is that many times people try to cover these
"nervous" body symptoms, hoping no one will notice. Meanwhile the
symptom intensifies. This is hard on the body. The face (which is a
primary covering) will be often most symptomatic, with tight lips,
mouth turned down or frozen into a nice smile; jaws that are set;
eyebrows that are perpetually raised or lowered, a forehead that is
furrowed; a little tic or twitch.

A man in one workshop began by saying that he was "all nerves."
His eyebrows seldom came down the whole time we spoke. He admitted that he had been self-conscious all his life. But as he sat back
and purposefully worked with his raised eyebrows, he could actually
feel the nature of that self-consciousness. As he sat there, his eyebrows
finally dropping, he reexperienced a childhood scenario between himself and his music teacher in seminary; a man in front of whom even
lions would cower. Suddenly he burst into tears and laughter and
came out with a volley of words that would have burned the old
man's ears; and from that point on, the work he did was deeply
empowering. When we take even the smallest risk, the unconscious
opens its gates—the mask we wear begins to yield its rigid cover—
and our voice returns.

Accessing personal power, however, never implies we rid ourselves
completely of fear. We may have fear until the day we die. What
works is to experience the fear, without judging or covering it.

Finding power in the voice, particularly if it means confrontation
or anger, is another task for some of us. Once in a group a young
woman spoke about how difficult it was to have the courage to stand
up to someone in the face of intimidation. She said she had been
furious recently at the owner of a garage where she had taken her
car to be fixed, but could not express herself to him or stand up for

herself. *"My car broke down last weekend. I took it to a garage and I was told it would cost about four hundred dollars to fix. I didn't have that kind of money so I went someplace else for a second opinion. The guy there told me it was my clutch plate and it would be a simple fix. I got furious with the men at the first place where I had gone. I'd like to go back and give them a piece of my mind. But the thought petrifies me."*

I ask her if she can role-play with me, talk to these crooks at the first garage. She starts out on the angry side to confront these men, but a big smile crosses her face and she laughs out loud and falls over. Collecting herself, she starts again but the anger is gone and her voice becomes almost inaudible. I ask her to begin again, to feel the anger and then speak from that place. Once more her voice trails off and her voice becomes weak. I tell her that her anger sounds like a mouse fart. We all laugh but there is an urgency to this piece of work, since so many of us have this problem of backing down from our feelings. I imagine that the other women in the group have some ideas that might help her find her voice. I tell her I'm leaving the room and she has five minutes to brainstorm with the group to think of a way to face these men who have ripped her off. I leave to go to the bathroom, and loud sounds of laughter and excitement follow me down the hall.

When I come back in the room a wall of bodies surrounds and encourages her. Everyone has drums, rattles, bells, rain sticks—the whole place has come alive. She stands in the middle and beats a drum, looking fierce in her assertiveness. I begin the role-play as the village cheat: *"All right sweetheart, you owe me five thousand dollars for a lousy job on your car. I know you're a poor student, but I've got to earn a living. So fork it over."* In the role-play her response comes out strong at first. *"You ripped me off and I'm angry. You have no right to do that. I'll turn you over to the better business bureau, you swindler!"* Then she falters.

I ask her what she feels in her body. *"Stronger, but my legs feel weak."* Suddenly she says, *"I can say the words, but inside I feel scared. I feel like I'm going to faint. My legs are going out from underneath me."* I tell her she has crossed an edge and it just *feels* like she's going to faint. I hold on to her and let her lean into me.

This faltering happens whenever the conscious and the unconscious mind clash. The conscious mind experiments with a new behavior, confrontation; the unconscious mind throws us the taboo from childhood, and we get weak in the knees. When this woman saw through the unconscious side of the taboo, she realized that long ago she had made a silent pact with herself never to be furiously angry like her alcoholic father. *"I promised myself I would never get angry like that, never want to hurt anybody like he did. All this time I've been afraid of my anger."*

The edge one crosses here is a tough one for any of us who have grown up with strong family rules about the expression of anger. The early childhood taboos have to be met head-on. When we have the will, as this young woman did, to clash with the unspoken rules in the family system, then we liberate the victim and empower the man or woman who needs a little Hercules energy.

The Warrior in Exile

When power has been abused, or when we have no models for authentic strength in childhood, we have to go to the source of that wound for the answers. We ask, *Why is my strength in exile? When did the power in my voice go into hiding? Where do I need that energy now in my life?*

The work of transforming our childhood wounds never happens overnight. Most of us don't even wake up to ask the right questions until mid-life. Once we do, we realize that these problems have been here for a lifetime. Our archaeology will predictably be slow going, but there is always a right time for this deeper work.

When there has been abuse of power in the past, the ego has a number of protective defenses it assumes. In some cases it overcompensates and forms a strong defense against being vulnerable (this is the false warrior we discussed earlier, the trickster). Or the ego compensates by hiding, running away from power, going into a passive stance.

A colleague of mine told me a poignant dream that he had when still a student in his early twenties. It seemed a collective dream as he told it because it clearly voices the problem of personal disunity, of a painful severing in the ego that happens to many of us as children.

In the dream he is standing on the top of the student union at a university campus. He is looking out across row after row of cornfields. A narrow dirt road goes through the field, and a man on a motor scooter drives along it. Suddenly the man is struck by a car, and in the force of the impact, the bike disintegrates, and the rider, still holding the front wheel between his legs and riding on it at breakneck speed, is ground in two. *"I run downstairs and out onto the field, and I run as fast as I can to the scene of the accident. Then just as I'm approaching it, a young woman steps in front of me and looking straight into my eyes, she says, 'You are about to see the death of a man.' To my utter horror I see that the man has been cut right up the middle, from his crotch all the way up to his neck. I am horrified. He is still alive and I can hear him moaning in the most incredible pain. I throw myself down on my knees and I scream, No! No! No! No!"*

At the time the dreamer was in a difficult period of emotional pain. His relationship to both parents had often been a great source of humiliation. He grew up being ridiculed (in often subtle but degrading ways) by a brilliant but demanding father; and he was, he felt, emasculated by his mother (who rejected sexuality and disdained men). *"I didn't know it at the time, but I was fractured. Split apart from myself. It was only later that I realized the man in the accident was me. I've never been able to be in my [masculine] body, to trust it, to feel good about it, or at home in it. Up until these last few years, I've had trouble asserting myself or really asking for what I want of life. My whole life I've been picking up the pieces."*

Almost invariably, when we work with the past (with the intention of changing some present behavior), we are going to run into a major conflict. On the one hand we are tired of our fears, of the blocks to courage we experience, and on the other, we can't yet move into the new territory because something in the past blocks it. The power of the warrior often means the ability to hang on in strong winds like the Buffalo Nation; it means holding the container of the ego together while we go through the business of "finding the pieces." When we can work consciously with the warrior archetype, we look for ways we can transform the original wound inside, in order to release the creative energy trapped there.

One of my clients had worked for quite some time on an issue of sexual abuse. Although he thought he had worked it through, forgiven himself, forgiven the uncle, the abuse had gone deeper than he had imagined. He had been meaning to make some important changes in his life, yet hadn't been able to get to those changes. He had been meaning to confront his boss at work, and hadn't done it. He wanted to set some limits with one of his kids (who thought he should keep lending her money) and he hadn't done that. He had been meaning to join a men's group, and hadn't made the call yet. We were talking about willpower in the healthy masculine, and he said: *"I've never been afraid to face the outside world, to leap over big mountains, or to go places it was dangerous to go. I've had a reckless kind of bravado for years. But where I find my courage lacking is when I have to face the changes I know I need to make. I have trouble confronting people, especially authority figures. I look at the assertive behaviors in other men who can be confrontive, even aggressive. I just don't have that kind of testosterone. I back down when it comes to saying where I really stand."*

This man had trouble with confrontation because he also had a deep wound to his masculinity as a boy. He knew what the problem was and what he had to do; his warrior simply wasn't showing up to help him because the energy was trapped in a complex. *"What if somebody feels hurt when I say no; what if they get angry? What if I get fired? What if when I say no to one of my kids, they commit suicide or stop loving me? All those things run through my head. But I am afraid of outcomes. I want to change this and I know I need to. But that's where I get stuck. I know what's wrong; I just can't follow through."*

I asked him once where the fear was coming from. He thought for a while, and then said, *"It goes back to the time my uncle molested me. I was unable to tell anybody, afraid that if I did, he wouldn't like me anymore. I was afraid my whole family would reject me; maybe I'd be blamed. My whole life I've done just about anything to make people happy. Where I need the warrior is to help me confront my fear (that if I speak, a catastrophe will happen). But I don't even have any men friends."*

The will to change was there, but the power serving the will was locked up in a childhood complex. The sexual abuse, terrible as it had been, was only one of the catastrophes in this family. The fact that he feared rejection and sensed that no one would listen or care tempts me to think that this family was not only ripe for incest but had all the makings of a toxic environment. The ego in that kind of family has a hard time getting the message that it has the right to be.

The power that sits in the North is, indeed, the Grandfather with the cleansing wing. Sometimes when we are caught by a complex and we can't get to the pure energy in the archetype, we have to do two things. We have to go where there are people who are stronger than we are—or who can be good models for us. And we have to pray and wait while the conflict deep inside us has its winter season. It's purification time. For men who have few or no real male friends (and no strong identification with the masculine), the brotherhood in a good men's group can be tremendously transforming.

A few years ago I worked with a group of women who were exploring personal empowerment Most of the women felt their role models for power and authority (as adolescents) had been either too strong or too weak. Those with dominant fathers or mothers had compensated by avoiding a show of power and assertiveness; others had needed a show of strength and independence to protect themselves. Most of us can identify with one or the other of these scenarios.

One woman said that she had a desire for relationship, for love and tenderness, but that she also had a need to protect herself from being too dependent on anyone. If it looked as though someone might get the upper hand, she ended the relationship. The false warrior that had lodged in her fear made her invulnerable, unapproachable, aloof. Her father had been a military man whose control over the family was somewhat obsessive, although not abusive. *"All my life all I wanted was his approval and his attention. It didn't matter what perfection I created for him in my life, nothing quite impressed him enough. Consequently I never felt deserving."* She started to cry, and then said: *"I don't feel okay with these tears. They make me feel small. What scares me is that, right here in the midst of all of you, I am totally isolated."*

As her work progressed, she was able to rage at her father for the abandonment she felt. She was also able to go into her voice of self-judgment and perfectionism, and confront that too. Once or twice she stopped herself and said sarcastically, *"I sound like the bleeding heart here!"* When she realized that was her father's voice, and not hers, she could go on with her anger and her tears. Toward the end of her session, she was able to ask the women for a group hug. Asking for this kind of affirmation, especially from a group of women (whom she had never really trusted), was a new experience. When the false warrior digs its heels into the psyche, male or female, it betrays the feminine gift of relatedness to others. But she had reclaimed her warrior in exile by supporting her right to be vulnerable and real and by asking for what she needed.

Releasing the Inner Warrior

To confront defensiveness is difficult, but critical to unmasking the authentic inner man or woman. A man I worked with in an ongoing group began to call himself honestly on what he saw as the "stones" over his heart. He half jokingly referred to one character as Stoneman: an adaptive figure from his childhood that had developed a rigid, controlling side; one that had no room for the wild man. It was a side he no longer wanted. Once he could identify and "voice" Stoneman, he decided to ask the others present to do a ritual with him, something to transform this rigid side of him. Since a long stretch of the Pacific Northwest coastline was just adjacent to our weekend cottage, he led us all outside; we would make up the ritual as we went along. Soon all of us, shoes off, were running down the beach, splashing through the waves in the cold November afternoon. For the first half hour or so we sprinted along; running, hugging, and tackling one another until our energies were spent and the sound of surf had penetrated us.

Then a spontaneous ritual emerged in which Stoneman laid himself out on a slab of dark rock along the shoreline, announcing that this would be his altar for the "letting go" ceremony. It would be the place for the breaking through to the wild man inside who wasn't so rigid and invested in outcomes. As he lay on the slab, the group began picking up stones from the beach. As though each of us were in a play with no script (yet knowing what our parts were), we glanced at the ground, stooping to see what the tide had brought in. Gathering handfuls of small colored stones, red, ochre, rust, jade green, and picking up larger stones, round, black, shiny, rocks of every size and shape, we took them toward Stoneman. Humorously at first we laid our rocks all over his body; one by one we placed them over his arms, hands, legs, stomach, genitals, solar plexus, chest, neck, forehead, until he was fairly covered. We laughed like drunks do when they have given up all appearances; then we fell silent, aware only of the surf once more, rolling, singing, and pushing herself onto the shore. We formed a circle around him and joined hands.

"These are the stones that have held me prisoner inside myself. This stone on my forehead; too many thoughts, too many worries; too much controlling, there it goes! This one over my throat; for all the times I kept quiet and couldn't or wouldn't say what I felt; the times I held back anger

or tears—it goes too! These stones over my arms and in my hands; too many responsibilities, too many concerns. All the people I have held up, all the cares of the world, there they go! This stone over my chest; holding my feelings, holding back passion, it goes!" Each time he cast off a stone the group shouted and cheered some hail into the cold wind.

Because this culture has made a virtue out of independence, some stones are hard to part with. To surrender the habit of being self-sufficient, or having the right answer, is no easy feat. Most people will walk away when they can't control something (or someone), because most of us fear being powerless. The problem for many of us is that there are often few models for authentic inner strength.

Years ago I worked with a man who had been depressed for several months. Although the root of depression is often varied and complex, this one seemed symptomatic of an impasse between the old role he had played in life and the new one wanting to emerge. He said he had no idea why it was coming up. He had a nice family, a good job; everything on the outside was fine. Yet he knew his depression was affecting his family, and his relationships at work. He wasn't sure where he belonged. As we continued to talk, what began to reemerge was a memory of having been physically abused by a step-father. His mother, an emotionally distanced woman, had little contact with him and apparently never knew about these incidents. Sensitive as a child and often ridiculed for his feelings, he soon withdrew into himself. *"I don't know whether I've ever really known what it was to be a man; I'm not sure I've ever really believed in myself."*

I asked him if he could remember a time in his life when he did feel strong, if there was a time he did believe in himself. After a bit he said he'd once had a grandpa who had been there for him. As he remembered their relationship, his expression changed, his energy shifted. *"My grandfather was different from the rest. I used to stay in his house sometimes, I remember him as a big loving man. A strong man. We had good times together and he was there for me. I think he was the only man I really could be myself around as a kid."* A deep sigh seemed to rise up out of a long silent place inside and tears came to his eyes. *"I remember when he died. The one man I really loved, who would have protected me, was suddenly out of my life. There wasn't anybody who loved me like that."* He stayed with his grief over his grandfather for a while and I sat on the floor with him.

"What was the gift your grandfather gave you as a boy?" I said.

"He was strong; just being around him made me strong. He made me believe I was okay." He wept openly.

After a while I asked him to imagine that his grandfather was in the room with us. That they could talk, catch up after all this time, that he could be any age he wanted. He chose the age he was when his grandfather had died. Already able to visualize this scene unfolding before him, he began to vibrate slightly; his whole body gently shook as he lay on the floor feeling the presence of the old man who had touched him so profoundly as a boy.

"So what's he doing now?" I asked.

"He's got my hand in his. He's walking with me and holding my hand. Now we're walking in the field by his farm and we're barefoot. We're going down by the creek where we used to fish. He's baiting my hook." I ask him what his grandpa might have to say to him now.

"I'm proud of you and I love you." Big tears ran down his cheeks. In the ensuing silence, they sat together by that creek, this man and his grandfather, and the old man validated the masculine strength in the boy. After a while I asked him again what was happening. *"I am standing in a field now, a plain. A dark elk is standing before me, looking at me, just looking at me."* Then his body began to shake like a leaf. It was a holy moment, something rare and sacred. In that moment all I could do was sit still on the floor by his side; we sat there with that elk, or so it seemed, on the gold grass blowing in the summer wind, a thousand miles from my office.

Within a few weeks we met again. He spoke about the pressures he had been feeling in the past months, and about the confusion, but his voice was calm and steady. He recalled with clear eyes the old man's reappearance in his life; a reminder that someone had believed in him and had loved him unconditionally. As he spoke he began to draw a circle around himself on the rug. He told me he was carving a place around himself where he could feel the elk. From that ground he could speak to his grandfather, he could feel again the power of the old man who said, *"I honor you."* From this place he could touch base with the seed in himself that held the power of the old warrior.

The appearance of these powerful figures brings insight and courage, and it is these inner archetypes one must access to awaken the inner warrior. From within the circle of his sacred place, this man's grandfather arose, an archetype for strength and wholeness. Gradually, from that circle, the faces of his family began to emerge; a sense of longing for them rose up, a desire to be there for them as his grandfather had been there for him. His soul had been fed by feeling who he was as a man, and through connecting to the powerful grandfather who had believed in him. All of us have an inner warrior somewhere, a *Wizaya* figure that tells us to look up at the stars and to remember where we came from.

Magnificent Vulnerability

One time a young woman came to a women's group I was a part of. For the first few weeks she sat quietly and said nothing. Not long afterward, each time she came to the group, she wept. It was clear something very profound was happening. One evening during a storm, sitting as close to the fire as we could, we began to share our stories. This woman spoke after a while, and as she did, several of us wept. Of itself her story was not tragic, but the guilt she felt over her life touched some chord in each of us. At one time in her life she had been a prostitute who had lived much of her life in the shadows of night, and something deep within her was simply opening up and seeing itself; a voice inside her was groaning. She wept for the betrayal of herself, for the loss she felt; for her young son who had seen so many men with her; for the years the locust of self-hatred had stolen from her.

Each time she wept in the group, her guilt dislodged itself a little more; each new surrender brought its small gift. In time she said that the tears that rolled down her cheeks were not so much for the past, but about some grace she was feeling in the present moment.

I suspect holiness is not how much we have done that is right or good in the eyes of others; but rests instead on our ability to use what we have done (or failed to do) as an open window through which we long for God. At the close of one spring evening, during which there had been another shower, the group walked outside and stood looking up at the sky. The air was warm after the storm, and luminous clouds, soft red and mauve from the lights in the city, blew gently overhead. Directly over the building where we had gathered, the clouds suddenly seemed to part, and a window opened in the night sky. It opened, no doubt, because we were all inside doing our homework about being real; and because Somebody thought we were beautiful in that stripping.

The Indians say that the dark road is the path of our trials. We all walk on it at some time or another, and each of our struggles will be uniquely our own. The fortitude to confront what stands before us is there in each of us. Archetypes of power in the psyche are always present to some degree; but there are levels to courage that one must find and embrace in facing these winds from the North.

A valiant woman I worked with once, struggling with a mother's grief over the death of her son, told me that for years nothing had been able to shake her pain. She had the strength to endure her tragedy, but there was another level of courage for her to come to. Pointing to her heart she said, *"There's a hole so deep in here, nothing can touch it."* In our talking together, she shared the following dream. *"I go into a house with a friend of mine. In the sink is a small baby, but it's slipped under water. The child is blue and barely breathing and I run to pick it up. I cover its mouth with mine and begin to breathe into it, and slowly the baby revives. I hold it close to me, grateful it is alive. Then I come into a huge coliseum filled with people. To the North hoards of buffalo stream down through the stands, yet no one can see them but me. I keep looking at the buffalo and then at the others and asking, 'Don't you see them?' One of the buffalo comes up to me and has a red robe. As he comes closer, the red robe, which is draped over his massive shoulders, suddenly becomes like a fluid gently falling over the contours of his body, completely covering him. I woke up feeling there might be some hope for this child I had revived. But I don't think it was my son, I think it was me."*

This woman, whose grief went so deep, was asking for the strength to release her son. Since his untimely death some years before, she said she had tried but had never fully been able to let him go. Although intellectually she knew better, she still felt remorse for not being able to save him. Her despair over the years had caused her to feel a gaping hole in her side, a numbing emptiness.

As we worked together, all of us wept when she told her story. Most of us were mothers who could understand and feel her loss. I knew there was no special sort of therapy that might relieve her pain; I sensed the only thing to do was to surround her in prayer and wait for some direction from the Holy. We remained in silence with our collective tears and the ache inside, just waiting.

As I sat there I could suddenly imagine her son experiencing a deep grief too, not unlike her own; perhaps for the pain she held on to. I asked her if we could pray; if we could ask his spirit into our circle, so they might speak to one another. She nodded. We prayed for guidance, and I choked back tears, feeling an intensity hard to describe.

After a while she imaged him standing in front of her, tall and strong and handsome. I asked her if she could allow him to lead her to a place where they could talk together. She nodded. *"We'll go to the mountains, to the place where I scattered his ashes, facing the Sangre de Cristo mountains."* In the silent grace of her meditation, they spoke. In a windless afternoon, suddenly a breeze gently pulled on the chimes that hung outside the window. After quite some time she straightened and sat full upright, and a smile crossed her face. *"He's all right now. He's really all right."* There was a definite shift in her countenance, a movement from piercing grief to peacefulness. The look in her eyes when she opened them was clear and deep, and I could see the whole world in them.

I never knew the whole content of their conversation. But whatever shape it took in the late afternoon on the mountain where they were, it was the healing she had longed for. Even when her conscious mind couldn't surrender the events surrounding the death of her son, her unconscious and the Spirit of life in there was preparing a robe of courage for her. The dream had sent her the message that she could breathe life back into the drowned infant (her own faith in life). The dream had also given her the long-standing strength of the buffalo; the help she would need to release her son. Our Hidatsa teacher used to talk about the red road of courage; but this woman, although half Cherokee herself, had not known of it.

When we have these images, they are medicine; they don't just symbolize power, they embody that power. When we work in reverence within the realm of the Spirit, we don't just "see" these things randomly; they don't come "from the imagination." The imagination is merely a doorway to an inner realm. These images have transformational power.

The Medicine Heart of the Warrior

Ho beloved, offerings come
when the mind stone is broken into.
There are sounds in the wind
only the heart can hear.
Voices whose howl is pure praise,
whose spirit refuses the trap of words.
O dreamer that listens, stay awake!
You are alive in that wind.
—Djohariah Toor

Whether our words are weak and faltering or powerful and to the point—to "take heart" is a medicine all its own. Heart medicine, the courage to speak and to be, becomes especially strong when we have stood in the wind and faced whatever cleansing has blown our way. "Magnificent vulnerability" is not just a concept from the medieval church, but a practice of opening our deepest wounds, cleansing them, emptying out the ego, and giving ourselves to the Big Wash.

People who have been able to withstand the winter in the soul begin to have an inner strength that doesn't break in a high wind. When any of us does the difficult work of mending the divisions inside, picking up the pieces, healing long-buried wounds, the Spirit within us has more room to breathe. When our human will is cleansed of self-interest, the mind clears; the coverings of the false warrior are removed. And the essence underneath our fears and self-doubts peers up at us. Some holy voice of authority within us says: *Take this talking stick and don't be using it to stir the soup. Hold it carefully, speak with a bold heart, and stand for what you know. Say your needs and let them be known. Be yourself. Be your essence. Be the seed. Strip yourself down to the bone, and be the bone, but don't be what you're not.*

In most people, the voices of fear and condemnation don't easily give up. Old voices and programs tell us we are not enough, that we have no power and beauty, that we have no right to speak. No matter what shape it comes in, fear makes us afraid to be who we are. It helps to remember that in the heart of the warrior there are no words of condemnation. The warrior heart, when we give it room, spares no occasion to give us bold words of encouragement; it empowers us to tell our own story. The story we speak becomes our medicine because it magically connects us to the truth inside. That voice we can trust.

In the beginning of the chapter I talked about the message I heard on my vision quest that first year on the mountain in Colorado. In that message the stars—or something hanging on them—spoke to me. Voices out there on the mountain said, *Listen now. The Spirit is bigger than your fear. Make yourself humble and transparent and stretch your senses into the wind, and you will hear and see and feel what you need. Be strong in your spirit so that when you are tested, you can stand. Make yourself one with the Jesus in your soul.*

6. The East and Birthing Wisdom

The second year's fast had an altogether different nature to it. I chose to be alone this time, and as it turned out, I wound up on a reservation in a remote area of Montana. The mountain I went out on was a cinder cone that had been the site of many prayer fasts in the old days. The sky on the first night out had been full of stars. All night long I watched the constellations in their slow move across the heavens; feeling secure on the dark mountain that I was being looked after, that all was well. When the sun rose the following morning, it seemed immense and red. I burned sweet grass to stave off my hunger, to lift my spirits. The weather was warm and the Montana skies were an endless blue. I sat below my campsite on a patch of soft green cedar boughs, grateful for sun that touched my body with its shafts of gold light. I felt things and people come and go aimlessly through my mind. I wept, half out of joy, half out of a restless longing for the wisdom the elders say the East brings.

Later that day I hiked up to the top of the mountain. The climb up was steep, and often the trail disappeared altogether or went in more than one direction. I was weak from the fast and my heart pounded hard in the climb. In spite of the light-headedness I felt, I was excited, as though on the verge of something. At each resting point I turned and looked for the spotted eagles, hoping they would come. I spoke to them in my climb. *Ho Eagle! How shall I see like you do? How shall I catch the currents like you, rise up high on the winds so my world becomes not so all-important? I am stuck without wings here! I am without a vision here. Lord, I am small and fragile and I don't know how to give birth to you in lasting ways. Ho Eagle, teach me to fly!*

To catch my breath, I sat down with my thoughts and stared out across the hills and plains to the east. The ache inside was intense, and I lay back and tried to feel its meaning. I recalled a dream I had years ago in which I had become an eagle in flight; yet on my wings were long strings that weighed me down. I could fly but I wasn't soaring. At the time I knew the strings were attachments, things and people I hadn't let go of. But over the years, attachments have a way of coming back, especially when we're addicted to some of them. I began climbing again, mulling over what might still be weighing me down.

It was exhilarating to be alone; to have these days for reflection and solitude. There seemed an intensity in the landscape itself, a shimmering radiance in everything; the joy of sensing it, taking it in, was immense. Unlike the Lakota-style vision quest done the year before, in which I was confined to a small space, I had the whole mountain to walk about. Just before the top of the ridge, an outcrop of dark red lava rock caught my attention. The trail passed through it, dividing it in two. About thirty feet above the rock, the trail widened out across the top of the cinder cone. I stood for a moment, partly to catch my breath again, and partly to pause, as all wanderers must, to greet the spirit in such a landscape. The two magenta towers on either side of me stood like stone guardians, there for centuries, marking the passage to the top of the mountain. Pondering their greeting, and thinking of those who had walked this place before me, I suddenly heard a loud roaring sound on my right, like a great wind out of nowhere. I jumped back, caught off guard. Just feet away a large spotted eagle was diving with full force down the steep incline, its wings tucked into its huge body, its whole being driven in a downward plunge. About thirty or forty feet below where I stood on the trail it swung up again and circled over me. Then there were two, each peering down and flying in a wide circle overhead, crying out the way eagles do on the wind, filling the air with a shrill whistling. I raised my arms in a greeting to the pair in their majestic soaring. I stood there for a long time watching them with a profound stirring in my chest, tears running down my face, and deep inside a cry welled up and spilled out toward the sun.

Along the top of the ridge, colored prayer ties hung in the trees, robes from that year's Sun Dance. After exploring the remnants of the camps made by others in years past (whether there to pray or to hunt for deer or bear), I walked out on the point and stood on the southeast side of the ridge. I had received two signs to focus my prayer to the East. The rising sun had been bright red, and the eagles had come with their promise of renewal. One of the women who had helped prepare me for my time on the hill had told me, *"You don't go up there with any specific prayer in mind. You go up there empty. Don't have any formulas in your head about the directions. When you get up there you lift your prayers to God and you let go of everything else. Your best prayers are your tears. Maybe one of those (motioning to the Grandfathers in the directions) will come to you, and show you a sign. Then you can pray in that way."* I sang then eastward, asking for renewal, wisdom, vision; to birth and live from the truth inside.

"The East and Sees Far"

From the East comes the life-giving power of the rising sun. In many sweat lodge ceremonies, whether in the Navajo hogan or the tipi of the Plains people, the door faces East. The old people say that the Morning Star in that direction brings wisdom, that the Moon brings guidance. The East in many mythologies reflects wisdom, illumination, and understanding: the first light that opens each new day. In the Easter vigil, one stands in the early dawn after the long prayers and the silence of the night, and waits for the Resurrection light to break across the eastern horizon.

Morning light is always beautiful in the wilderness, powerful and life-giving. Whether we have had a restless night in our own bed wrestling with the powers of darkness and self-doubt, or whether we are sitting in the wild like monks or fishermen waiting for the blessing of day, first light is a sign that we can begin again. It says we are not bound to yesterday's dark dreams and fears and losses and that every moment is potentially filled with healing, with some new beginning.

When addressing the East, the Hidatsa woman often spoke of the sacredness of the eagle. When the third Grandfather spoke to Black Elk, he told him: *"Take courage younger brother, for across the earth they shall take you! Then he pointed to where the daybreak star was*

shining, and beneath the star two men were flying. From them you shall
have power . . . from them who have awakened all the beings of the earth
with roots and legs and wings. And as he said this, he held in his hand a
peace pipe which had a spotted eagle outstretched upon the stem: and this
eagle seemed alive, for it was poised there, fluttering, and its eyes were
looking at me. With this pipe, you shall walk upon the earth, and whatever
sickens there you shall make well."[1]

Once or twice in the sweat lodge ceremony with my Hidatsa teacher,
it seemed as though in the dark there was the sound of huge wings
flapping close by. I never saw anything, but clearly something numinous was present. Sometimes when the eagle enters a sacred ceremony, it comes as a healing presence. In the sweat lodge given for
me before my second vision fast, somewhere during the fourth and
final round of prayers I distinctly heard an eagle cry; or I heard the
sound of an eagle-bone whistle. It was loud and piercing and when
I heard it, all the wet hair on my neck and arms stood on end. I
clearly felt blessed, and I knew it meant something special.

The Hidatsa woman referred to them as the Eagle Nation, messengers of the Creator. In many mythologies, the eagle is a mediator
between heaven and earth because its flight means "prayer rising to
the Creator, and grace descending to mortals."[2] Among some Native
peoples it is said that the eagle has far-seeing vision, the ability to see
great distances. At the mythic level, the eagle symbolizes both the
ability to see from afar and the capacity to see intuitively: to be able
to navigate the inner world.

The metaphor for "sees far" refers to our ability to see objectively,
without sentimentality or attachment. It represents our ability to see
through denial, old mind-sets, blind spots, relationship tangles that
have too many strings attached. One who has this kind of clear vision
possesses the knowing of the crone midwife or the wise old man, the
wisdom figures in the psyche who can bypass the labyrinth of too
many emotions.

There is another way of seeing connected with the East. This is
one's ability to work with discernment, with a "third eye" vision that
comes to us intuitively. This is our ability to see inwardly as though
to observe life, as Saint Augustine puts it, with the "eye of the heart."
Inner seeing describes the realm of intuition, gut-level knowing,
dreams and visions; it is being able to tap the vast storehouse in the
collective unconscious. The "eye of the heart" is the Spirit of life

within us looking out of its apartment, bringing us information that the conscious mind doesn't have yet.

Many of my clients, for instance, have had strong intuitive experiences in which, through a dream or a vision, or a sense of inner knowing, they have seen things before they happen. Many mothers have this sixth sense for their offspring. My grandmother used to sense whenever my mother was sad or distressed, even though they lived a thousand miles apart. My mother-in-law used to dream the answer to the mathematical equations my husband had been working on while he was a student at the university. I met an elderly German doctor once on retreat in Taize in eastern France who had this gift. He could simply intuit the world around him; whenever he needed to know something, he sat still and closed his eyes, called on God, and there it was. Many Native American elders and third-world people who don't live outside themselves (in the fast lane) have this gift. They may know when you're coming before you arrive; they sense when the rains are approaching or when something is about to happen. Just before my father was diagnosed with cancer, I had a picture in a dream of his white buck shoes and they were empty. The image was distinct and real. A month or so later I received news that he had lymphoma. Many of us, when we're not going too fast, have access to this deeper realm of knowing. The East is that quadrant in the circle that governs our ability to open the inner eye.

The East and the Midwife

A second theme that comes from the East is the symbol of emergence. Its season is spring; meaning gestation, birth, openness, and change. The archetype to explore here is the midwife: the Great Old Man or the Old Wise Woman that Jung spoke of who is like a true grandparent in the soul. I chose the symbol of the midwife to symbolize the wisdom figure in the East because it is the midwife that helps us birth new life. The vignettes in the last chapter illustrated the hard work it requires to change, to heal. Since healing is a slow process, it is like gestation, a time in which things must cook in the dark. Something new is coming, but there's always the labor first. People who have to sit day after day and hold the tension of the opposites within themselves, to hold the conflict between the old complex and the new life, know this kind of labor.

The archetype of the midwife opens for us the door to creativity. She (like green buds in the spring) is our energy for new life. I sometimes ask my clients (and myself) what it might be like to imagine life without the old scripts, without yesterday's self-fulfilling prophecies chasing us. What would it take to imagine that we are free to experiment with our life dreams? People who long for something real in life, in relationships, in their work and career—people who long for change, for something new—are in the process of giving birth. Male or female, all of us have some creative fire we can work with. In the East, we ask, *What is the wisdom I want to give birth to?*

In circling through the directions, it's helpful to know that the work in each of the quadrants significantly overlaps. Each of the archetypes in the directions has a role to play. By the time we get to the East, we have the novice and the warrior right behind us. The novice keeps us honest about what we see and feel (and signals us when we may be back in shadow or denial). The warrior lends us not just the courage to go into the deeper wounds and to heal them, but also the endurance it will take to see us up to this part of the labor.

Birthing itself demands our full participation. Nobody should go into the labor of therapy or healing and recovery work imagining it's not going to require immense effort, profound concentration, an acute devotion to each contraction. Inner work, by the time we reach the eastern shore of the psyche, means we're about ready to give birth to something big. In that phase of the work we make a commitment every day to hold the pain and the promise, and not give up or anesthetize. People at this point in therapy are often right in the middle of a crossing, a crisis, or a change of some kind, but they don't know what awaits them.

One woman put it this way: *"I feel split from my old life, my old friends, the familiar roles I've lived, the things I've done. Every day I wake up feeling, 'There's got to be something more.' There's an ache inside to run away and start my life without all these old identities. I want to disappear into the woods and paint and swim naked in the creek and make love to the moon and stare into a campfire and just feel the shape of this new beginning in my soul."* This is a crucial point, because it often means that when departing from the old life, or at least from some parts of it, we waver. Some of us go back to the old identities, the old addictions, the old lifestyles.

The person who clings to old habits and ways of seeing may stay safe, but the labor stops. One woman said to me, *"I don't live my life like other people, because they haven't suffered what I've suffered. I can't accept love like other people because something in here feels I don't deserve it. Intellectually that's stupid, I know it's not true. Once in a while I feel what it's like to let somebody love me, give me support. But I sabotage it sooner or later, because at the gut level, I don't feel like I matter. I don't feel like I have the right to be."* This was a self-fulfilling script this woman carried with her. She didn't like it, but it was part of her family album (which she took with her into her relationships). Her family had indeed given her a message—*You don't have the right to be*—common to many men and women, particularly those who have suffered an abusive environment. The good news is that she realized she had enough faith in life to *choose* having the right to be.

In the East, we have an opportunity (or the need) to humble ourselves and "cry for a dream." At some point in our labor, if we are serious about healing our wounds, we will go into transition. Like it or not, the soul then demands we push. This is where the old midwife comes in and holds us up (right at the point when we want to give up) and says, *Yes, you can do this, and you will! The sun is rising! Breathe! Push!* All of us in the throes of transition need to hear this message.

The symbol of emergence represented by the East means we have the power to transform our lives, because every moment is pregnant with possibility. It means we don't have to be stuck in our attitudes, in our way of seeing the world, in convention, in a bad relationship; we don't have to stay in the soup of the past forever.

Seeing with the Eyes of the Past

The power in one's personal vision is dramatic. We are literally spellbound by what we see in life, or by what we think we see. Ultimately what we see and believe about ourselves determines our fate. A woman tells me she sees all men as untrustworthy, because that was her experience of her father. A man sees all women as objects because he is a flaming narcissist. Often a person's view of himself or herself is a similarly fixed idea. I have known many people who see themselves as unworthy (consciously or unconsciously) and they run their life program according to a self-fulfilling prophecy that says, *You don't deserve to be happy; you don't merit too much success or love.*

A man in a workshop I attended once was asked to say his name, to say something about himself to the others in the room. *"I feel nervous about doing that. I don't see myself standing out in the crowd like this. I feel very self-conscious."* It was a simple enough response, and one most of us in the group could relate to. The group leader then asked the man to make a picture of an earlier time in his life in which he had also not stood out. The man thought for a moment, and his expression changed into a sullen frown, then tears. *"I am a small boy. I'm standing in front of my mom. She's leaving home, and I am powerless to stop her."* His memory took him back to a traumatic event in childhood in which he recalled a painful separation from his mother. Along with the trauma of the divorce, he took on a huge burden of responsibility around the house. Because he had been the oldest of three brothers and sisters, the care of his siblings had fallen to him. In such a role, he couldn't afford to "stand out." For the sake of caring for the rest of the family, he had to fade into the woodwork.

The problem really has little to do with whether we have a "good" self-image or a "bad" self-image. Someone who has a "good" self-image generally has this image only consciously. In other words, people who have a high opinion of themselves are often very invested in keeping their image intact. In one workshop setting a man told me he wanted to work on feeling his anger, on the incongruity between his outer man (who was nice, who always acted reasonably) and the deeper wilder man that stormed inside. In the beginning he allowed himself to feel the wild man. He screamed and pounded the floor and we wrestled and he cursed at life and me and I cursed back at him. People around us held their breath and braced themselves or jumped out of the way. But at some point he couldn't go on. His self-image was coming back, and the work to release the wild man stopped. Having these raw feelings was exhilarating, they made him feel free for a moment. But almost immediately they became unacceptable feelings, and the old censor in him reclaimed his territory.

The struggle he felt reminded me of the woman who had the dream of the snow goose; in her heart she felt a longing to be like that soaring bird, but she had to wrestle with a self-image that had trouble experiencing that much freedom. This is a scenario I have entertained myself over the years. Inside something tells me I am a spotted eagle with a great wingspan that effortlessly catches the wind; but another voice tells me I still haven't paid my dues to mankind, and when I listen to that voice, my wings are clipped, and my soaring stops in midair.

Many individuals cannot let go of themselves because of a loyalty to the adaptive roles picked up in childhood. Whether that means being responsible, in control, enduring, nice, patient, clever, not to be messed with, brilliant, beautiful, fragile—all these imprints of childhood roles hang suspended under our hats.

Some contemporary advocates of personal growth say that we can consciously choose to believe a certain thing about ourselves. Change our perception of ourselves, and we create new consciousness. I can say I choose to see myself as capable, creative, powerful. I can act that way at times; I can even believe it. When I do this, I am shaking loose some of my old beliefs about myself. But I may only be changing my conscious self-image.

The problem is that the conscious mind is always governed in part by the unconscious. The self-image is divided, its good intentions on one side, and its past impressions on the other. The conscious mind might say to itself, *I'm definitely going on a diet. Everything's going to be different from here on out. Now that I have this insight, I just need a little willpower.* But anyone who has tried over and over to stop compulsively eating, drinking, gambling, or spending, anyone who has tried not chasing perfection at work, or who has tried not to fall repeatedly into codependent relationships, will tell you a predictable story. Try to alter any habit, and it soon becomes clear that lasting change is not just about conscious choice; it's also about getting to the unconscious impressions that have rooted themselves deep in the child's psyche we still carry around.

Dialogue with the Split

I want to illustrate in a little more detail the split in self-image, because it's a gap people repeatedly fall into. A young woman in a recovery process had been in Alcoholics Anonymous for about five years. She had done well for the first few years, but then she experienced a series of relapses. She "worked" a good program, had a loving sponsor, and couldn't understand her recent failure to stay grounded in recovery. *"I have no reason to use. I have a good job, I've come a long way. I'm headed someplace. I've got my life in order. I'm a lot stronger than I used to be. But every time my boyfriend and I have a fight, I want to forget recovery. I just want to use. And I can't understand it, after all the work I've done."* The outer personality does well for a while; her recovery and its rewards seemed to carry her along. Yet the unconscious self-image has its own story.

Eventually she remembered that at about the age of twelve, she had been sexually molested. Initially she had pushed away the shame and humiliation, the terrible sense of diminishment she had felt, until gradually her memory of it ceased. Although she managed to forget the incident consciously, whenever she had a fight with a significant other, or a major setback to her self-esteem, trouble followed. Part of the problem was that under pressure, she unconsciously identified with the twelve-year-old victim; each time a major threat to her self-esteem came up, the victim child came up too. To escape the pain of these old feelings, she drank.

A man who had smoked dope for years had begun to recognize that he had a problem. Yet once he started to talk with his addiction, he began to see that the reason he had trouble quitting was that it was giving him something he'd been missing. *"When I smoke dope my mind literally feels free—something in my head just expands. I can talk to others when I'm high, I can be myself. I feel connected to the world. I can even feel God, or definitely something bigger than I am. When I'm not high, communication is hard for me. I don't feel free to be myself."* In this case, the outer personality doesn't like the addiction and wants to quit; on the other hand there is a man in the unconscious who is afraid of the outer man's rigid and controlling ways. The only time he can get the rigid man upstairs to loosen up is when he can talk him into using. The outer man and the inner man had never seen eye to eye.

In the dialogue that ensued between this man and his symptom, he was able to experience how the inner man was starved for contact, for feelings, relationship, closeness. The inner addict wasn't interested in control, didn't care if he made mistakes, wanted to quit body-building and become a sculptor. As it turns out, this man had taken care of his mother as a child, because she was entirely dysfunctional and "needed" him to be there for her. Growing up, he had very little connection to his feeling world or his wants when his mother was around—because they fell headlong into the Grand Canyon of her needs, which automatically diminished him. Later on in life, substances became his connectedness to others, the elixir he used to feel his needs being met. When he found he could engage in a dialogue with the *unconscious* self-image (the boy who felt he had no rights), he could then consciously practice being honest and clear in relationships, without actually smoking dope. The difference was that he had begun to image himself as having the right to ask for contact, playfulness, for affection and closeness, and his inner wild man could emerge.

In this quadrant, each of us must ask if what we "see" in ourself is really a reflection of the breakthrough work we've done, or whether we are still recycling some museum piece from our past. Childhood complexes, which are not so rare these days, are going to trap the energy for change, because of the painful and often invisible disunity in the ego. The question here is: *What are the healing images I need? What will feed the soul?*

Let's turn once more to the wisdom of the dream. A friend of mine, recovering from an abusive and incestuous father, and struggling to deal with the ways she had for years dissociated from pain, told me the following dream: *"I was traveling with a young man in a red sports car, and it was very sleek and close to the ground. I wondered if we were in a race, but then I found out we weren't. This young man and I came to a church. In church a celebration was going on. We wanted to go into the front, because it looked like that was where the service was happening. But I had to go to the bathroom and so I went looking for one down the hall. I found the ladies' room and it was all dirty; kind of dingy like a subway station, with graffiti written all over the walls. I thought, This can't be it. But it was. So I looked for a toilet, but all there was, was a hole in the ground. I could see way down to the floors below. I felt reluctant but finally sat down on this hole in the floor. Then I thought, 'I have to go down this hole.' I thought, 'No that's crazy,' but I went anyway right down into the basement of the church. I wasn't hurt at all. Then I saw the young man rushing for a train and he wanted me to come too, but I knew I had to go back to the basement of the church, so I let him go on, and I went back to what I had to do."*

This dream signaled her what her next move was about. In order to face the unconscious elements that would have disempowered her healing work, she had to leave the upstairs of the church. The upstairs, where there was a celebration going on, represented the nice world of appearances, the respectable or religious side. Her route was instead through a dirty bathroom written all over with graffiti: a place in the church that had a dark shadow side to it. Her family had all been devoutly religious, and in particular her father who had molested her and her sisters on a regular basis. Part of this woman's survival had been focusing her life on other people. Her animus (the young man) had her running around compulsively caretaking others in a driven way (speeding along in a red sports car). This was how she had outrun her pain.

She began to have a dialogue with the split inside her, and to dive headlong into the painful rift between the victim child of incest, who had turned into the adult caretaker, and the real woman underneath whose soul wanted to heal. Her vision of herself (once she got free of seeing herself as a victim) could begin to transform.

A woman I worked with wanted to change her codependent relationship to a man she had been engaged to marry. Tired of being self-effacing and being second in his presence, she wanted to stand up to him. She had already done some degree of her own inner work; she knew her blind spots in the relationship. But she hadn't been able to heal the conflict between her conscious intention (I know I can say the truth) and the unconscious self-image (I don't count enough to say my feelings).

Then she had a dream in which she saw both of these sides clearly. In the dream there were two female children walking with her in a mountain setting. One of them was beautiful and healthy, the other one was crippled and frightened. They were walking together and suddenly a huge shadowy figure tried to kidnap the lame child. *"You can't do that,"* she shouted, and ran after the man who had stolen her child. *"I felt terrified but furious and I caught hold of him and wrestled him to the ground until he loosened his grip on the lame child. Then in the light I saw the face of the intruder. It was my father's face. When our gaze met he relinquished the lame child to me. Then he became a small child himself, with a lame leg. I realized he had passed his inferiority, his brokenness to me as a child. On the outside he was critical and blamed everybody, but on the inside he was frightened and paralyzed to be himself. If I'd let him steal the lame child, he would have taken my wound away;*

then I would have had no awareness of her. I had to have her back. She is part of my healing."

Now she was ready to confront her fiancé. She had seen where the father complex (her wound) had kept her from being true to herself. *"I knew what I felt but not how to say it. I just went ahead anyway. I told him, 'I love you and care for you, but I'm not willing to sacrifice myself anymore. I want equal footing here, instead of continually sliding into an abyss around you, giving in to what you want, what you think. I count too and I'm here to say that from now on, love is either going to be reciprocal, or the deal is off.'"* Here was the intuitive side of her, working instinctively from the dream symbol. She was both seeing and speaking from the inner woman whom she had begun to distill.

The ability to be "far seeing" means we can use the power of the image in practical ways, as this woman did by bringing her conflict (and her dream) into dialogue. Once we can reach through the complex that has our creativity bound up, we can pull some of these vital images through.

The Creative Process in Imagery

The metaphor of facing East is about conforming our self-image to the new life we want to create. Clearly there is healing and guidance in the images that come from the soul: the question is, How do we bring those images to birth? How do we get a vision for our life that feels real?

The roads to the creative unconscious are pathways that are, for the most part, mostly unexplored; yet images can heal and change lives. The energy of the old crone midwife is important here, because we have to lure the images out, to coax them out to consciousness, and it takes some wisdom to do that. Images don't just come because we want them to. We have to make a place for them, prepare in some way—perhaps by living more meditatively, or creatively. Once we get an image, it has to be given time to take shape. We have to talk with it, draw or paint it, write about it, act it out (perhaps in a role-play or creative ritual). It has to be made concrete and given shape through art, clay, dance, poetry. The old crone midwife (our creativity) helps us birth the image. If we meditate on the symbol as it comes, the Spirit can illuminate and clarify its meaning.

Consulting the spontaneous power of our waking images is another distinct way to open up to the creative side of the mind. A man whose wife had left him had become depressed and had thoughts of suicide. The root of his depression, however, was not that she had left him, but that his own identity had never fully developed. He had fused with his mother as a child, and he had simply transferred that dependence to his wife. As long as she believed in him and needed him, he was all right. When she left, his strength failed him.

In one session I asked him if he could image the way he was feeling. He closed his eyes for a moment and saw a small boy, completely alone and frightened. We worked with that for a bit, then I asked him to give me an opposite image. After a while he saw a red-tailed hawk in flight. I asked him to be the hawk. He stayed with that picture for some time. After a while he said, *"I feel something. I can see the small boy down there but I don't feel his fear. I'm soaring. I feel something like—I feel wings under me. More moments passed in silence. I feel tears but I don't feel sad. I feel free. I've never been alone and felt free. This hawk is alone, and it's okay."*

Maybe for the first time in his life, he had an image from his possible self. His identity had been wound up in his wife for years, and with her gone, the abandoned boy in him was lost. Yet had he remained identified only with his pain, he would never have found the hawk. All along, the makings of the red tail hawk had been in this man; but he had never accessed them. It wasn't until she had left that he could feel this power, could feel his aloneness and not be afraid he was "nothing."

No matter what our crisis or trouble is there is always at least one door that opens in the present that gives us a glimpse of the truth. The Greeks used to call this sort of visual image a gift from the "eides," a little visit from the gods. The eidetic image contains tremendous power to transform and heal; the archetypal healing forces that come to us from the wisdom in the unconscious are powerful. They open our eyes to the present moment. In the French classic *Abandonment to Divine Providence,* the author says we must embrace the present moment because it provides "an ever flowing source of holiness."[3] When we don't cling to our personal history, we clear the way for new, more potent images.

One of the women in a group I once did had a profound experience along these lines. Initially she told me that although she had done a lot of work in her own recovery, she periodically felt discouraged. *"I can only go so far, then the voice of doom rears its ugly head and I'm done for."* Somewhere in the middle of a weekend workshop, she told us the following story: *"I was sitting outside in the grass just meditating and feeling a lot of what had been coming up for me this weekend— when I heard a kind of chatter behind me. I looked around and saw a black squirrel. As soon as it saw me it ran away, scurried up a tree, and hid behind one of the large branches. I thought suddenly, 'This is exactly what I do to myself.' Like that black little squirrel I creep up on myself from behind and chatter at myself. No matter what I've healed or accomplished, a little voice goes off inside, chasing me, scolding, saying 'You're not good enough.'"* The power of this discovery came about because she had been awakened to the old self-image as it manifested in the shape (and the "voice") of the black squirrel.

Eventually I asked her if she could go around the room and say something truthful about herself to each individual in the group. She hesitated, *"That would be too humiliating; like disrobing, taking off all my clothes."* The dilemma she faced in her mind's eye was that she had always seen herself as a person who should have the protection of self-control. Self-image, when it digs its heels into the unconscious, is often reluctant to do something "out of character" with the original image. I told her I thought she was right, that this was like disrobing. But if she could disrobe and expose her deeper need to the group, then she wouldn't have to listen to that little black squirrel forever.

She began facing each woman in the circle, talking to them. The latent power of the old image—bearing the message *"You shouldn't be doing this"*—brought her a racing heart, tears, and intense fears of rejection. The old self-image felt outraged, shamed, self-doubting; yet the new one (to which she was trying to give birth) went on addressing the women in the circle. In effect, she was challenging her old taboos, opening up the abyss of her shame, facing the voices of discouragement, shame, and self-doubt, and she was magnificent.

As she finished the circle she suddenly felt an intense lower back pain. I asked her if she wanted to lie in the middle of the circle and be held. As she leaned back into the laps and arms that supported her, she felt what she described as labor. There were about fourteen women holding her; gently massaging her stomach, torso, her arms, hands, feet, chest, and solar plexus, all of us humming quietly, waiting, sitting with her. After quite some time the process ended, and when she sat up the pain was gone. Several women in the group said they felt as though they had witnessed her giving birth to herself. This work is like a woman's labor: on one side there's immense fear and trepidation, on the other side something beautiful comes.

This drama of transformation came about because this woman allowed the struggle between the conscious and unconscious personality to emerge. She chose to confront the old self-image within, and therefore dispelled its dark hold over her. With the help of this kind of vulnerability she exercised her worst fear, and in the breakthrough that ensued, gave birth to more of her original self. Contemplatives of all centuries say that inner peace happens only when we touch the present moment; then the dark of the past dissolves. Any self-image we identify with too strongly needs this disrobing. If my friend with the black squirrel had identified too closely with her fear of being vulnerable, with the thought of being humiliated, she never could have done this piece of work. But she chose the eagle instead.

The eagle, in many mythologies, not only flies closest to the heavens, but has the power to mediate the inner world to us. About a year after the bear dream, I had an encounter with a golden eagle. My husband and I had returned to Alaska for a wilderness fishing trip with our son and daughter-in-law; and we had boated and walked through some rugged country to get to a remote lake in the Alaskan interior, famed for its fleshy pike. I had been listening to the rain pelting my tent, aware of how hard the ground had been; feeling deep inside how tired I was. Over the months back home I had finally managed to take on fewer commitments. I had also fired a number of time-consuming obligations (and the acquaintances that went along with them). But caretakers can always find some problem to wrestle down, even when the conscious mind knows better. I knew my dreams were signaling me that the artist and the mad poet inside longed for more wilderness behaviors, more time spent with the Great Old Woman, the mother of visions.

I rolled out of my sleeping bag, glad to get off the hard ground underneath it, and pulled on my rain gear. I had spent the first few days of my vacation doing strenuous walking, poling a heavy boat laden with gear up a shallow creek, stepping in potholes of ice water up to my hips, cooking in the rain, cursing like a Dutch sailor over the burning socks I hung too close to the fire to dry.

Still early, the rain turning to a light shower, I took a long walk along the shore of the island, and headed toward a southern point where I had seen some eaglets nesting the day before. Rounding the corner, not far from the point, I saw another golden eagle, this one perched in the branches of a huge black spruce. I slowed my pace, but kept steadily walking, expecting him to take flight any second. I stopped finally, just feet away, and stood staring into his dark eyes, amazed he had given me permission to come so close. A light mist continued to fall in the cold morning above the lake, and the two of us continued to gaze at one another, sharing for a while the patch of ground between his reality and mine.

In the long moments that ensued, I stood still beneath the great bird, not daring to move much, talking softly and singing some praise or another. I had been walking that morning clad in a pair of old yellow rubber boots, covered over by a ponderous black umbrella half a century old that had never seen an eagle. Perhaps the golden had never seen a black umbrella with yellow boots either. Maybe that's why he hadn't taken flight. We had caught each other by surprise in the early morning; neither of us seemed compelled to move. Out of the corner of my eye I could see tiny pink wild roses, and random stalks of white iris glistening with dew. Loons across the lake made their plaintive cry, and I spoke softly to the eagle, telling her I wanted her wings to soar on the currents with; her eyes to see long distances with; her heart that drew so close to the Creator. And an inner voice said, *"You want to know how to fly? Let go of the branch."*

I walked back to camp in my yellow boots, loaded down with purple wildflowers, sure something powerful had just happened. For the next few days I was awakened each morning by the sound of huge wings in a swooping descent near my tent, a piece of the sky diving down just as the dawn began to spill its silver light on the lake. I sat by its waters each day, relaxing a little more, gradually unwinding, filled with the promise that the coming year was about midwifing some important changes. Less work and more poetry, more nights sleeping under the stars, more painting and less compromising. I decided that the Great Mother caretaker in me would have to move over for the artist, the village idiot who didn't have to be responsible for the cosmos; for the emergence of a wandering monk rattling her bones and singing in public more and taking life less seriously.

Working with the Power of Vision

And at the end of woe, suddenly our eyes will be opened,
and in the clearness of our sight, our light will be full,
which light is God, our Creator....
—Julian of Norwich[4]

Native American traditionals say that when we face the four sacred
directions in prayer, each direction is alive with a gift for us. As I
point myself in that direction, I am in touch with a sense that the
gift has a twofold nature. The gift is "out there" and simultaneously
"in here."

When I stood facing the West in my first vision quest, I knew that
the shape of the clouds I saw, the sunset in swirling circles through
the aspen, and the figures in the trees were also shapes within my
own heart. If the red clouds in the West shaped a horse and rider,
brightened by the falling rays of the sun, it was a gift for me to ponder
within; not a phenomenon out there in the distance unrelated to me.
Since the first vision fast (when in the North I saw the great warrior in the silhouette of the trees) I have read Lakota and Oglala
stories that talk about *Waziya*. Perhaps the traditional people would
say this was a vision of the Grandfather in the North. Still others
might insist that it was not a vision apart from me, but a living
energy within me: a voice that said, *"In your life, don't be afraid of
anything."*

Along with many Native traditionals, I personally believe that the
directions are sacred powers without; they are the "robes" that house
the spirit world. I believe that, from time to time, the eye of the heart
can see into that world. I have talked to people who have had visions
of angelic forces, a deceased friend or relative, and to several people
who have had images of Christ, or a great light, or swirling patterns
of light. I knew a man from Nigeria who used to be able to see a
bright light around certain people. He didn't see this all the time;
but, being a holy man, his eyes were sensitive to these things. Whenever there is leisure time, I pick up Julian of Norwich's book, *Showings;* I read there of her profound vision of the passion of Jesus, and
of her revelations of the "motherhood of God."[5] I am always touched
by these revelations, certain that in my work and play with others, I
have also often seen the Mother God at labor. Clearly there is a spiritual

world that most of us won't know about until we see it or hear it or feel it breaking through to us.

Yet no matter how profound the images or how stunning the vision, these things often remain like fragile shoots underground unless we put them to work in some way. One might spend all summer on the mountain contemplating life, or one's entire lifetime having insights, dreams, intuitions, and glimpses of God. But unless we actively use what we've been shown, our vision will have no power. Black Elk found that he had to share his vision with the community, for instance, in order to affirm the truth of it. Julian of Norwich, after receiving the "showings," spent years pondering them, meditating on their meaning, and writing about them.

Spring means giving birth to new life, to new vision, without the burden of our old attachments. It is important to ask ourselves from time to time, *Without the past weighing me down, without my old self-image, without my limits, who am I?* Asking that question is the first task.

Bringing these interior images to life is the second task. To do that, we have to contemplate them; to keep them close by to refer to; we have to write and draw and dialogue with them in order to bring the power out. We have to sing over them. And we have to practice them.

I want to give one more example of the creative process in imagery, because it illustrates what can happen when we are open to the Spirit in our work. The woman whose experience I am about to talk about had been in therapy for some time; one of her most painful issues was a mother and father who both effectively abandoned her. She was from a large family (ten children); her mother was distant, cold, strict, and talked over her children's heads most of the time. Her father was a naval officer who was gone most of the time, but when home, although more affectionate, was also a strict man. This piece of work began with an image this woman had of being a two-year-old child, suddenly alone in the wild. We took this image and amplified it.

"I am left alone in a meadow, and no one is there to take care of me. It's dark. There's a lone wolf nearby in some trees. I also see some people standing some ways away. I know I have to choose whether to go with the wolf or to go with the people. But how can the wolf take care of me? So I go to a clearing near the edge of the forest, and suddenly all these

people are standing around me. I desperately want to be picked up and held, but no one comes to me. They all stand around talking, as though my being all alone was something they could solve by talking. How can they just stand there? I feel utterly alone. I leave there and I walk along.

I see a small village. There's a man sitting under a street lamp on a stool, and I approach him. It is my father. He's all dressed in his Navy uniform, and he is young and handsome, and I know that I love him. He picks me up and sits me on his lap tenderly, and he says, 'I'll help you, I'll teach you how to be a little girl.' But as I sat there on his knees, something was wrong. I knew that what he meant by that was that he would teach me to be his little girl, or to be the kind of girl that would be pleasing to others. But that's not me, and so I get down and leave him. I'm walking by a café and in there I see an older woman. I see her through the window, and I think maybe she can help me be a little girl. But when I approach her, she is cold and unkind. Her face is bitter and it looks burned out, and I know she can't help me either. I feel sad that she can't teach me how to be a girl child.

Now it's daylight and I'm leaving the village. I go back to the forest, and the wolf is there; she welcomes me and she is kind and gentle. She lets me play with her fur and keeps me warm. I feel safe for the first time. Then she takes me up on her back and we go through the forest to her cave in the woods." At this point in the imagery she stopped and became silent. Then I asked her what she was experiencing. She said, "*I'm entering the mouth of the cave, and I can see an object some distance away. It is a gift from the mother wolf, but I can't make it out.*" Then suddenly this woman burst into tears and cried out, "*It's a doll! It's a girl doll! And it's me!*" She sat sobbing and rocking back and forth, and several of the women in the group gathered around and held her, while she held her doll. The doll of herself.

She said some months later that the healing images in that piece of imagery had stayed with her and had been very nurturing and empowering. For one thing, the image of her father as a handsome young man (before his alcoholism) gave her a sense of forgiveness toward him. When she saw the face of the older woman in the café, whom she later recognized as her mother, she could also feel a new empathy toward her, and for the life her mother had failed to live. The power of the image shifted something for her. "*I had always expected my mother to be a mother, or to be strong or to be there for me. But when she wasn't, I used to be there for her, to be strong, to care for her; I was a mother to her. We were completely enmeshed. I felt abandoned and angry that she could never be a mother to me, but I suddenly understood when I saw that old woman's face. I can't explain it, but I felt a real acceptance of her. And the doll in the cave. I never expected it. It just took my breath away. That was me in there that the she-wolf had led me to. That was her gift to me. She was giving me back the gift of myself. It was amazing. I still have that image in my mind, and it still feeds me."*

From the initiations and dreams that jar us awake, we begin a path toward change. The long work with the polarities and tensions in life that stretch us, the shaking loose of old attachments, all this prepares us for psychic birth. We dream about it long before it happens, as though the unconscious signals us from the first moment of our breakthrough, that it's time to begin the labor. Images from the soul are alchemic; they can strain the impurities from the mind. Images that take us to these depths reconstellate the healthy side of the unconscious, because they open our capacity to see beyond our limits. They take us into the realm of light.

7. The South and the Heart

Southward from the top of the ridge, endless fields of rolling wheat spread out below as far as the eye could see. Miles away the tin roof of a barn flashed silver in the sun. Somewhere in the distance I could hear the droning of a sawmill. Next to where I sat were three or four piles of large stones, rock cairns that had been many generations on the mountain, each stone a prayer offering by someone who had been there before. July in the mountains on the ridge was shared with hundreds of buzzing creatures of every shape and size. At times I welcomed them and tried to share my patch of ground with them as they crawled over me, hummed around my ears and darted into my face. I thought of the monks, East and West, who used to sit meditating, unflinching at the biting and stinging of little insects. At other times these little creatures were a nuisance, a seeming endless distraction I had little patience for.

Of all the directions, this one seemed the most enigmatic. Facing the South, one prays for humility, for patience, compassion, for love and healing. My prayers went out from the mountain for those things, for all the people in my life, whether I loved them or not. The sun gradually grew hot and by noon a warm wind rose up. I took my clothes off and circled all the directions in prayer, then lay down in the warm sun to let my thoughts wander. I began to feel exposed up there with no clothes. Weaving in and out of my meditations came fantasies of intrusion, derision. Once or twice I pictured someone coming and felt in advance my shame; a little surprised at the strength of my inhibition. I tried to put such thoughts out of my mind but they persisted in coming back, even worse than the small black gnats that kept up their steady visitation on my bare skin. One of my teachers had told me once to look for the teaching in such annoyances. I stopped my prayers and listened to my fears without trying to push them away. I thought to myself, I'm sitting here naked and exposed and I'm afraid of this kind of undoing. I'm praying for an understanding of love and I have fantasies of being shamed, laughed at. I have unconditional love for others in their vulnerability; but when it comes to my own nakedness, when it comes to this sort of utter transparency, here love falters. I thought of Saint Francis, who once ordered one of the shiest of the brothers to the altar to preach. When the terrified monk faltered and stammered on the altar, and people in the audience began to laugh, Francis suddenly rose up, stripped himself of his cassock, strode to the front of the church, and preached on the power of nakedness. Tears streamed down my face.

As I walked back down the mountain to my camp, the loose shale and precipitous slant of the trail made me fall hard three or four times. During one tumble I reached up and grabbed a tree limb with my left hand. As I grabbed for the branch, a finger broken years before suddenly shot through with excruciating pain. I folded up on the trail and held my sprained finger, suddenly afraid of being alone with this much pain; my escort back to town was not scheduled to come until the following day. I began to wonder if some malevolent spirit wasn't trying to oust me from the mountain. I was tempted to wonder if my fall had something to do with not being grounded enough, or whether it was just the shale and the steepness of the trail. It occurred to me, however, that when I could be naked like Francis, when I had that much trust toward being vulnerable, then even loose shale wouldn't be an obstacle. Once back at camp, I rested, prayed over my swollen finger that throbbed with pain, wrote in my journal with my good hand, and waited for night to fall.

When we go on the mountain, we take our burdens with us. We go up there not just to pray for a vision, not just to purify ourselves, but to pray for others as well. I had taken many hearts up there. For years I have listened to stories about how love is often misunderstood, abused, squandered, withheld, lost, turned to hatred; how it brings even to lovers a strange blend of wild ecstasy and unfathomable pain. I regularly hear tales of love turned to violence, incest, jealousy, craziness, to the covert tyranny of an apartheid in our own homes. On the hillside one's mind wanders, recalling randomly the faces of clients, friends, relatives past and present, remembering the poignancy of souls that have touched us. One never goes up there alone. I thought of the reservation whose ground I was camped on; of the people there struggling under a bad system of politics; of the ones who spoke day after day of some tragedy, yet struggled to stay bold on the land. I felt, too, a portent of things stirring in the Persian Gulf, an uneasy prompting that the men of war in my country were preparing for a brutal display of power. I was certain I heard voices of fire in the wind. I thought of the earth and its painful abuses. On this mountain, in the wind, in the rocks, the trees, from the ground up, I felt an anguished cry for love rise up within that felt as though it would tear me off the mountain.

Late that evening, just before sunset, a lone wolf howled close by, and night came bringing a soft covering of clouds. If the wolf had arrived, surely Francis was somewhere nearby. A wind had come up, warm and filled with smells of pitch, ozone, and smoke from a forest fire far away. I sat up in my sleeping bag and pulled myself under a tree as the first few drops of a light rain began to fall. The shifting pattern of clouds in the night sky stretched out like a coverlet under the galaxies, covering the stars, the moon. And under a swirling blanket of red sky I felt involuntarily swept into the center of an enormous broken heart that seemed to cover the planet.

South and the Lover Archetype

The direction of the South represents the season of summer, symbolizing fullness and the verdant power of nature. For the Hidatsa, the Power in the South governs love, compassion, healing, and purity. To the Cheyenne the power of the South is for innocence and trust, and for perceiving closely the nature and the "things of the heart."[1] According to Black Elk's vision of the four sacred winds, the South is the direction of the flowering stick, symbol of the "power to make grow."[2]

Each of Black Elk's visions of the sacred directions (and the powers that reside there) has its own symbolic meaning, but this one has always struck me as one of the most beautiful of the symbols. As the power of the South spoke to him, he said, *"With the powers of the four quarters you shall walk, a relative. Behold the living center of a nation I shall give you, and with it many shall you save."* Black Elk went on to say, *"And I saw that he was holding in his hand a bright red stick that was alive, and as I looked it sprouted at the top and sent forth branches, and on the branches many leaves came out and murmured and in the leaves the birds began to sing. And then just for a little while I thought I saw beneath it in the shade the circled villages of people and every living thing with roots or legs or wings, and all were happy."*[3] I have never looked at this passage without a profound sense of awe. A flowering tree is a beautiful image for the heart and, indeed, for the wounded heart among the nations of the world. When the "bright red stick" (the power in the heart) is flowering, then what comes from that center is life giving. Love is a healing medicine, a fertile thing, alive with the possibility of empowerment for the whole planet. If we can hold the flowering stick, it becomes a sheltering, powerfully rooted tree.

Yet facing South on the mountain that second year of doing the vision quest, and struggling with the enigma of loving, I felt none of this. In the early dawn I had prayed for myself and my family and loved ones, my clients and friends. In the afternoon on the ridge I prayed for the people in El Salvador, Guatemala, Iraq, Ethiopia, East Oakland, for the people in the street. I wandered the streets of the nations and in my nakedness I stamped the ground and raised my arms and cried out for the tree. Love is medicine. Yet so far, the way of the heart is still unknown to most of us.

The Flowering Stick

Hildegard of Bingen, in her *Book of Divine Works,* spoke of the fullness of creation as a "greening power." She saw creation in full bloom as a flowering of God's hand not only over the earth, but over the human soul. *"For . . . the Holy Spirit poured out this green freshness of life into the hearts of men and women so that they might bear good fruit."*[4] In this vision, Hildegard saw that the energy behind creation was a divine heart with a living fire that moved through all things.

The "green" Hildegard talks about, similar to the "flowering stick," is a potential within the heart; it sends out buds only when we have spent time nurturing the tree of life inside. When any of us honors the flowering stick, we ask for the ability to trust our growth; we ask for the ability to stay in touch with the heart of life and not run from it. This is the archetype of the lover.

I've heard it said that "there is only one sin, and that is not to love enough."[5] Yet most of the people I talk to, including the people I prayed for on the mountain, often lose sight of loving because the "green" in the heart is blocked. The heart and its potential for aliveness are on hold because for many of us love was painfully conditional, measured by what we did or failed to do.

People who walk into my office in relational conflict are often anxious, confused, depressed, fearful, or angry. The pain they experience is a symptom that says they have lost the great tree. The problem is that all of us have an original wound around loving. Somewhere early on, the green doesn't bud out because the trust we arrive on the planet with is betrayed. When we are met with parents or peers or institutions who don't have a flowering stick themselves, there is little or no vitality to pass on. Consequently most relational behaviors are defensive, reactive, bound sometimes by fear or a notion of exchange and reward. If love and attention come to us initially as black and white and there is no green, then love goes dormant.

Parents who bring in their children or adolescents for therapy often look to the therapist to fix something that has gone wrong, not seeing that the problem is the family tree as a whole. They do not see that somewhere along the way the sap in the tree has dried up. One young boy I worked with repeatedly created a sandtray that featured a tree without any green leaves. Each time we came into my office he painstakingly stripped the toy oak trees of their branches and set them, bare and empty, in the middle of his tray. His play told me that something in his life was a wasteland. His own internal center, which should have been in full blossom, was barren. He should have been tearing into adolescence and young manhood with some fire and wildness, with his hopes and dreams running ahead of him, with his strength intact; but inside he felt depressed and powerless. Each time he left my office, I painstakingly pieced together my dismembered oak trees, trying to think through what he was trying to show me, aching for him.

If love and trust have been wounded, if the past and the people in it have knocked the buds off the flowering stick, then love gets tangled up with motives aimed at relief, gratification, or some other kind of emotional revenue. The good news is that when we are young, the seed of authentic love is always there in the soil somewhere; the green is always a potential that can take off and grow, whether anyone has bothered to nurture it or not.

Jungian analyst Marie Louise von Franz said once that relational squabbles are the same the world over because the problem is that people don't really *see* one another. They blot one another out by projection; or by needing to see in one another what they fail to find in themselves. People in marital struggles come into my office mad and disillusioned because their partner has not compensated for some parental wound or another. Or the family ghosts have all come out of the closet and are having a clash: a woman discovers the man she married is suddenly acting just like her father, or a man finds himself face to face with his wife's father's ghost. Relational issues live on and on, whether our ancestors are here or not.

For the Navajo, the South is the direction of the Corn Mother, the nurturer and provider of sustenance, keeper of the sacred pollen that is the kernel of life. In one legend farther south, from the Huichol of Mexico, a young corn maiden is compelled to grind corn for her relatives. As she is grinding, her arms disappear, then gradually her whole body. Her willingness to grind herself away symbolizes her maternal desire to become substance for others. When love and kindness are given unconditionally, the result is food, bread for life. However, until we can learn to be substance for ourselves, we can't be bread for anybody else.

It's true that some of us give ourselves away in the process of misunderstanding love. People get caught in projections, games of pursuit and distancing, romantic inflations, boundary problems, wild ideations. But when love is authentic, the real thing, one can't "love too much"; we're not supposed to be miserly with genuine love. Love's nature is to be lavished. The task in the South is to find the source of authentic loving: to experience the tree of life at the center of each of us; the one that the Spirit in Black Elk's and Hildegard's visions was trying to get across.

The Problem of Self-Approval

In the South, one of the key ingredients for awakening the green is being in relationship to ourselves. The wilderness in the soul we long for is accessible only because we have opened our feeling world. In the fourth direction we turn to the taproot in the heart and explore what has wounded it, and what restores it. One of the best salves for greening the heart is the practice of self-acceptance.

The green power of the heart is unconditional love; but that works only when we have a genuine relationship with ourselves; and it works only when we patiently welcome every aspect of ourselves—when we say yes to the whole package. Self-acceptance is conscious self-love, and in heartwork, it's like the sap in the tree itself. Self-*approval*, on the other hand, stems from an unconscious need to justify one's existence on the planet. Self-acceptance is the ability to be in good standing with ourselves, to accept ourselves exactly the way we are in the moment without judgment and critical self-rejection.[6] Self-accepting people are people who can laugh at their mistakes, dance with their shadow, and be infinitely patient with the unknown. They are slow to anger, quick to forgive, and can lift their skirts at a White House picnic. Self-approval works differently, and in it we can see the great wound in love.

Self-approval, which is the opposite of self-acceptance, springs from a deep-seated need to compensate for loss. Self-approval aims only for relief from pain; it's not about loving, really, but about gratification. A man I know works constantly to be somebody, because as a kid he never measured up to his father's expectations. A woman gives herself away in relationship to her children because she's convinced her giving will buy back the losses she knew as a child. An adolescent girl strives to be pretty and accommodating to others because she thinks her looks and her niceness will keep her from rejection. Most early relational experiences forgot to teach us anything about self-acceptance. We grew up measuring ourselves by what others thought of us, often with a rubber yardstick.

If we grow up learning self-acceptance, then we grow up with an internal sense of what's true. When there were safe laps to sit on, and affirming words, and a shared trust that life was an experiment, there was life in the family tree. Kids who grow up without that kind of trust in others don't have access to the root of life within themselves. Clearly self-approval is one of those building blocks in the personality that, even early on in life, undermines the power of trust.

Someone told me once, *"I've always had problems being myself in a relationship. I'd like to be able to open up ... to feel like I could let somebody in here. But as soon as someone gets close to me and wants to love me, I do something to make sure they don't. I lure them but then I get scared and run. I don't think I trust anybody at close range. I've done enough therapy to realize that all this started when I was a kid. I chased my father all over the place trying to get his attention, but he was always out of reach. I know how it happened, but I don't really know what to do to shake this fear. It's big."* When trust is hurt or exploited in some way in childhood, self-rejection always follows.

Another person's early memories of relationship had been blocked for years, but when he started to remember, he recalled scenes between himself and his father that would have extinguished anyone's capacity to trust. *"He and my mother both drank, but he drank the most, and he was violent. I remember night after night lying in bed listening to them fighting. I lay there terrified, afraid for my mom, for myself. I longed for somebody to come in, but nobody was there for me. My real feelings never were validated. I grew up basically alone. I'm still alone."*

The archetype of the lover, when it's healthy, always implies that we can be in honest relationship with ourselves. If I trust myself and honor my own feelings, needs, and the spirit of the green inside, then I'm not going to fear closeness and intimacy. What I see operating oftentimes in relationships, however, is not trust, but fear. When fear governs our response to feeling, to the things of the heart, we arrive in relationships with a barren tree. A man convinced that intimacy meant too much risk and vulnerability once said: *"Relationship is a paradox to me. I get close, begin to move toward some kind of intimacy, and suddenly I feel overwhelmed. Like someone's trying to control me, take away my independence. The bottom line is, I feel unsafe."*

Because this man didn't trust his own feelings, and because he had no intimacy with himself, he "saw" the other person as taking something away from him. If he had been in good standing with himself, he might have had room to trust others. Instead he was tangled up in his own fear; he could relate to others only from a safe distance. His control was a remnant from a childhood in which his mother needed to control him. Like so many parents, she didn't do it with any conscious malice, but in order that her son might find approval in the world (from his teachers at seminary, from his father, and, of course, from herself). His impulses, feelings, his wildness, his shadow and his radiance, all were sacrificed to fit father and the church. His natural relational self, the wild man in him, the seeds of his passion, slipped through the cracks.

A man told me that at a seminar weekend he attended, he had a very self-defeating experience. On the first day the participants were asked to break into groups of two, so that each person in the dyad could share something of him- or herself with the other (but not be exposed to the whole group). Unsure of choosing a partner, this young man lingered in the back of the room, feeling a bit awkward. Then suddenly he discovered that everyone was in pairs but him; because the group turned out to be an odd number, he wound up being odd man out. *"I felt rejected. Old feelings of being forgotten, not good enough, powerless, came up for me. When I stood there alone I thought, 'Here it is again.' I went home feeling, 'What's the use?' "*

This man's experience in the group had been an unfinished fragment of his relationship with his own father; a nightmare of rejection that followed him wherever he went. From the looks of it, this father had wanted the best for his son; but his desire for his success was a little bigger than life, and it created a huge ambivalence in the boy's ability to trust himself. The father had been caring and approving when his son met his expectations, yet judging and rejecting when he had not. As a child he had picked up his father's shadow side (a fear of failure and a buried self-rejection), which he then carried right on into life with him.

Not surprisingly, most of us internalize the people we grow up with, since they're all we've got to begin with. But for many of us, self-rejection begins with the unconscious shadow of the parent. Once trust in ourselves is wounded, self-approval and self-judgment become the Achilles' heel we walk into life with: the whole package becomes part of our self-image. On top of that, the rejecting (but sometimes also loving) parent figure we think we've left behind comes along with us as well. Eventually, the ghost of that parent and his or her need for self-approval will take up half a football field of psychic space. He stands across the room and avoids us; she sits frowning in the audience. He wears himself menacingly on the face of an authority figure; she gossips about the way we look. He can't wait to take advantage of us. The internal judge—the voice of self-doubt, self-condemnation, discouragement, the wild fear in the back of the mind that we won't measure up—creates these endless projections. Worse, they become the lens through which we experience relationships.

Another problem with seeking self-approval is that there is always a temptation to compare ourselves to others. We soon get lost because someone else always seems more talented, more deserving, more intelligent, more in need. One woman in a group said once, *"I really don't have much to complain about. After listening to everybody else's problems, mine are pretty small in comparison."* This is not a greening thing at all, but the kiss of death to self-acceptance. At another workshop one of the participants left early and just walked out. I noticed her spot vacant and called her later to see what had prompted her exodus. *"I just had too much pain. I couldn't say my pain because I felt it would be too much for everybody. I wanted to spare you that. I feel such disappointment in myself for not being further along than I am."* It was clear that "sparing the group" meant that she had projected her internal judges onto the others. But the rejection she feared was hers. The moment she compared herself to "more deserving" or "more needy" women in the room, her goose was cooked. Some people spend their whole lives looking for approval, but there's a flaw built into that kind of looking.

Over and over again people cancel themselves out by self-judgment. In the most subtle ways, we doubt ourselves: we undermine how we look, minimize what we're feeling, criticize what we've done or failed to do. Not only do we condemn what we perceive as our faults or any part of the shadow side, we also judge and reject our radiance. For the most part we tend to notice radiance and shadow in others, but when invited to acknowledge these characteristics in ourselves, many of us would rather read the morning newspaper. Devotees of self-approval all have one thing in common: they unknowingly nurture the critic in each of us whose lifelong task is to cut down the flowering tree at the root.

Some of us did not have critical parents, but I find wounds of self-judgment in all of us. Many of us, for instance, learned to do things only for the praise or affirmation that followed. If getting love and approval was based on some act of pleasing, a subtle tyranny is established inside. The tyranny is that gradually we learned not to count on ourselves for validation. When others have loved or affirmed us only if our room was clean, our hair was in place, our grades were good, and our underwear was changed, we are going to acquire a bias toward performance. When love is conditional, it will be experienced as a subtle kind of oppression.

Families that have good intentions for their offspring, and most do, also have generous expectations of the next generation. Yet in the family where convention is served before creativity, when there is a reputation to live up to, more than a life to be lived, there is no greening. All families have a persona that expresses the way they want to be seen in the community. There are rules, spoken and unspoken, that either overtly or covertly tattoo the family dynamic into place. In some families these rules are healthy and negotiable; in others they are not. When the family persona doesn't make room for the person *in the circle*—for differentness, for real feelings, for the child in the tree—self-approval offers itself as the next best thing. In the South, the task is to begin to name the places, the people, and the events in childhood that first spawned self-approval.

A friend told me, *"In my own family, my sister and I were carefully (sometimes even lovingly) prepared for social acceptance. But these tender manipulations didn't affirm much self-worth in either of us."* In most cases our parents weren't intentionally trying to ruin us when they conditioned us to seek approval from others, when they advised us to seek acceptance from others first and to consult with ourselves last. But they did strip the leaves off the tree. When we are told to think of ourselves in terms of the conventions around us, we diminish the possibility of knowing ourselves at all. Self-acceptance can happen only when we put away external referencing.

The work southward is to practice genuine relationships to ourselves. The power of the green is about embracing our wounds, our shame, our losses, failings, weaknesses, our passions and deep feelings, our nakedness. If any of us is merely covering these wounds, we're still seeking only approval. And if we're still seeking approval, none of us will ever measure up. Which is what I was struggling with stark naked on the ridge.

Self-Acceptance: The Power to Make Grow

Royal dignity was yours from the day you were born,
on the holy mountains,
royal from the womb,
from the dawn of your earliest days.
—Psalm 110:3

During my last visit to the Alaskan interior a few years back, I met an old man in one of the villages, whose bearing and beauty caught my heart at first glance. Standing out in the warm sun during a village gathering watching his many grandchildren play, his leathery dark face etched in a smile, he chatted with me about the old days now long past. Years ago, to pass the hard times and the worries that came often in the long Alaskan night, he, like many of the men in his native village, began to drink. He says he drank for years. *"But it was no kinda good for me,"* he said, *"and one day I just quit."* He recalls that long ago, when he was a boy, when the old people of his tribe spoke, *"it was like medicine."* We watch as the children play in the cold creek shining against the dark blue mountains, and both of us become silent. In the back of my mind I am thinking that now in his old age, tall and proud and beautiful in his simplicity, he is like medicine. I fell in love with him because I think he suddenly stood in for my own father who died an alcoholic, who never had a chance to be medicine for anyone. But there was this old man, standing in power in the afternoon sun with his humor, his beauty, his gift of aliveness, a rough gem I wrapped up somewhere in the folds of my memory and have kept over the years.

I've heard it said that our wounds come from the same source as our power.[7] To have been bruised, like this wintry old man, and yet to grow from that trial creatively, is to turn the wound into potency, into wisdom. Self-acceptance is about regarding our experiences in life—and our response to them—without judgment or self-condemnation.

Greening is impossible for people who insist on taking weaknesses or trials personally. In my life I have made a fair number of mistakes; I still struggle with a list of incongruities myself. I am still given to finding loose shale on the ground (sometimes even on flat city sidewalks). I still have a huge shadow and the remnants of an enormous father complex I lug around. On some days I still get tempted to feel intimidated by certain authority figures. There are times I forget self-loving and judge something I've done; there are days I have far too many expectations of myself and the world. I forget laughter and how to be medicine for myself.

As I reflected back on my second year out on the mountain, I could see how self-acceptance gets handicapped in life. The resistance I felt toward being naked on the mountain began to make sense. For one thing, my fear was not really about being without my clothes for a few hours; my deepest fear was about being too vulnerable and open; it was about being exposed and then being suddenly humiliated. In my journal I opened up a little dialogue with that fear of exposure. I began to write about the times I have been open, honest, and self-disclosing in relationships; times I'd let the inner child or the gypsy or my shadow out and somebody had judged or misunderstood that. I wrote down every incident I could that recalled being shamed or humiliated or doubted or misunderstood. I saw I had some old scars there that wanted attention; but I also saw that these past wounds in trust had moved (bag and baggage) into my own psyche. They each had their own room and they were self-doubt, self-condemnation; fear of humiliation, mistrust of intimacy; and they were a whole jury of old bearded patriarchs who did not approve of my wild side. What a lot of tax collectors they were. Thank God that our wounds and mistakes, our fears and shortcomings, are not permanent possessions. Thank heavens that the moment we stop judging ourselves, and start accepting the most abandoned side, healing begins.

One of my friends talks about her own recovery from alcoholism as a time of learning the art of self-love. *"I used to think there was something wrong with me for all the craziness I suffered in my life. But now I know that I was not to blame, I just walked into a set of insane circumstances. I finally caught on that God was not my judge; I was. These days I work at seeing myself as acceptable, as worthy, as someone who has permission to make mistakes, and to grow from them. I laugh a lot and I'm beginning to know a real patience with myself. My recovery isn't about being dry; it's about learning to love myself."* She had begun to discover the kind of dignity the Psalmist had been singing about; that quality of royalty that comes as part of the birthright.

Self-acceptance is a skill, and it takes time to develop. It is the practice of saying yes to our contradictions, of quieting our need to have all the answers; it's about releasing our expectations about what we should be able to do, or where we feel we "ought" to be in our life. It is accepting exactly where we are without judgment. It's especially about embracing the side of us that hasn't made the leap to freedom yet.

A woman I worked with once in a group said to me, *"I want to warn you, I don't cry."* As soon as she said that, huge tears began to roll down her cheeks. She was shocked, but she just let them come. Then she had a spontaneous memory of her mother walking away from her. *"I was about seven years old. My mother used to come into my room every night and kiss me goodnight. Then one night, maybe it wasn't long after my seventh birthday, she said, 'You're getting too old to be kissed goodnight.' That was it, she just said, 'Goodnight, dear' and then turned and walked out of my room and closed the door behind her. I cried myself to sleep, and never cried again."* This experience had not only sealed her tears; the message was, it wasn't safe to grow up, to have needs, or to ask for anything from others. In that family one had to be self-sufficient. This was no atmosphere for self-love and acceptance. The breaking through of her tears started a deep healing that gave her a new trust and compassion for herself. In pieces of work like that, it is awesome to see the sudden melting of the stones over the heart. This is not a dilemma reserved only for the Stonemen among us.

Whenever I am privileged to sit with someone and witness this cracking of the shell that has frozen our self-compassion, I am always amazed at the strength of the fragile shoots in the heart. No matter how long they have stayed dormant, they are always ready to push through whenever there's the least permission and the time is right.

When people ask me how they can internally check on how self-approval works, I tell them to look over their dreams. Look for the shadow figures in dreams, and watch for the characters you dislike or mistrust in the dreamscape. They are loaded. One man dreamed repeatedly of being chased by masked men and shot at. These were his own internal judges on his heels, masked and armed and dangerous, firing insults and killing words and thoughts at him from behind.

A woman I worked with at a weekend workshop told me she had had a dream of a child who had been completely blue. *"I feel like that child sometimes, like there's no life in me. That there's no reason for living.*

I sometimes feel I never had a life at all. Except for my recovery, I don't know what I have." In a piece of profound imagery work she did that day, however, she went down to the river with that blue baby and put the infant in the waters, and started to cleanse it. She let the waters flow over it. I think the Spirit must have started to pour over her, because things started coming out of that baby: old hurts and wounds, times she'd been abused and neglected, discounted and yelled at, slapped and blamed. I lost track of just how it happened, but I went there with her and together we cleansed that baby and wrapped it up in a blanket; I think we sang to it. She wound up having the image (and the accompanying feeling) of really holding herself as a baby, and she experienced a change. The whole group responded to the image, to her, to the infant in the blanket. Somehow in the alchemy of all that, she walked away with a new sense of herself as a person.

Just at a time when I was struggling with self-acceptance (which has been most of my life), I had a disturbing dream. *I had been walking along an underground subway that led out onto the ground, onto a dirt path. It was as though I was walking along a long tunnel in the belly of the earth. Several dark East Indian men passed me, all looking rather menacing. I felt afraid and suspicious until they got close; then I could see their faces and they weren't frightening at all, just impoverished. I walked a long way and eventually I came to a huge brass bed covered with a colorful quilt. I was tired because I had walked a long way, and I lay down on the bed to rest. Directly on my left, to the side of the bed, I saw a tall disheveled man with wild blond hair staring in my direction. He was standing inside a barred door, like a prison door, just looking out at me. I felt a genuine distaste for him, for the weakness and depravity I saw in him. Behind him I heard a woman in labor, groaning and crying out in the dark cell in which he apparently stood. Then suddenly I heard a small cry issue forth from the dark, a newborn baby. Taken aback, I asked myself whether anything so filled with new life could really come from such a dark hole in the ground. In the dream I thought to myself, How could anything so beautiful come from such a dark hole of Calcutta? I woke with a feeling of disgust.*

When later in my journal I had a talk with this man, I began to realize that this fellow was the opposite of anything I ever liked. He was failure; I don't like failure. I like challenge, a good show of strength, the feeling of getting things done; there he was, all weakness and inability. I take pride in how I appear to others, and I am attached to controlling my destiny. But he stood clad in rags behind bars, ignoble and helpless. At times in our inner healing work we *say* we are patient with our faults, but inwardly dream figures tell us we are not, because somewhere inside of us, these characters are locked up; we don't want them to come out. In the dream, just behind this man, birth was happening. A baby was coming. I realized that when I could eventually love the weakest side of myself, without rancor or judgment, when I could give up my own ideals of perfection, goodness, rightness, a nobility born out of the false hero myth (the false warrior), then something real could be born. But not without embracing the man behind bars.

Wounds are inevitable. The way in which we walk through them, however, makes a difference. Some of us stay in the wound. Some of us make our home there; we think and feel and relate from that place. Victims or aggressors, caregivers or passivists, the "power to make grow" is lost to us. Others who have faced the abyss and stepped back from it have done so because they have reconciled with the wound; they have discovered a power and aliveness within themselves. They have found some compassion for their experience, and, at some level, their old life of self-approval has died.

Elk and Deer: The Greening Instincts

The Hidatsa woman in her prayers often called attention to even the smallest things. She said even the "creepy crawlies" (little bugs and the tiny creatures on the ground) are related to us. In her circle, we all gradually became students of these creatures. Like the twelfth-century mystics, who "made use of creatures in order to rise to the state in which they could contemplate the Creator . . ."[8] she saw every creature as an expression of God.

The "four-leggeds" I mentioned earlier represent that side of the heart that describes the feminine feeling world. Meditating on the South one tries to think of kindness, compassion, patience, forgiveness, tenderness, things of the heart. All of these creatures would teach us about the ways of relationships. She also spoke of our need to be alert, to use that sixth sense the animals have.

Some years ago some friends and I got up well before dawn in late October to hike down a trail in the Colorado Rockies, toward a meadow where a large herd of elk was feeding. Freezing cold, stumbling down the trail in the dark with only a little moonlight shining in and out of the trees, we made our way to a hiding place near the meadow and sat for some hours waiting. The elk had come down from the mountain above and were grazing on the green grasses in the meadow; sounding their deep-throated cries and clashing their great horns in some mating ritual. In the dark we could only listen, spellbound. Sitting down there in the cold morning as the sun mercifully began to rise I saw something I thought was distinctly a lesson for me. The moon, now pale with the light of dawn, began its westward falling, and I became acutely aware of these animals. Watching them filled me with awe. Every now and then one would look up, stand completely still, sniff the morning air, not a muscle moving, every fiber in that great body attentive. Seeing this stance of sheer instinctive watchfulness gave me a profound sense of well-being.

Reflecting on the qualities of some of these "four-leggeds" I have sometimes shared the woods and plains with, I'm reminded that their medicine is often a finely tuned connection with themselves and their surroundings. When I have seen them in the wilderness they walk quietly, attentive, listening; heedful of the scent in the air, alert to distant sounds, to changes in the weather, to the feel of the land they walk.

The elk I began to dialogue with told me that my own instinctive nature, the ability to be alert and sensitive to myself, was imbalanced. As a therapist I had plenty of this gift for others. I often knew what other people needed, wanted, sometimes were thinking even before they spoke. But there were times I wasn't alert to what I wanted or needed. My instincts there faltered. The elk told me that if I could practice this sensitivity toward myself more often, I would know what I was feeling, sensing, experiencing inside. *"Have this kind of intuition toward yourself,"* she said.

Compassion, the ability to "feel with," is crucial to self-acceptance. It's an instinctual response to life that many of us have but tend to use exclusively on others. A friend of mine said to me once, *"I walk around as though I seem self-assured, on top of it, together at some level, but inside there are needs I don't say. I take care of others but often don't give that attentive regard to myself. Sometimes when I get hit with something, instead of saying, 'Ouch, that hurt,' I toughen up and say, 'It's nothing.' Other people can have difficulties and I'm right there. When there's some pain in my own life, something that's hard to look at, I have a hard time being there."*

In the circle of the directions, one has to practice feeling and sensing at deeper and deeper levels; that means retreating into the backwoods in the heart, into the intuitive senses where we ask the instincts what *they* see.

I worked with a man not long ago who had fallen into a deep depression. Ordinarily a religious and often cheerful man, he had lately been feeling very separate from himself; detached from the Spirit and quite empty inside. After a bit of conversation, we decided to drop inside, to try to intuit what might be going on. Several images from childhood came up for him, one of which was an experience of sexual abuse by an uncle. He had worked on that before in therapy, but somehow there seemed to be a piece missing in the healing process. In the long run he hadn't forgiven himself.

In the imagery work we did, he had a powerful experience. *"I stood at the edge of a huge cliff. I stared down into dark flames, and columns of smoke rose up around me. I cried out, 'Lord, where are you?' A voice said, 'I am here.' But I couldn't see anything. I kept turning around to find the voice but I couldn't find it. 'Where are you? I can't see you,' I said. Then a voice again, 'I'm here, inside you. You can't see me because you have to see yourself first; you have to be in relationship with yourself if you want to be in relationship to me. You have to love yourself like I love you."* A few moments later he had an image of the child within himself. *"Maybe this seems funny,"* he said, *"but I see myself pregnant. That's me in there."*

It didn't seem funny to me, because in the silence of our inner journey I had seen the same image. Here was the Holy Greening at work, the voice of compassion inviting this man into relationship with himself, inviting him to forgive himself, to look within for the answers. His depression lifted and he left filled with a sense of affirmation.

People who forget the green don't stay in touch with themselves. At a practical level, learning to sniff the wind means learning to be aware of one's needs. Genuine wants (different from the needs connected to gratification) are vital to personal and spiritual growth. In matters of the heart it is important to ask ourselves what our innermost desire is about.

In greening the instincts, it's important to give ourselves permission to design our own life program. On some days we must make promises and commitments and plans, but the elk-in-spirit will nonetheless stop and sniff the wind. On some days the elk-in-spirit may decide to stay put or get a massage, write a poem or putter in the garden, marry the frog prince or not marry at all, or quit the corporate life and run a bakery or a soup kitchen.

The Rag Doll: Greening the Inner Child

During the second year of my studies with the Hidatsa teacher, just before the first vision fast, we were asked to bring our childhood dolls to the next sweat lodge, if we still had them. *"When you come next time, bring the doll that says something about your own childhood. Or bring one that reminds you of that time. This will be a lodge for your own inner child."* At the time, I felt disconnected to the idea of bringing a doll to the lodge. I had a rather sorry-looking bear I sometimes slept with at night, but the idea of bringing a doll struck me as odd. After all, I had dealt with my inner child already. I put it out of my mind until the morning of the lodge. About dusk I went quietly into my daughter Sarah's room, perused a dusty array of dolls lined up on a shelf, and chose a rag doll to take to the sweat with me. As I left through the front door, I stuffed her well under my towel, and we set off.

As I was driving the stretch of redwoods to the coast where the lodge was to take place, it began to dawn on me that small passenger beside me looked like the rag doll in a dream I'd had. In the dream I had been living in an unfinished house with my family. *The place was only half built and we were suddenly expecting company. I told my daughter Sarah, who was five at the time, "Clean up this room! What a disaster area!" When I came in later she was mindlessly playing in her toy box and the room wasn't picked up. I lost my temper, and began yelling at her to clean up her mess. In the back of my mind I worried about what the company would think. When I came back later it was even worse. Furious, I grabbed her and spanked her, but suddenly she wasn't a child at all; she had turned into a rag doll, sitting with her big empty cross-stitched eyes staring blankly at me.*

Handmade of calf leather, somewhat flattened and drawn on over the years, with a mop of thick faded white cotton string for hair, and green string eyes that criss-crossed like Raggedy Ann, she was not only the doll sitting next to me in the passenger's seat; she was the rag mop inside I didn't want anyone else to see. I didn't like her very much. I felt a wave of impatience recalling the dream, certain that I had already worked it through. On the other hand, I knew I wasn't finished with her, because I still made excuses for her messes, her feelings, her weaknesses. I still tried to dampen her spontaneity, to talk her out of her passion and intensity. And I still drove her to perform.

Before we went into the lodge, the group of women sat out in a circle around the fire, all of us silent, holding these babies. I sat solemnly holding my own self as a child, my face turned to the heat of the fire, listening to the sounds of Mother Nature in the rising morning. In the heat of the blaze, water and old tears lined the rims of my eyes. Images of a divine wilderness wove themselves through my thoughts. Standing on the edge of that kind of passion, I knew that's where that little rag mop still hesitated. That's why she'd come for me again.

I sat thinking of the rag dolls my clients have brought in over the years, of the collective problem of self-approval. I thought of the times so many of us have been offered the flowering stick and have resolutely held back. Just at the threshold of experiencing our fire and creativity, some fear of rejection paralyzes us; an old voice judges us unworthy; the worn voice of expectation echoes in the back of our mind—and into the toy box we fall, lifeless. Still sitting by the fire outside the lodge, I looked at my rag doll again, her big green crossed eyes suddenly alive and looking straight into mine. *"Oh, but they won't understand my passion, they'll misjudge my wildness,"* she said. Just then a voice rose up inside me as I held her limp little body. *"You are a child of the universe, what could you fear? Why do you hold back? Remember who you are! Remember you are a part of every living thing, the stars, the winds, the shining waters, the earth under you, the green things, the animals. Remember where you came from, and when you ask for help, it will always be there."*

In the lodge I became aware of some of the other voices in the dark heat. Going in a circle we spoke one by one to our dolls, to the oddest assortment of little faces, some scrubbed and clean, stylish and well dressed; some in tatters and barely intact. Some of the doll faces were soft and infantlike, smooth and pink and almost human; others were stiff and rigid with fixed little smiles and unblinking eyes, with every shining hair in place. Some looked brand-new. Others looked like they had been through at least three generations of pioneers (one or two looked as though they hadn't circled their wagons in time).

Terrible and joyful memories of childhood filled the lodge. We groaned because of the intense heat, cried over some of the most painful memories, and sweated almost beyond endurance. One woman said to her inner child, *"I love you and I want to tell you you don't have to feel bad about yourself anymore. The things that happened to you were not your fault. Your parents didn't know what they were doing. They just didn't understand because they were wounded too. Come out of that hurt now. Come out into the light. You are beautiful and you were meant to walk in the light. Others may have hurt you, but I'll always be there for you."* One by one we went around the circle giving those dolls words of consolation; we hugged them, spoke to them, affirmed their broken little bodies and their beauty. When the tears were finished, there was laughter too. Red hot, muddy from the earth we sat on, purged of the past, we and our sanguine little dolls emerged from the lodge.

This was a turning point for me. Unconsciously there was a rag doll in my self-image. When I made demands on myself, compromised my feelings, anger, and passion, she went limp. When I tolerated no messes, no imperfections, and wanted approval from the world, she fell into a heap in the toy box. No wonder I hadn't liked the idea of bringing a doll to the sweat.

The "power to make grow" that Black Elk saw in his vision as he looked toward the South animates a sacred branch within each of us. The branches of this flowering stick are love and self-acceptance, personal transparency, trust, and a four-legged instinct to sniff the wind. The moment we are willing to reclaim the lost or wounded child we've run from all these years in our chase after self-approval, the divine often manifests in unexpected ways. When we hold out a welcome hand to ourselves, no matter what our past has held, forgiveness toward ourselves goes into wild bloom. The inner lover thrives on that kind of relationship.

8. Our Mother, Sacred Earth

You never enjoy the world aright
Till the sea itself flows in your veins
Till you are clothed with the stars.
—Thomas Traherne[1]

Turning in the fifth direction, one simply touches the earth and gives thanks. The Indians say that the Earth not only protects and feeds us, but listens to us very personally. We are her children. If we honor her, she will care for us. In most ceremonies I have participated in or observed, the earth elements were always revered—the stones, the wood (greening things), the water, the fire, and the smoke that takes our prayers. These are a gift from Mother Earth, and they are given freely.

Over the last few years I have sat on the ground much more consciously. I have given myself to the Great Lap many times, and always she has patiently borne my tiredness, my tears and tensions, the deep thoughts that I cannot speak to anyone. I have walked or lain on her in all my moods and always she is welcoming. Under the tall Doug fir in the Sierras, wading stony creeks and rivers, gazing up at the constellations, I know I am related to all things. My dialogue with the earth over these last few years has made me more sure of the flesh I live in; more aware that the ground I feel under my feet is something not apart from me. Sitting one day perched atop a granite boulder on one of her magnificent mountains, she told me the theologians had it backward; that God is not exclusively in some high place, but is enfleshed in the soil of the earth and seeded in the deep ground of the body.

I think, like John Muir and the mystics and the children I have known, God takes shape in the mountains, along the sea, in the desert, in the shining stars and swirling galaxies, in the eyes of all devotees, no matter what their path. Those are the altars I most deeply trust. When I sit on the earth to write or pray or rest, I sit with the elements that give shape to the divine. Without sky, sea, water, wind, without this vast solitude, God would never really have made sense to me.

Mothering Power

Luther Standing Bear, an Oglala chief and teacher on the Rosebud reservation in the late 1800s, called the earth a "mothering power."[2] Among her many lavish gestures is her power to draw us back to ourselves, to our roots, our beginnings. On the edge of the city, in gardens, in small groves, or in vast stretches of wilderness, there is a potency in her that heals us, a salve in her for the bruises of our technical world. To my Hidatsa teacher, the earth was Grandmother; it was always to her that we returned to purify ourselves in the sweat bath. In the fullness of her green robe, she is the one we honor when we turn and touch the ground.

Standing Bear spoke of the reverence the Lakota people had for nature: *"It was good for the skin to touch the earth. . . . The old people liked to remove their moccasins and walk with bare feet on the sacred earth. Their tipis were built upon the earth and their altars were made of earth. The birds that flew in the air came to rest upon the earth, and it was the final abiding place of all things that lived and grew. The soil was strengthening, cleansing, and healing. . . . The old Lakota was wise. He knew that man's heart, away from nature, becomes hard; he knew that lack of respect for growing, living things soon led to lack of respect for humans too. So he kept his youth close to its softening influence."*[3]

I am touched by the image of keeping the young people close to the "softening influence" of the earth. To walk the land and to revere it is to return to something deep and natural within us. Young or old, we need this humbling kind of "softness." I remember once arriving for a sweat lodge in a downpour. Climbing the hill to the lodge in the slippery mud and not liking it much, I greeted my teacher with a little whine about the rain. *"Oh, but it's beautiful! I love it!"* she exclaimed, proceeding to stretch out her arms and receive the downpour. *"This is our Mother. She's nurturing us, blessing everything that grows."* We were quite a contrast in that moment; I was huddled under a damp rain tarp, scowling; and there she was smiling, laughing, praising. Keeping soft.

The land is like a shrine to the Indians, an offering place. Dineh Navajo Medicine man Jack Hatathlie says, *"Our Land, where we are known by the Spiritual Beings, is where we pray. It is not possible to practice our religion . . . in some strange building."*[4] Although all land is holy, some places by their very nature take us more deeply, more immediately inside ourselves; it's as though the very features in the landscape begin to live for us. Special insights and healing events can happen in these places because they awaken the sacred within us. Finding one of these hallowed places, even once in a lifetime, is to feel one has come home.

The earth is a storyteller, an Old Woman who weaves our human threads together with the fibers of trees, water, stones, clouds, and all living things. I have a friend who says, *"Even when I was a young child, I knew the wind. It told me things. It spoke my name. When I held rocks and stones, little branches covered with lichen and moss, when I sat in the wheat fields and studied the clouds, I knew who I was."*

In some childhoods, when life felt chaotic and people were angry or unpredictable, Mother Nature with her welcoming meadows, her deep forests and surging seas, her green arbors and dark brown limbs, was a refuge we could count on. When no other welcome found us, there was hers. In the spirit of Job, who says: "Speak to the earth, and it shall teach thee," some of these sanctuaries have "spoken" to us a whole lifetime.

Whenever I am alert to nature, she usually has something up her sleeve, a message, a teaching, a spacious solace that draws me to a thought or feeling that's been waiting to come. I often hear people say that when they drop the high life and get off into the woods or get out under the big canopy of the sky, they remember themselves again. Most of us need nature to remind us that we are not supposed to be identified with our work or the persona we wear. We can work hard and even love what we do, we can serve people and love them unendingly, but we're not supposed to so strongly identify ourselves with these things that we lose sight of the uniqueness in our own soul. We need to know that we are also sea and wind and sky and stars, and we are the brown clay of the land. When we feel the solace and renewal of our connection to all created things, we know the reality of being keepers of the Flowering Tree.

Even the Trees Have a Voice

Holy Mother Earth, the trees and all nature, are witnesses
of your thoughts and deeds.
—A Winnebago saying[5]

Tatanga Mani, or Walking Buffalo, a Stoney Indian from Canada,
once said that even the trees themselves have a voice. *"Did you know
that trees talk? Well, they do. They talk to each other, and they'll talk to
you if you listen. Trouble is, white people don't listen. They never learned
to listen to the Indians so I don't suppose they'll listen to other voices in
nature. But I have learned a lot from trees; sometimes about the weather,
sometimes about animals, sometimes about the Great Spirit."*[6] It's true
that the trees talk, but it's not true that non-Indians don't hear the
messages in nature. Creation-centered people, whatever their ethnic
origin, do listen to these voices.

In the book *The Sacred Landscape,* Fredric Lehrman says of walking
through the redwoods, *"These trees are teachers and healers. Walking
among them changes the body."*[7] A friend of mine on the Oregon coast
has a huge grandmother cedar on the hill behind her house. We have
walked up there many times and just sat in silence under the majestic
branches of this salmon-colored matriarch. With the sea sounding
itself below in the rain, we have sat releasing our burdens there,
soaking up the strength of her five-hundred-year-old roots.

One of my friends told me that in the midst of a troubled relationship (in which she and her partner were at a painful impasse),
the best therapy was a tree in a field near her house. *"Somehow the
tree was the only place I had that was my own. It welcomed me sitting
there every day. The ground felt like the only solid thing I knew. In spite
of what I was facing, I took deep breaths and relaxed under its branches.
I could hear myself think, my feelings calmed, and I could feel God out
there under that tree. It steadied me."*

Trees, green or otherwise, have a life inside that is old life; life
that goes back centuries. I was feeling sorry for myself one time after
a hard blow I experienced from a friend of mine, a misunderstanding
that took us into some primitive territory. I took a walk and found
myself in a grove of old aspen. I headed for the biggest one and leaned
hard into it, moaning and cursing and finally dousing the tree with
some tears. Suddenly I distinctly felt a kind of spirit in the tree (I

don't know what else to call it); I saw the tree as an ancient woman, old and wrinkled but strong from her years, infinitely wise. I heard no words from the tree, but I had a thought out there, sitting at the feet of this old tree crone. I realized that what had happened between me and my friend happened because each of us was judging and mistrusting the other, and because neither one of us had enough heart wood.

One of my friends on a vision quest once experienced a profound sheltering sitting under a tree during a violent storm. *"I was soaked, hungry, everything I had was wet, and I got cold. I got so cold I thought I'd freeze, then I got scared. I remember being told that when we got out here, if something went wrong, to pray for help. So I prayed that the tree would keep me warm. I stood up and laid my whole body against it and just asked for warmth. Suddenly the tree grew very warm. I couldn't believe it! I could feel warmth running like a stream down the tree. It got so hot I had to stand away from it!"* When she told me this story I remembered a passage from Revelations 2:22. The author in the scripture talks about the sheltering of the heavenly tree . . . *"and in its branches shall be a healing for the peoples."*

I have never heard voices in the trees as such, but I have sensed messages through the sounds of nature. Things that we have too long silenced are going to speak to us out there. They will come in muted whispers, in quiet syllables stirring in a breeze, or in the voices of winds that sing through the long pine needles. When the mind is quiet, the truths we have in the unconscious will have their say.

Rain and Sweat and Sister Water

Water is by nature healing. As one of earth's most powerful healing elements, it can evoke feelings and insights that have eluded us at a conscious level. A friend of mine told me: *"When I'm near the water, I slow down inside; the thoughts I'm usually running from are—right there. Kayaking or rafting pulls me into myself like nothing else does."* Rain storms along the coast in the winter and thunder storms in the desert or the High Sierras in the summer months are awesome displays of nature's passion. *"I can feel myself in a storm,"* one mountain-loving man said. *"My feelings are right there: excitement, joy, anger, my tears, my worst fears, the wild man inside, everything comes up for air. I know the weather is external, that it's out there, but on the other hand—there's weather inside too. It's just that I usually don't let myself feel it."*

In many cultures, water is used for sacred ceremonies, for healing and purification. The Pueblo tribes and the Hopi still annually dance for rain in the spring, praying that they will have good crops. Rain to the indigenous peoples of the Southwest is the giver of life and fertility, an inseminating power that replenishes the earth.

On a hike through Mesa Verde ruins in Southern Colorado one day I overheard a guide conversing with an old Hopi man and his wife who had been sitting on a bench outside the ranger station. When they got to talking, the ranger asked them what had brought them to the park. The old Hopi told him they were just passing time until they could go to their sacred place to pray. The ranger had heard of a spring and thought it had been a shrine in past years for the Hopi. But when he asked the old man where the site was, the old man only grunted (possibly because his wife had just given him a poke in the ribs). Waving his ancient hand in a generous sweep from north to south, he said, *"Over there somewhere."*

In her teachings, my Hidatsa teacher often spoke about the sacredness of water. Water is life for the land, sacred to the people; it purifies and strengthens us. When she spoke of the sweat lodge, she often said the water that came up as steam was like holy water; it renews each time we go in. Whether water from the steam, our bodies, or our tears, all these had the power to purify us. It always seemed to me that there was something about the intensity of the heat, the dark, the solitude, the pouring of water off my body in what seemed like waves, that demanded no less than an immediate return to myself. The gift of water that soaked me from head to foot was a renewal of my depletions, a constant kind of baptism. One could sleep through a bad sermon, monotonous rhetoric from the temple, or the wise words of a guru or teacher after a good afternoon meal. I never went to sleep in the sweat ceremony.

Oftentimes, working in a group I use elements of nature as a part of a healing ritual. Because the mind is very receptive to nature as a healing force, elements of nature make an excellent container for ritual. In one women's group, which had nestled for the weekend in a small mountain cabin in Colorado, I asked the participants to pair off and to create a foot-washing ritual. This ancient ceremony of forgiveness not only symbolizes a cleansing of the past, but often reconciles us with the part of ourselves we have exiled. Those receiving the foot washing were "sitting in" for their own inner child whom they had abandoned, neglected, not listened to, been embarrassed by, or silenced in some way. The women giving the foot wash, quite on their own, took up soap and oils and lotions, and rubbed and forgave and sang to the feet they held. Those whose feet were being bathed were releasing tears, old memories and hurts, and were forgiving and welcoming themselves—a sure sign that the Spirit on that snowy afternoon was the Foot Washer. I sat by and watched this group with tears in my eyes. They must have found the sacred spring.

A woman I know, wanting to release the painful memory of a relationship that had ended, and wanting to give a symbolic closure to it, walked down to a stream nearby her house and sat for a while with her grief. Eventually, as the time felt right, she took some small stones which symbolized her past, the man in it, and the memories she wanted to release, and threw them into the water, one by one. Then, stripping down, she immersed herself in the creek and bathed, forgiving herself, forgiving him, telling herself she was ready to move on.

In many cultures water represents the life-giving energies in the womb. In Islam, water is creation: "From the water We made every living thing." In *Canticle of the Sun,* St. Francis wrote praise for sister water for being "useful, precious and chaste."[8] John Muir echoed Francis when he praised the shimmering rivers and streams of the Sierra Nevada for allowing him to feel the solemn wonder of the Creator. Endlessly fascinated by the intricacies of nature, water, in the form of snow and rain, mist and dew, vapors and springs, was for Muir a "song of creation."[9]

A young woman took a walk on the beach along the Mendocino coast of California. She had been working to unearth a more spiritual and more playful side of her personality. She recognized that the perfectionist side blocked her from her spontaneity; she worried even that the soul and the child within her was too deeply buried. We had been walking along the coast one early morning and she suddenly stopped and stood staring at a little creek that was cascading down one of the nearby cliffs. We had agreed to keep silence, so it was a long time before she spoke. After our walk, as we drove back to our weekend house, she said: *"I saw that creek come winding down the cliff, over the rocks, making its way down to the ocean. Then I noticed it disappeared under the sand. I followed where I thought it might come out near the water, and there it was. When I saw that little creek come pouring back out from under the sand, I realized that this side I want to connect with is not gone, it's just been running underground."*

Walking by the water, one walks very near the edge of one's own unconscious; close to the other side of one's intentions. Water, like other natural phenomena, is not only physically nurturing and renewing; in the mind, the metaphor of nature is itself a powerful restorative.

Stones and Things that Talk

The rivers of northern California in the late fall are always magical, and at the turning of the season especially more so. The snow on the tops of the coastal ranges, powdery lace over the deep green of redwoods, fir, and pine, clearly marks the change toward winter. When I walk along the shores of the big rivers during steelhead season, I am drawn to the stones along the bank. In the drizzle one can expect on some late fall mornings, I am drawn to the beauty of their dark lustre, slick and wet and deeply colored in the rain. They spread themselves out along the canyon like river mosaics, as far as the eye can see.

What fascinates me about rocks, I don't know, but I have always experienced them as though each one had a life of its own. I carry them home from my travels the way some people collect souvenirs. More than once the trunk of my car has been mistaken for a river bottom. Stones are for me like natural icons that symbolize special events, transitions, meanings; sometimes they mirror my thoughts exactly. Once sitting by a riverbank and writing in my journal about what it might mean to love others from a pure heart, a small white rock in the water caught my attention. Bending down to pick it up I saw that it was a perfect heart shape. Signs of an ancient time, stones remind me that my stay on the planet will be brief by comparison. These little shards from the earth, even when they bear no symbolic message, are one of the better masterpieces of the Great Hand.

In myth, stones (and mountains) are an *axis mundi:* a fixed point or center where man can regain Paradise or receive enlightenment. In Greek tradition, certain stones, such as the omphalos at Delphi, were said to be prophetic stones (baetylic stones: "the stone that speaks") because they had fallen from heaven and contained a divine message. The baetylic stone of Jacob in the Hebrew tradition was the meeting place between heaven and earth.[10] In the New Testament, addressing the disbelief and scorn of some of the pharisees, Jesus rebukes them by saying, *"If I do not speak of these things, surely the stones themselves shall speak."*

Like the trees that have a voice, stones to most nomadic and hunting tribes are the bones of Mother Earth. To most Native Americans, stones have life because they have been touched by the Creator. Before entering one sweat, we were told: *"These stones here, they are sacred. They have life. In the sweat lodge they pray for us to the Creator. If you can hear them, they have voices. We call them the stone people."*

More than once in the sweat lodge I have been gazing mindlessly at the red hot rocks and a clear shape has evolved from the stones in the fire pit. Once last year at a friend's house, on a reservation in northern Montana, a bear's face appeared, as clear as an artist's pen might have sketched it: round and full, a long nose, little beady eyes, slightly laughing, mirthful. When the stones get red hot, they can often assume such shapes. Bear had come to say something to me about my introspections, which had become a little too somber: *"Don't be hard on yourself! If I can laugh, you can too. Even in the dark there is joy. You can make mistakes and feel sorry if you want to. But in the end if there is no laughter, that would be the worst mistake!"*

Nature often greets us right where we are; she mirrors us, draws out our thoughts and feelings, our best and worst sides. She talks to us when we listen, through whatever happens to catch our attention. This is the kind of synchronicity Jung was so tentative about discussing with his more scientific colleagues (for fear of censure). It's the idea that the things and people, and the events in the natural world, will often mirror something we are experiencing in our own life.

Once a friend of mine sat down after a long trek up a desert canyon, a kind of medicine walk in which she had been asking for some spiritual guidance in her life. She had closed her eyes and was meditating for some time before she finally opened them again. When she did, she saw a tiny gecko peering up at her with one huge dark shining eye. She felt she heard it say, *"Listen friend, you worry about so many things. Now let go and don't take yourself so seriously."* The gecko people.

Being in relationship to the fifth direction means learning to sense whether or not we're walking in sync with our own nature. Reading the language of the earth simply means we learn to engage everything we see, the things we hear, the stuff that presses in upon our senses. Nature will, if we let her, wake us up in the midst of her wild rivers and pounding surf, in startling sunsets and thunders, in shafts of lightning and soft rains. In tiny objects on the ground.

Hiking in the San Juan mountains in Colorado, one of the women at a weekend workshop who had been on a medicine walk saw a tiny talisman on the ground. *"My eternal struggle seems to be that I'm very 'doing-focused,' and I get fragmented whenever I fall into that mode. I was thinking of my sister who loves to fill her pockets with rocks. She says they keep her grounded. I was laughing to myself about the ones she carries in her backpack, when I looked down and saw a plain little rock half buried in the dirt. When I picked it up I noticed it had a perfect bear claw mark on the surface. I took this as a reminder that I needed a cave like the mother bear. I keep it as a kind of prayer stone. When I feel scattered and disconnected, it reminds me to turn and come back to myself."*

The synchronous appearance of objects in nature symbolizing or paralleling some psychic process of ours is always a mystery. These objects seem to find *us.*

A woman told me once that she had seen a strong image in her mind's eye during a guided meditation. *"I saw myself walking out into a wooded area, then up a hill. I knew that I was looking for something specific on the ground, a symbol for the direction I should be taking. Suddenly I saw a dark arrowhead on the ground, carved from obsidian. When I picked it up, and felt it in my hand, I knew it meant I needed to get down to something more earthy and basic in myself."* As a clinical psychology student, she had complained that her studies, which she liked, kept her in her intellect too much of the time. The symbol had been a reminder not to abandon her earthy, feminine side.

A few days later she took a walk through a wooded area not far from her home in the foothills of northern California, and walking up a hill she saw a black shiny object on the ground. Bending close she saw it was an obsidian arrowhead, identical to the one she had seen in her visualization exercise. The power of that symbol had suddenly come to life.

Time after time I hear these stories of nature's elements showing up on our doorstep, and I cannot help but feel awe. It makes me more and more certain of the thread of connection between all living things in creation. I cannot pretend to explain it, but I am always humbled when I hear these things. A friend and colleague of mine took a sabbatical a few summers ago to work on her own issues (always a good idea for people in the helping and healing fields). She had gone to Hawaii to attend a workshop centered around healing the heart and empowering the Spirit. She told me the following story: *"I knew I had work to do on my heart. For one thing it liked the safety of staying closed; and it had these trust issues. After days on this island, working at therapy, looking at the stones in my own heart, eating guavas, chanting in volcanoes, dreaming dreams, I began to ask myself if it wasn't time for a new heart. I put everything I had into this work. Then one day, walking along the beach, asking the Spirit for a sign that I wasn't nuts to drop this many defenses, I suddenly stumbled over a beautiful coral heart. The amazing thing was I had been working and praying for an opening in my own heart, and this white coral stone had a hole in it."*

Earth Dreams and Healing

When objects of nature (or nature itself) appear in dreams, these nature symbols are energies in the unconscious trying to surface. A man I know had a compelling dream which clearly paralleled his own inner conflict. *"I was walking once by a huge snowcapped mountain. A distant rumbling caused me to look up and suddenly I saw an avalanche starting down from the summit. A tiny hut at the top suddenly disappeared underneath a mammoth wall of snow and I began to run for my life. I woke up terrified."* When this man, a lover of Muir and a hiker, worked on the dream, he began to realize that the mountain was himself. *"I've stored a lot of feelings over the years. A lot of my anger and resentments, a lot of my hurts were in that mountain. On the outside it looked majestic, powerful, impenetrable. But in the dream, the whole thing came tearing down, ripping out everything in its path. I've got some digging work to do here."*

Earth elements in dreams are often manifestations of something within us that wants our attention. Stones and rocks in dreams and imagery can symbolize immortality, strength, protection, support;

often they are sacred objects that possess healing and divining power. Rocks and stones can also represent impasses, blocks, obstacles, rigidity, or spiritual hardness, as in the Old Testament where Ezekiel speaks of men (and presumably women) with a "heart of stone" (Ezekiel 11:20).

In one such dream a man walks down a road and sees a tall fortress standing off in the distance, a castle. *"I know I have to get inside to find what's in there; I don't know what it is, but it's vital to me. Just outside the fortress is a huge wall of boulders and I am unable to pass. I try everything, but I can't climb, smash, or get around it. I sit down, exhausted, and don't know what to do. A storm comes up and rain begins to fall. Suddenly a huge bolt of lightning strikes the wall, and it splits the stones apart."*

The wall was his defenses, his drivenness, a will to make things happen his own way. Only when he "gives up" his own efforts does something bigger than ego come into play. Help comes from above to pierce his old way of doing things: to show him that when he lets go, the lightning (an intervention from the divine) can break the stones.

Water dreams often not only reflect the power of our emotional life surging up to consciousness, but also symbolize the deeper reservoirs of creativity wanting to surface. Certain kinds of psychological or spiritual passages in dreams often involve water, symbolic of a renewing baptism. One of my colleagues once dreamed: *"I'm walking along the side of the sea. All of a sudden St. Ignatius comes to me and says, 'The person who loves God is not afraid to drown—because it's just looking into the face of God.' When I woke up I was very moved by this dream because water is very meaningful to me; it's always the place where I go for renewal and inspiration. At the time I was teaching physics and had been for a while. I'd always enjoyed it but I knew that wasn't 'it.' I had asked a Sufi teacher of mine some months before about my real work and she said, 'When you know what your heart wants, then you'll know what your real work is. Otherwise, it's just your ego.' After the dream I stayed in quite a state of peace for three or four days. I realized that what I wanted to do the most was to help people come to themselves."* In the dream language the one who is not afraid to drown is the one who is not afraid to let go. The dream reflects the promise that when we can be strong enough to throw ourselves into the drink, to abandon all our old strongholds and securities, we will see the meaning of life, the "face of God."

Trees, forests, and the greening things of the earth are likewise symbolic of our psychic processes; they reflect our creativity and aliveness, our "power to make grow." A woman in a deep healing process once dreamed: *"I was walking through a forest and noticing how beautiful it was, how the light poured in and covered the ferns and flowers on the forest floor. How peaceful everything was. Then suddenly I was led to a large tree. When I looked closely at the tree I saw that there were no leaves at all. It was completely barren. A feeling of incredible sadness came over me and I woke up unsettled, melancholy. I felt sad the whole day. As I journaled, sitting with the image of the tree in my mind, I realized that I was that tree. Outwardly I look more or less together. But inside there is a wound. A deep scar from a time in childhood I was molested; something I've never directly dealt with. My whole life I've had this fear and shame about my sexuality, like a barren thing inside. I know it's time to heal this piece."*

In some mythologies the Tree of Life grows in the center of paradise; at its center a sun is often depicted, the power of the heavens descending downward to the earth. The Bo Tree, under which Buddha received enlightenment, represents the sacred center, the place where all the different parts of our human nature meet.[11] In the same way, the Flowering Tree represents the life of the people, one's relationship to God. The tree, because it represents the axial center of one's self, is a powerful dream motif.

A woman who experienced being molested in her past spontaneously imaged this part of her childhood as a tree with a grave split down its center. In an ongoing group, she worked on this for several months, remembering how the incest happened, then dealing with her rage, her sorrow, and the immense betrayal she felt. Gradually the work she did brought her to another image; a tree with its broken midsection beginning to heal; a tree with small buds beginning to open. The split inside her had begun to close. In a piece of work she did some months later, she became the tree. We sat in a circle around her trunk and asked her to bless us; she called us all by name and blessed us with her arms, now great leafy branches, stretched in benediction over those of us at her feet.

The Gift of Earthiness

Eight centuries ago Hildegarde of Bingen wrote: *"The truly holy person welcomes all that is earthly."*[12] There is an innate wisdom in creation-centered mysticism that says holiness is not just reserved for God; it is reflected in all of creation. To the individual at one with herself or himself, the handiwork of God lives in nature: in trees and grasses and flowers, in birds and wolves and worms, in waters and streams and fire and sand and light. You and I are that handiwork, no small piece of genius.

Western theology claims God and matter are separate; this is a problem for anyone interested in redeeming holiness (as defined by Eckhart, Julian, Hildegard, Mechtilde of Magdeburg, Thomas Aquinas, and many other innovative writers and theologians, past and present). In a traditionally patriarchal view, God is object, man and nature are subject; and creation in that myopic view is split. In the traditional Judeo-Christian view, God has, in six miraculous working days, created the universe, the earth, the animals, and man and woman. In this most banal of traditions, God then moves to heaven and rules the earth and all created matter (or *mater*, meaning *mother* in Latin) from on high. Creation theology, on the other hand, doesn't see it that way. When matter is seen as "less than" God, less than perfect, less than sacred, that kind of theology condemns human nature. It talks in a theistic language that separates God from creation. But this is a language foreign to the human soul, because the body *is* the house of the soul.

In the illuminating classic *Original Blessing,* Matthew Fox talks at length about the need to recreate our religious experience, to move on from the fall-redemption theology into a more creative spirituality that includes and celebrates human nature. In creation-centered spirituality, God is often expressed in maternal images. In one passage, praising Julian of Norwich, Fox says of her theology: *"For her the maternal side of God is enveloping, embracing, welcoming, inclusive, cosmic, and expansive."*[13] To the creation mystics, God is all things.

Many of the men and women I work with are most deeply wounded in the realm of the body, in their sexual self-esteem. There are deep scars in the psyche of the child whose body and sexuality were abused or negatively imprinted by fear and guilt. In the creation-centered view, there are vital energies in the body that are lifegiving—provided they have not been affected by abuse. Although healing physical or sexual abuse is a long and complex process, we *have* to redeem the body. Yet this work is generally only accessible when one has done some introspection, when we have found our voice, our vision, when we have at least some self-acceptance. If healing the sexual wound is begun before these other directions are walked through, however, the work can get too painful or feel overwhelming. If a woman who has been abused, for instance, hasn't dealt with guilt or fear or denial, if she has never gone into her dark side, she won't go into her body willingly. If a man has too much pride to admit his fear of sexuality, if he has never gone into his false warrior, he won't tell his secret; and the therapeutic process dead-ends.

The task here is to look and feel honestly within the body, then to ask what part of our sexual nature is in exile, to ask how we have disowned our flesh. Whether we are hurt because of abuse, negative modeling, parental inhibitions, or cultural bias, the body, for most of us, has been betrayed. In the fifth direction, when one can connect with the body (with the *mater*) in exile, tremendous help comes from that reunion. The symbol of the healthy, life-giving mother literally begins to come alive in the disowned flesh. The following is an example of what I mean.

At one woman's seminar I taught, the group exercises and the sharing we did were focused on healing the feminine. All weekend long these women were courageous in challenging their defenses. Each person spoke of the wounds she had suffered to her feminine self-esteem and sexuality. One woman's work was particularly poignant. She said, *"I have never liked my body. It's too demanding, it's always wanting something. I can't satisfy it and I constantly abuse it. I want to feel at home in it but I can't love it enough."* During the course of her work on childhood abuse from her parents, her unconscious began to flood with images. Like a film running in the back of her mind, memories of childhood rejection came to her—double messages around sexuality, demands for perfection, and critical judgment for any failures to live up to her parents' standards.

At the end of her session, after she had cleansed this long-forgotten memory, she decided she wanted to do a ritual to reconsecrate her body. Knowing that she had also split off from her inner child, she sat silently for a time, then held that child. She sat rocking back and forth, holding the image of the child in her arms. After a bit she straightened up, decided to shed her clothes, wrapped up in a blanket, and went outside. Choosing a spot by the creek, she then lay on the ground, her skin touching the earth, spreading her blanket over her. *"My mother wasn't there for me, my father wasn't there for me. But this Mother is here for me. I want my wounded child to be healed. I want my body back."* The rest of us sat around her on the ground, covering her whole body with a loving touch (which she gave us permission to do). The ground was a mother to all of us in that moment.

In the fifth direction, one begins to experience the maternal side of God, the "mothering power" in the earth that welcomes us. One gets down and simply lies on the ground. The disowned body, its senses, its natural passions and instincts, wants to come home. This is hard work, but men and women who are struggling to heal the sexual self find that when they can penetrate the fear and rage in the wounded body, it begins to heal. The emotional body (the feelings at the cellular level still identified with abuse and rejection) begins to heal. The creation at our own physical center reaches up for an anointing.

Healing the grave wounds to our sexual self, we need to know that when we go down that deep, there is a "mothering power" that welcomes and soothes, that cleanses and affirms us. To consciously walk in nature, to touch the ground, to sleep on it from time to time, to lose oneself in her compassion, is to experience not just the healing earth, but the feminine side of God. That mother is alive in everything. When we go to her she simply receives us right where we are.

People who are working in therapy, or in a supportive group to remedy these hurts would do well to remember, however, that this work needs a lot of spaciousness. It takes huge stamina and courage to work without giving ourselves the boot, sabotaging ourselves with impatience, shame, or criticism. Our thoughts and attitudes toward ourselves need to be expansive, accepting, "soft." It takes an act of faith just to trust oneself here, let alone anyone else. Therefore it's crucial to agree to suspend our fears and inhibitions, and to be aware of how shadow might like to shame or distract us. The trickster in this particular work around sexuality is formidable.

In the midst of this process, hopefully we will keep company with people who are nurturing and steady, who have a little Grandmother or Grandfather in them, or who can help us to see ourselves beyond the past we may feel bound by. We also need to humble ourselves before the body and its innate wisdom—to become its student. That means we agree to feel it, occupy it, open up to it. It takes some doing to get there, but when we do, the only thing to do is let go and trust.

In the fifth direction, we pray that our sensual nature can rejoin the cosmos around it. That our body will be alive like the trees that talk and the stones that speak, like the rivers and streams that find their way down to the sea. Sitting on the Great Lap, we ask to feel the "mothering power" in wind, sun, rain, pleasure, cold, in the pulse of sexual and spiritual energies, and in the blessing of all our senses.

> *Holy persons draw to themselves all that is earthly....*
> *The earth is at the same time mother,*
> *She is the mother of all that is natural,*
> *mother of all that is human.*
> *She is the mother of all,*
> *for contained in her*
> *are the seeds of all.*
> —Hildegard of Bingen[14]

9. In the House of the Grandfathers

Wavering about whether to do a vision fast that third year, I took a day off to hike in the Sierras to clear my thoughts. My mother had just died, there were things to settle about her house, and there were issues at work that needed attention. In spite of all these things, I felt called to go. I knew a vision quest was more than a few days of fasting and prayer; it also often encompassed the days and weeks beforehand. Long before one arrives, there have already been little tests, and obstacles. But regardless of the roadblocks, if one is meant to go, the doors open and the adventure is on. So it was for me. I returned to Montana early in the fall of that third year. When I arrived at a friend's home on the reservation, a wild electrical storm was brewing. I sat up late writing in my journal, thinking of my mother, missing her, listening to the loud cracking of thunder and rain. Lightning struck the hill not far from the house, illuminating the dark night outside.

When I went out that third year, everything seemed contrary. For one thing, it was already September, and I had ingeniously arrived in the peak of hunting season. For another, local well-wishers had warned that some "weather" might blow in from Canada. Out where the temperature can plummet 40 degrees in a few hours, that forecast was not welcome news. By the time I got out on the mountain, the wind was howling and cold; the temperature had been dropping and was altogether inhospitable. I had brought long underwear that, as it turned out, was the wrong size, and came just halfway up my thigh. The evening I arrived I had a frightening episode with four deer hunters. They had been looking at me through field glasses when I first spotted them. Later they hiked up the hill to ask if I was alone, and, of course, I told them I had friends along. On the second day out I became dehydrated and had to endure a splitting headache.

Not surprisingly, I had some moments of what might be described as panic. It was a far cry from the warm star-filled nights, the peaceful and at times ecstatic solitude, of the year before.

My fantasies of disaster shamed me completely, but I had to entertain them anyway. I tried to reassure myself that everything was going to be all right, that God knew I was out there. That I wouldn't be killed by flying bullets or attacked by cougar or freeze or dehydrate or break a leg. My conscious mind was able in some cases to calm my fears, to convince me to have some faith that somebody was looking after me. But in the pitch-dark night, I realized I had no control over my fate, and I felt utterly vulnerable.

By the next day the storm had blown over and the day warmed up, bringing with it a sense of profound relief. But I had not come alone this year; dogging me was a furious and skeptical six-year-old who had absolutely no interest in visions. Like it or not, there was a child in my psyche whose deep fears reason failed to impress. During that first night she had been with me constantly, tearing the lid off my piety, and stripping me to the bone. We were a pair: I in my willingness to throw myself onto the mercy of the mountain, and she with her mistrust of herself as a child of God.

It was clear that the direction I needed most to face and pray into was the direction of my relationship to the blue robe, the Creator. I had always had a relationship with God, but there were some basic ingredients missing. During the long hours of dusk the following evening, I remembered my first vision fast in which, sliding down the hill all night long, I had broken the stick fastened to the blue robe. I recalled the humiliation I felt when my Hidatsa teacher said it had broken because I lacked trust in God.

As children, when we have a sense of connection to the divine, we are still in the circle. Yet once life pulls us outside that kabir, some of us take the innocence of that relationship and replace it with an intellectual understanding of the Godhead. I had begun to see that the wound of trust had come as a result of learning to identify God with holiness and good conduct, with various works and behaviors, with caretaking and causes and certain supplications. I never meant for it to happen, but my relationship to God had become identified with what I could do, not who I was. Not that God disdains these things. These forms of loving are our initial training; and for a while they are the only holy connection we know. But these forms are not God.

On the second day of the fast, after I had sat up all night with a terror-stricken child, it dawned on me that the reason I had signed up for the Hanbleciya in the first place was that something inside me longed for an adventure with God. I wanted to go out on the mountain because up there, there were no familiar religious containers. I would not be secure or comfortable or in control; above all I would not be masked. God and I would have to talk, not through a mediator, but through the heart of the inner child who had reservations about divine love.

The Above and the Orphan

In the sixth direction, we enter a relationship with the unseen world of the Spirit. An ancient man robed in the traditional white wool blanket of the Taos Pueblo once said to Jung, *"Does not all life come from the mountain?"* Standing there under the majestic Sangre de Cristo range, Jung just nodded and, like the old man, continued gazing in the direction of the high snow-capped peaks. When we turn toward the Spirit, we come to the mountain, where "all life comes from."[1]

No matter what our religious background, without some sense of what our place is in the universe, without a firm sense of connectedness to the divine, we have a spiritual wound that paralyzes the heart. Most people on a healing path acknowledge the existence of something sacred within themselves. But many of us have a religious wound that has cut us off from holy ground. Many of the adults I work with have serious distortions in their image of God; the betrayal and abandonment some have experienced in religious institutions (and from parents who have forgotten a loving Creator) goes deep.

For many of us there comes a time to meet ourselves in the wilderness; like Jacob, we have to wrestle with ourselves at the soul level, and with the God who resides there. Without this sort of labor, our relationship to the divine stays in a prolonged adolescence. Whether one chooses a retreat, a vision quest, therapy, spiritual direction, or a workshop spirited enough to do this kind of leveling with one's religious roots, the "mountain" symbolizes our intention to confront how we have closed the doors to the Spirit.

Each time I go out on the hill, I am never without some shadow remnant from the past. If my ego had its way I would be out in that vast beauty with my dignity and my religious devotee intact. I would want to look like Jesus or an old Tibetan lama out there. As long as I'm going to all that trouble, there should at least be some profound and numinous experiences. But instead I am often pestered by the orphans in my psyche I have ignored, and all the hungry ghosts I have never completely loved.

These shadowy figures, much as we don't like to experience them, often become our guides to spiritual breakthrough. They are curative figures; they take us almost immediately to the blocks in the ego that isolate us from God. In dreams these are the characters that are often wounded, hurt, imprisoned, depraved, angry, threatening, or disempowered in some way. I used to dream of a young man in a wheelchair (a symbol of my powerlessness), but on the mountain, I met him face to face. He and I had to talk about what false strength meant.

Once we get near the sixth direction, it helps to imagine that the Above and the orphan are never separate. One old man in a sweat lodge once said, *"We are really pitiful people. We have many needs. We have to look to the Creator for everything."* He was—just then, in his need—suddenly an altar, a skin and bones ground where he (with his broken heart and his imperfections) and God could draw the same breath.

The Axial Mountain

Without the energy that lifts mountains, how am I to live?
—Mirabai[2]

Our work with the directions so far has led us into the sacred wilderness. All along, the healing archetypes in the directions have counseled us to go into the dark honestly, to "see" in there; to stand and speak, to be ourselves; to dream dreams and birth a vision, to hold the flowering stick; to trust we are part of creation and to let the "mothering power" of the earth heal us. All along we have been approaching the mountain. Some people, even when they begin introspection and "sees within," already have a religious practice or a strong sense of the holy. But the task in the sixth direction is forgoing what we think we know of God. Ultimately it means yielding to the experience of communion (dialogue), kenosis (emptying out), and mystery (letting go to the unknown).

Any honest encounter with the soul requires resolve and patience, and a willingness to see how some of us have broken the stick that holds the blue robe. In this direction, one begins a relationship with Spirit that is not based on projection or on contracts or compensations, but on transparency.

John Snelling, after a climb in the Himalayas, wrote: *"In some ancient cosmologies, a great axial mountain is said to lie at the centre of the world. In fact, any mountain that is regarded as sacred . . . is a symbol of the Centre. . . . The true Centre, however . . . resides in the heart of man. Here then lies the key to the strange power that some mountains possess: their ability to fascinate and draw men to them, magnetlike, across hundreds or even thousands of miles, and in spite of all manner of danger and difficulty. The devotee who, with a pure heart, undertakes such a pilgrimage goes through a process of intense spiritual training that may, if he is lucky, open his own heart/mind and initiate him into the great mystery enshrined therein."*[3]

The power and enchantment of the mountain always has an inner dimension. One sees something out there and feels an intense stirring inside. The soul is amplified in the wilderness because we are alone out there without agendas and distractions. Wilderness is both challenge and solace; its openness is fertile. It invites us inward.

Yet whether we go out into the wilderness or not is not so much the point here. Although such a venture can be a powerful initiation, the main task in the sixth direction is to be aware of whatever keeps us from an authentic relationship with God. The originator of Self-Acceptance training, Dick Olney, used to say that we may have a good relationship to God, or a bad one, but one way or the other, we have a relationship. One can reject the idea of a Godhead, but we cannot dissociate from our soul.

Wilderness Encounters

While living I want to live well. I know I have to die sometime, but even if the heavens were to fall on me, I want to do what is right. There is one God looking down on us all. We are all children of the one God. God is listening to me. The sun, the darkness, the winds, all are listening to what we now say.

—Geronimo[4]

Theologian John Dourley comments that both Paul Tillich and Carl Jung were aware that religion, when not brought to consciousness, has a destructive side. That is, when one relates to God unconsciously—when God is seen solely as a power outside the self—religion loses its spiritual sustenance.

Tillich and Jung both felt that once we can experience ourselves in the image of God, we have a direction for devotion that does not pull us out of ourselves. If we pay attention to the "native language of the soul" (to our dreams, symbols, or to the natural world), then we will simply know we are made in the image of God.[5] Like Geronimo, we will know not only that we are children of the one God, but that someone out there is listening to what we say.

In a day and age where religion has become predictable and bound by hierarchy, I find a number of people who want to leave their traditional religious practice, or at the very least, to make it more real. The metaphor of a wilderness encounter is about getting back to something essential, something nurturing and powerful in our relationship to the divine. Many people I talk to don't want religious concessions or contracts (I'll do what you say if you take care of me); they want the real stuff. They want to know that God is not only "looking down" on them, but has a voice. Yet it takes some intense listening to hear it. And we have to get past ourselves first.

If Moses can wander in the desert forty years, if Jacob can wrestle with the angel while in exile, if Jesus can go off for forty days of fasting and solitude, if our ancestors on this land can cry for a dream, then there is an important message here. No one of us can be "soft" (open, welcoming, inclusive, expansive, accepting, experiential) unless we have experienced *some* kind of initiation. The wilderness encounters in these following vignettes illustrate what happens when, indeed, we give ourselves to this *kenosis* (emptying out).

The first thing that happens on the mountain is that our religious persona begins to wear thin, and the psychic luggage we've hidden away suddenly reappears. The pain that we'd rather not think about suddenly magnifies under the looking glass of the stars. One of my friends said of a time in the wilderness he spent camping solo, *"I never realized how much I've held on to my grief, or to the losses I've had these last few years. I honestly thought I had dealt with that stuff. I thought I'd worked through it. But out there under the stars, I knew I was hanging on. I knew then I had to let go."*

A woman who had decided to do a one-day fast and an overnight in a remote setting said: *"I felt bored and restless, full of chatter. I wanted to pray but my mind kept spinning. I felt powerless and unable to impress myself or God and I hated the cold. Then I hated myself for hating the cold. I was Jell-O out there. That's a side of me I never see in church."*

People tell me all kinds of stories about their wilderness encounters: some frightening and difficult, others peaceful and ecstatic. A friend of mine once told me she had gone out to the Three Sisters wilderness, feeling depleted and tired, and very unsure of herself. The moment she arrived she had a remarkable experience. *"The moment I got there, I just went way in, deep. Those Three Sisters are very female mountains; they really felt like sisters welcoming me."* Just setting foot in that place had not only ignited a sense of acceptance, it had the effect of restoring her confidence. Indeed, these places are holy; they take us past our failures because they mirror the soul.

Another person who had gone on a four-day fast in the Canadian wilderness recently told me: *"I wanted to test myself. I was determined I could do it. I also felt incredible fear. Things came up from the past that I felt I couldn't bear to look at. I wasn't sure I could last the whole four days without eating. I was afraid in the dark. I felt at some point I was going to lose it. I thought they'd find me just wandering, a basket case in the woods, grasshoppers in my hair. But one night I had an incredible dream. Or maybe it was a vision. In my delirium I wasn't sure. St. Francis came to me and offered me his robe. The minute it fell over me, I felt myself again, and deeply peaceful. My fear and exhaustion vanished totally. The beauty I began to notice then was overwhelming."*

One common denominator we experience in the wild is that we're always going to have an appointment with that element of ourselves that is normally out of sight to us. Whatever we don't "see" consciously about ourselves is suddenly amplified. The unconscious, when exposed to the elements, will cough up the last of our denial, resistance, inflation, fear, and sorrow. In verbal therapy, inventory, confession, or even talking to friends, people can mask what's really going on. But in the wilderness, there is no one to seduce.

A woman talking about her first solo mountain overnight said: *"I never felt so utterly small and alone. But I never felt such a longing for God, either. In my fears and apprehensions I felt suddenly diminished. I pride myself on being pretty self-sufficient most of the time. But huddled under my blanket out there, I felt like a dwarf under the stars. I walk around life with a lot of padding. Up there, I didn't have any."*

A young woman I had been working with for a while went out on an overnight in the wilderness. She had fasted and prayed and was sitting out on a cold mountain waiting for a blessing. *"Suddenly I looked up and I saw this huge cougar standing in the trees. I was terrified. All night long it prowled near me, crying and howling. I was sure it was stalking me. Somehow I managed to keep praying off and on throughout the night. Once in a while I would think it had gone away, then I'd hear it cry again. I've never felt so afraid."* Now, as it turns out, this cougar had started its evening out as a tomcat from a neighboring ranch. It was a good-size tom, however, and had a formidable cry.

The fact is, this marauding lion was a projection of this woman's negative father image. In a piece of work she did later, the fear she felt about being attacked by this cougar was an unconscious remnant of a judgmental father (who used to verbally attack her). Because she hadn't adequately dealt with this fear at a conscious level, it had leaked out of the unconscious in the pitch-black night. And it happened to land on this passing cat. *"I think this mountain lion creeps up on me sometimes in relationships. That's when I get scared of rejection, when I fear that what people say is critical or judging. It's also the anger I feel when I think I'm hearing rejection. Then I want to attack them, or run away. What a revelation!"* She also had a vision of two dark horses. As she began to meditate on these two figures, what she was shown was this: *"One horse was my 'work horse.' He's the side of me that's driven and wants to do it right, and doesn't want to let go. The other horse was like a companion, a guide to remind me to run free and to play and take chances and be a little wild. Then I felt him running under me in a huge field of flowers, taking me for a ride."* She had made a descent to her worst fear, but she had also ridden the Great Horse.

Before that third year of "going out," I had already wrestled with the dark plenty of times. I had struggled with religious mind-sets, with demons and angels and doubts and passion. I had stood up to the patriarchy in more than one religious tradition. I knew about shadow and abandonment and father complexes, but I had never said, *"Look God, I've always loved You, longed for You, but I don't trust You. I can't let my defenses down utterly; I'll be naked. I can't show this much need for anything; I'll be crushed. Give me holy causes to do in life, brokenness to heal, tough hombres to deal with; let me experience humility, let me see into the crevices in the heart. But don't ask me to trust You."* That's what the mountain does to us; it strips us down, empties us out.

In the book *Psyche as Sacrament,* John Dourley cites Jung as saying that when the ego undergoes such a transformation, then "God can be born in the soul of man."[6] The poet Rumi, in his search for spiritual wholeness, also felt that the workings of the heart and the mind could be a sacrament. In one of his quatrains he said:

> *The Way of Moses is all hopelessness and need*
> *and it is the only way to God.*[7]

In this song (many of Rumi's poems were originally sung) Rumi assures us that the only way to get to God is to honor exactly what we are feeling. Pain, loss, helplessness, rage, sorrow—when felt with intensity and not denied—are all sacraments. On this sort of psychic ground we enter a struggle that is terrifying and yet clearly empowering. It is an abyss, and it is exhilarating beyond measure. The mystery intensifies when suddenly we realize we're in that dialogue by the courtesy of our instincts. By the seat of our pants.

When any of us goes onto the mountain, it is breathtaking to experience how suddenly our fears, our reservations, and our childhood complexes will surface. A savage struggle goes on; the adult ego with all its defenses and fortifications pitches in wild discontent. The ego suddenly becomes a judge, demands we get hold of ourselves. The false warrior springs into action, certain that he must defend us from that stripping.

Sliding Off the Mountain

There are always reasons some people never venture to the mountain, never get to a genuine sense of the Spirit. Sometimes our religious heritage has been a bad experience; other times it's been too ordinary, never fiery or moving enough, and we stay in a safe complacency, too bored or self-satisfied to go.

Many of the people I know say that as children they knew how to talk to animals, stars, sea shells, imaginary friends, deceased relatives, and angels. Until someone taught them to, they didn't step on ants. Children live in the numinous world of images, symbols, the sense-felt world of the instincts. Our relationship with the Spirit, however, has diminished by adolescence. Imagination, intuition, faith in life (and sometimes the people in it), the feeling world, the power of metaphor that many children can so easily occupy—these things have all receded.

By the time most of us begin our religious programs, a terrible but subtle polarization sets in. The divine wilderness—the profound sense of oneness some of us felt as children—begins to slip away. God is identified with something outside our world. A client of mine once said: *"When I was a child, God was something big and powerful and holy, and I was not. It was clear that we lived in two different worlds. I was on the outside of paradise, and He was on the inside."* This psychological split says one of us is in exile.

Most of us have heard that we are children of the Creator, but one gets other messages along the way that leave a different impression. *"We had to kneel every day before the cross and recite our prayers, and we knew God meant business from pretty early on. We were forced to do this every day, and if we didn't we were shamed or punished."*

Sometimes the Spirit is lost to us because we have experienced grave betrayals that scar the heart, and our center is devastated. A woman healing from sexual abuse told me that as a child she hated to go to confession because the tiny cubicle reminded her of the closet where her father locked her while he sexually abused her older sister. In the mind of a child who has been hurt and abandoned in some way, God is associated with the betrayal. One woman who had been ritually abused said, *"I was certain God didn't care because he didn't intervene."* A terrible feeling of personal insignificance, a sense of isolation, begins here and takes hold of one's soul.

A woman I know stayed in a destructive relationship for years because she thought divorce was a sin, and because her pastor convinced her that she would be in grave trouble if she left her marriage. After two of her children were later molested by her husband, the pastor responded by blaming her for not fulfilling her "wifely duties." This tragic story has many sequels. Men as well as women are subjected to this kind of negative projection of God. The danger for both is that sooner or later God gets identified with this abuse and winds up looking like the perpetrator.

Some of the people I work with don't have such deep wounds in relationship to the Spirit, but most of us have been taught that God lives on the other side of the fence. This dichotomy creates a rift between what appears to be good, acceptable, safe, what looks nice— and the realities in our own lives (which may look very different). Albrecht Durer once did a wonderful etching of a man kneeling in prayer in the middle of a pigsty surrounded by barnyard animals (and other things that presumably one might find in a barnyard). It inspired me for years. I often felt that if I were God, that's exactly where I might be—in the sty with that man with the fervent heart.

One way or the other, the figure of God ends up carrying enormous projections. And as long as we relate to the divine as "out there," God is in exile. A friend of mine said once, *"The more I got into my recovery, the more I saw that real relationship was about honest confrontation, intimacy, about trusting I could be myself. But I had no models for that in my childhood; men weren't available, didn't show feeling, didn't like to play. I danced the dance of a good girl for God the father for years, trying to imagine I fit in somewhere."*

If, by some good fortune in life, we have been able to remain centered in our faith and have not lost ourselves to projection, then we have kept some measure of holy ground. Yet without even knowing it, even devotees can miss out on authentic dialogue. If we're going to explore relationship, we can't do it outside the circle, looking in.

In my early twenties, I followed a spiritual teacher named Bapak, who taught a particular kind of prayer exercise that I followed for many years. His wife, Ibu, and he traveled together every few years to teach and visit the international groups he had begun. Ibu (which means "mother" in Indonesian) used to pray with the women, and Bapak with the men; the two groups were always separate for worship.

In this prayer exercise there were Christians, Muslims, Jews, Buddhists, Hindus, Sufis, people from all religious backgrounds praying together.

The exercise itself was always spontaneous; one might be seen dancing, another singing, shouting, weeping, another silent. Sometimes we took different prayer postures, standing, sitting, kneeling, moving, leaping; all spontaneously directed from within. It was a wonderful emptying of oneself, and a receiving. These two people were good teachers, simple loving people with a clear message that always pointed in the direction of God.

One evening when a large group of women was practicing this worship I suddenly thought, *I have to be near Ibu. I know I'll have a better blessing if I can just go stand near her.* But God was watching all this in the meantime. It was toward dusk and the lights in the large room were dim. Ibu was a long way across the room. I pushed myself into the crowd, trying to dance and bob my way to where she stood quietly in her own praise. What I didn't see was the Moslem woman kneeling on the floor. It was a holy fall, sudden, loud, and obnoxious. A tiny voice spoke to me as I lay dazed on the floor in a tangle of arms and legs and someone else's skirt over my face: *Where are you going? Am I not right here?* That was my first teaching about projection.

Many of us relate to God in the same way. With our child mystic out of the way, we set out to find the holy in others, or in some formula or holy book. When religious rhetoric subtly infuses us with the idea that God is just out of reach—it gradually disfigures our self-image. We then have no choice but to seek holiness outside ourselves.

From Projection to Relationship

Everywhere I go I meet people who are weary of rhetoric and ritual that constricts Spirit, particularly if it betrays and rejects the feminine. One woman, waking up out of a long history of this, commented, *"One day, after years of sitting quietly in front of long sermons, I realized I was stuck. Underneath this statue in the pew was a fiery, wild creature exhausted from her religious compensations, and aching to experience herself as an altar. I realized I am a vessel for the Holy Spirit; I am a chalice. I am the womb for holy birth."* This woman's insights are shared by a great number of women (and men) on a spiritual quest. Many of us are looking for ways in which we can experience the divine; for ways we can know ourselves as the chalice.

In most religious services, all one needs is a head. For many of us, God has been systematically reduced to a teaching. But religion without heart and tears and dance and color is empty. One of my clients working on a more authentic relationship to God said, *"My sense of Spirit as a child was healthy. Church was a sanctuary. I remember the warmth on my mother's lap, the smell of fresh cotton, a feeling of well-being against her flesh. Church was about songs and color and people standing close and touching one another. Later on we moved, changed churches; the songs got more formal, the colorful banners gave way to dark wood and musty smells, and mother's lap got smaller. God became more and more an event in history. I could still relate to the idea of God in my life, but I didn't feel the immediate presence or the wonderment I knew as a child."*

Once any of us experiences (not just understands) a *relationship* with God, once we taste that kind of intensity, we are hooked. God is meant to be engaged, not just talked about. A great drama is unfolding in front of us, a fire is being kindled in our midst, a birth is taking place, and in some circles we are only paying lip service to it.

I have a friend who had been visiting a church in another city. She had gone early and sat down to pray. *"I felt the most incredible sweetness move into that chapel. A wind stirred. I don't know whether it was inside or outside, but I could feel it. I was getting ready to teach a weekend seminar, so I'd been asking for some guidance. A voice said: 'Just love them. Don't worry about being prepared. I am the only preparation you need.' I let go of my concerns and just sat there feeling overwhelmed with relief and thanks. Then I heard the pastor coming in and everybody stood up. The manner of this man was brusque, matter-of-fact; in his homily, he was condemning. I held on to my joy throughout the service, but I couldn't help wonder about those who hadn't come a few minutes early."* When the Spirit is suddenly squelched, it is hard to accept substitutes.

Just before my mother died she asked me to give the eulogy at her neighborhood church. I agreed to this, and then spoke to her pastor about it. He wasn't fond of the idea, nor did he like the suggestion to invite people to sit in a circle around the altar. The crowning blow came shortly after I told him I wanted to invite other people to say a word or two about my mother, if they felt like it. He thought that sitting that close together, letting "just anyone" speak, even letting me give the eulogy, might get "too emotional." I asked him where he thought it might be appropriate for people to have emotions, if not in the church. We bristled, and the stale air in his little office began to stir. I sat on the edge of his big desk, he rolled up his sleeves, and we got into it. I told him that if he wanted to run the kind of church where everything was tidy all the time and everyone's feelings were in check, where all the chairs faced forward and everything proceeded according to his will, he could certainly do that. I said he could give neat little sermons in that church with everyone staring ahead unflinching, but that God wasn't interested in neatness and order. God was interested in relationship. I told him that people's hearts weren't there by accident, and that death wasn't something to cover up with a white sheet and forget. By the grace of God we did not strangle one another, and he agreed I should give the eulogy, and that our family friends could remember Charlotte out loud if they wanted to. She must have loved that.

In the early church, people had a relationship with the divine because God was not an intellectual exercise. Before the Logos became the sole focus of religious service, God was a holy wind in some gatherings, something people felt in their flesh. Before the dogma of the church fathers took over, the divine had a room in the psyche. In the first few centuries of Christianity, with the advent of the Upper Room experience (the coming of the Paraclete, the breaking through of the Holy Spirit), people danced and sang and wept and held one another close; religious fire and persecution does that. In the early church, as well as in some Eastern traditions such as the Bhakti movement in northern India in the twelfth century, religious followers experienced a relationship with the numinous through heart feeling, through the intensity of the whole-body experience. Worship was a celebration of the senses as well as a spoken word. Before it was delivered in the age of reason into the hands of the priest, Spirit was a shared experience of divine passion. The Bhakti poet Mirabai says:

"I have felt the swaying of the elephant's shoulders; and now you want me to climb on a jackass! Try to be serious!"[8]

When the Spirit speaks through people, God—in spite of us—is enfleshed. I suppose that's why I liked black and Hispanic churches and the sweat lodge so much. For me, God was enfleshed in these third-world places. In the black church I could dance and weep and sing and nobody avoided my gaze or shook my hand like a wet noodle. In the sweat lodge, nobody was telling me anything *about* God. There were no mediators in there apart from the earth and the stones and my sweat and the Spirit that spoke to me. That Presence never cared if I knew the Nicene creed or not; it only said, *"I am closer to you than your breath. Learn to trust that."*

Dialogue from the Circle

In the sixth direction, one experiences the divine instinct toward self-acceptance, a letting go and emptying out of oneself (*kenosis*). In soul dialogue, as on the mountain, we meet the sides of the personality that we least love. But in this circle of friends, it is love, not condemnation, that convenes us. Arrogance is, after all, only a thin covering for shame and fear; far better to let the coverings go and embrace the poorest side of ourselves.

For predictably good reasons, some people are doubtful about having a dialogue with soul, about releasing ourselves to the Great Wash, because it means that to some degree we have to let go of the rope— the one that says *"I'm in charge here."* Some people say that when they are depressed or angry or afraid, they feel isolated from God. Dialogue, on the other hand, means we volunteer not to be unreachable.

In soul dialogue, a window opens between us and our conflict, and we then make a choice whether to shut the window or leave it open. Letting go and breathing into what we feel is like a prayer; it has the power to dispel our defenses; to break the rigid hold depression has over us. When we can say our longing, God may suddenly be in the next breath. A woman wrote in her journal: *"I've never accepted this incested child in here. I've withheld her from the light because she shames me. I know I shouldn't feel this way, but there it is. I just have to accept my shame and not push it away. Feeling this much permission is scary, but I ache to bring that child home."*

Inside the circle, we go as we are, and we take all the orphans we've ever abandoned. We go in there with the bare flesh on our bones, with the body that's in pain, the heart we've ignored, the sexuality we can't reconcile with, the mistakes we've made, the people we can't stand, the losses we've endured; nothing gets left out. God isn't interested in our accomplishments, only in our surrender. One man struggling in his recovery said: *"I feel incredibly exposed. I feel enraged, and terrified, and I hate this much need. I want to tell God to forget it; the deal is off. But I say that because I expect to be judged; because I judge myself. And because I don't want to rely on anybody but myself for that."*

Relationship to the Holy is about confrontation, intimacy, passion. Dialogue that has that kind of transparence is a communion that's rich and vibrant and sensual, like making love in the sun or having a good fight in an Italian restaurant. It is a relationship without veils, stripped of at least some ego. Like it or not, this relationship means you stay in the circle, you and the Big Holy together, touching in there; you are engaged in a conversation, painful or ecstatic, and you don't leave that embrace.

A woman beginning a talk with her pain, and with her conflicting desire to open to the Spirit, wrote: *"How shall I contain You in this small form? How shall I hold You in the midst of my child's wounds? I am afraid and furious and abandoned—and my longing to see your face overwhelms me. In this dark place inside, in this pain, this is all I can offer you."* This is the abandoned child who has to stand with us on the mountain.

A woman religious dreamed once of a very seductive teenage girl, wild and free and urgently wanting her attention. As a teenage girl this woman had repressed her sexuality, fearful it wouldn't fit her image of piety or the taboos about the body she had been taught. This woman had gone on to become a model of religious life, but in the process had betrayed her body and denied the deep feminine-feeling nature within her. In the dream this split came up. *"There was a girl dressed like a gypsy; she had on a colorful skirt and ribbons and bells and she was absolutely wild-looking. She was dancing provocatively and twirling and spinning and she was beautiful. But suddenly I felt ashamed watching her, anxious that someone might see us. Then I got angry, furious with her, and I grabbed her and told her to stop dancing. When she refused and started to dance even more wildly, I began to beat her. The rage that came up inside was overwhelming. Then when I saw the look on her face and what I had done, I was horrified. I started to weep and felt this incredible remorse. Then we fell crying into one another's arms."* When the dreamer realized how she had abandoned her adolescent, how she betrayed an essential wildness in her inner woman, she could reconcile with her sexual nature. As she subsequently worked on the dream, she received an image of Jesus coming through a crowd to dance with her. They were at a wedding, and he was dressed like a gypsy.

The men and women I have worked with who have the deepest wounds are usually people who also have the deepest desire for the Big Holy. Where pain runs deep, so also does longing. God can spot these lovers, even when they are dragged kicking and screaming onto the mountain.

You Become that River

The Indians would say that it is useless to argue about whether or not God exists, since the presence of the Spirit is everywhere. Jung, who studied and mapped the unconscious, and the Indians who studied the beauty of creation, both say that there is a natural continuity between the divine and the human. In the sixth direction one becomes, like the "four-leggeds," alert to that presence, instinctively responsive to it.

This presence is under every leaf and rock, on every breath of wind, in every sunset. The potential for communion with the divine is in all things. When we are conscious of this relationship, God is no longer and can never be a dogma, a distant figure, a projection, a form we cling to, or resist. Inside the circle, the boundaries that have kept us from the divine wilderness begin to fade.

One old woman told me once that God was like a river, a stream. *"You can get into that stream or refuse. But if you get into it, you will be touched by it. When you are touched by it, then you get cleansing, guidance, help, maybe you get knocked down a little. You get what you need. After a while you know you are part of the water of life, that your life is in this water. After a while then, that Spirit moves in you like a river. You don't know where you end or where the river begins. If you really let your life go to the river, then sooner or later, you become that river."*

The dialogue we have done so far in this direction empties us out and begins to cleanse the impact of the world on the soul. When at last ego surrenders itself, our psychological work (to some degree at least) is done. Relationship now moves us in the direction of the unknown.

Meister Eckhart says, *"The best and noblest of all that one can come to in this life is to be silent and let God work and let God speak."*[9] But it is not a specific religious language or practice that this internal silence invites. To "let God work" is to let go of our known pathways to God; it is at this point we begin to experience the vastness of an interior wilderness. In the sixth direction, prayer is based on fiat, emptying out of our expectations. It is what the psalmist talks about when he cries, *"Lead me to the Rock which is higher than I."* We just go up there and sit.

In many ways this *kenosis* is not just for cleansing the ego; it is also a key to prayer. In prayer I am to lose myself from time to time; to loosen the seaweed I get wrapped in; to stay close to softness. I go into that circle to remember how to be alive and real, more divorced from my critic, more lavish in my loving.

Letting God work is an act of relinquishment. The presence of God comes through much more powerfully when we can drop our own prayer agendas. In this emptying the Spirit can come in images, words, sounds, sensations, or an utter silence that lures us into the best kind of embrace. God is continually shape-shifting, evading the forms we once knew, occupying all or none of them.

In a powerful piece of breath work I did not long ago, I had an unexpected visit from the Above. I had never done too much breath therapy, but an analyst friend of mine from Long Island insisted I have this experience. *"It will be good for you, just go,"* she said. *"It's a woman from Kripalu who studied for many years with Babaji. You'll like her."* I climbed four flights of ancient stairs on the west side of Manhattan to get to this woman's flat. There was no elevator, just these stairs that felt as if they might disengage any minute from the wall that held them. But I managed to climb them without giving in to the knot in my stomach. Somewhere deep into the exercises, which were surprising in their intensity, I quite unexpectedly had the experience of birthing. I could feel the force of labor moving through me in waves. There were strong contractions in my uterus, a tremendous pressure, but no pain. At one point I felt the bag of waters break and flow out through the birth canal. When the labor ceased, I was soaked with tears, and it felt as though I was wet from the birth waters. The whole event took me by surprise, because I had gone into that experience in a mood of self-doubt, feeling far away from my soul as though I had drifted a thousand miles from the

Holy. Or so it seemed. Now I picked up the infant and held it aloft. The two of us stood before a luminous yellow-white light which radiated a warmth I could clearly feel soaking into my wet skin. It seemed like the infant, however, was myself. I sensed that neither of us was separate from this remarkable source of loving. I distinctly heard the words, *"Nothing you have ever done, or ever failed to do, will ever separate you from the love of God."* Reflecting on this later, I felt the experience was somehow the soul of my inner child coming to birth. The labor I had done over the years had finally begun to come about. This profound experience took place about a year after my third vision fast on the mountain.

In prayer and dialogue we are always facing into mystery. Probably more than anything else, being on the mountain has taught me how to long for and to see God in the subtlest things. Up there where the syllable of the wind is Hu, this Presence speaks through the endless devotions of nature; through trees, sunsets, waters, rain, wind, and bright air; through the tiniest creatures, the soaring and crawling ones, in sweet grass and tears and hunger and hard ground; through starry nights and fears and doubts and cold mornings, through hot sun and longing, and sometimes in dreams and visions. God comes in both our weakness and in our strength, in our strongest faith or the lack of it. The more one releases the old forms, the more one notices that God is everywhere.

In relation to God, there is always paradox. There are moments in that relationship that seem to go utterly blank. In the seasons of prayer there are times we don't feel or see or sense anything; nothing comes back our way. Then, for one reason or another, we are forced simply to listen to interior silence. We are, nonetheless, still in dialogue.

Kenosis is most painful when there are questions on my heart that I want answered; sorrows and hurts and losses I want some accountability for. Like the emperor's new clothes, I try to make my demands as noble as possible; I bargain, make promises, I try reasoning with the Holy; I tell God I am desperate and that I can't possibly go on without him/her. And aside from the little voice that says, *"Why not? You seem to be doing fine so far on your own,"* there is only silence, and sometimes the occasional stirring of the wind.

I have seldom met anyone who likes this kind of intense silence. It is as though the soul itself shuts down, leaving no clue at all how to proceed. I have never felt this holy blankness without some sense that I have failed at something, and that I have taken a false turn somewhere. I have never stayed in that void without resisting it. Yet when I was out on the mountain that third year, sitting in the sort of silence that is anything but inspiring, I had a small revelation. It dawned on me that when there is nothing to do, when nothing fills us, when there is no stimulation, no light, no juice, no feeling, no passion, no interior voice, no sunset, no eagles, maybe this *is* God.

Later, in conversation with my resistance to these times of silence, I began to suspect that maybe there is no holy without the void.

> And yet I raise my hands aloft to God, that I might be
> held by God, just like a feather which has no weight from
> its own strength and lets itself be carried by the wind.
> —Hildegard of Bingen[10]

At the times one feels this void, there is nothing to do but be in it. We are standing under the Big Mountain, where "all life comes from." The substance that comes from that axial mountain is the life that comes from the heart, from the Spirit, from the House of the Grandfathers in each of us. We are on that mountain whenever we face ourselves and God inside. In that dialogue, when we are honest, undefended, open to tests and cleansing, willing to hang in the breeze suspended, not needing to know, not needing control, when we can open to mystery and not resist any part of the dialogue, then God takes every shape, even the shape of silence. Rumi's poignant verse comes from that kind of embrace:

> *O Lord, truly, Your grace is not from our work,*
> *but from your mysterious giving.*
> *Save us from what our own hands might do;*
> *lift the veil but do not tear it.*
> *Save us from the ego; its knife has reached our bones.*
> *Who but you will break these chains?*
> *Let us turn from ourselves to You*
> *Who are nearer to us than ourselves.*
> *Even this prayer is Your gift to us.*
> *How else has a rose garden grown from these ashes?*[11]

10. Coming Home: The Seventh Direction

Look for the Dawn Boy's house, the rising
red sun house, look for the tent where the beaded
sky lives, but don't go to the place
where there's no sound of laughter. Don't chase
after people who won't love God,
or you'll wind up in a house without doors. Seek
instead the One who births you
and don't rely on anything but that mercy. So many
people I talk to cover the soul
with dark compromise. Break away and don't look
back. Her hand lifts you
on Eagle's Wings. He is a rock that steadies.
Go there whatever way you can.
—Djohariah Toor

The beauty of the directions is that circling them is a process, an opportunity to practice the sacred on a daily basis. When I walk outdoors in the morning and I remember the world is wrapped up in the "robes" of Grandpa and Grandma, overlooked by helping spirits in the four corners, in the above and below, I can't help feeling that the communion between me and the next world is an ongoing event.

When we have walked the directions, sat in the Sacred Winds, and put flesh on the six archetypes within us, we are on the road home.

The seventh direction is the midpoint in the circle, the heart within each of us. In our bones is the novice and the warrior; the midwife, the visionary, and the lover. In our veins the rivers flow and the Spirit that made the rivers. In this chapter I want to briefly revisit each direction to illustrate with stories and meditations, simple ways to stay in the circle.

In the Tao Te Ching it says that we make many beginnings. That is indeed what one does in inner work. Bringing the directions home is a commitment. It's a promise to ourselves to be awake, alive, to keep our face into the wind, to stay in love with life, to sing up the sun every day. People who make an art of life will tell us that real creativity comes from trekking the inner world; from sitting at the fire pit in the center of the soul. The task in the seventh direction is to stoke the fire and not let it go out.

The danger for us in the Western world is that we value the technical side of knowledge so exclusively that we bury the creative side of the mind; we listen neither to the heart nor to the inner realm where the Spirit speaks to us. Some robes we take on in this culture are dangerous to the soul. Some of us wear the robe of sees-nothing. Every time I get too settled down in my ways, too comfortable in my world, maybe too self-serving (which happens), I stop seeing. Every time I bury myself in my own wounds or try only to protect my own interests, I don't hear the pain of others; I don't remember the Third World or the people on the street or the events of Wounded Knee. In the seventh direction, we try to stay in the circle; to be awake not only to ourselves and the Spirit, but to the world around us.

I want to emphasize again that one need not do anything fancy or exotic, nor must one travel to some remote cinder cone in order to be a seeker of holy ground. What we do need to do, however, if we're aimed at keeping the creative fire going, is be intentionally focused with our time. The problem we face when it comes to growth work is being consistent—being careful that our Western penchant for productivity, niceness, neatness, order (for convention) doesn't seduce us; that our childhood fears and complexes don't pull us back to sleep. Life is full of charlatans who will do their best to convince us that the *things* of the world are food for the soul.

I am coming to see that if I am going to persist at all in inner work, I need to carry a big talking stick that will automatically swing at me in midair when I forget, neglect, overlook, deny, or slide past in the fast lane the powerful truths of the inner world. Without careful attention to interior crossroads where the Flowering Tree stands, I am outside the territory of the wilderness. But in the seventh direction, the moment I remember, I begin again.

The West: Honoring the Realm of the Mothers

"Sees within," which is the opus of the West, is the practice of opening the door not just to the hidden side of the self, but to the *realm of the Mothers* we spoke of earlier. Whether we are male or female, right brained or left, linear or intuitive, the territory of the mothers is the creative womb in the psyche where our aliveness is stored.

When I keep my journal, write some verse, paint or sketch or daydream consciously, if I have feelings or thoughts that lead me to the truth inside, then I am in touch with the creative unconscious. When I record and talk to my dreams, moods, fits of temper, feelings and fantasies, when I can honestly own my own faults and not project them onto others—when I confront the hidden life in those things— a new energy is released to me. I am sitting at the fire pit.

In the West, everything is an opportunity for reflection; the novice is always watching, listening, waiting for what comes from the unconscious. When things happen during the day that seem unrelated, annoying, interruptive, or mysterious, the novice will stop to ask what might be going on. A colleague of mine once told me, *"Last year I had a terrible pain in my cervical vertebrae for about six weeks. It was so excruciating that even the stoic in me was in tears. I came home from work (after having to hold my head up during the day while talking to clients), fell on the rug, and couldn't move. I decided to talk to my pinched nerve. The words that came back to me from that pain were not sweet. 'Well, you asked for it. You've taken the world on your shoulders, you've satisfied enough obligations for two lifetimes, and you've left no time for yourself. Whatever you do, never say no. Keep pleasing the world until you drop.'"* That stunning little piece of enlightenment caused my colleague to take a long-needed sabbatical. She took her empty journal and her blank sketch pad and disappeared into the woods for a while. This kind of dialogue, which informs us there is a problem we need to confront, also begins to open the doors to our creativity.

A friend of mine told me she had recently gone on a rafting trip on an exciting stretch of western white water. *"I was in charge of the second boat and everything was going fine, when all of a sudden we lost control of the boat and it flipped and we all went in. It was scary. I went under and my shoe got caught in a rock. At first I was fairly calm, and knew that all I had to do was unwedge the shoe or untie it and get my foot out and everything would be all right. Then I realized my foot wasn't coming out of the shoe, and I couldn't breathe down there. I panicked. I really don't know what happened, but the next thing I knew, I was floating along in the current. I don't know how I got out of that shoe. I got to thinking about it later, and I decided to use that experience as a metaphor for my life. I asked myself, 'How am I drowning in my life?' "* In re-imaging the experience, she sensed that being under water with her foot caught was like being unconscious (being pulled under) in some of her relationships. The ordeal caused her to rethink what aspects of those relationships needed more attention.

No matter where we are in the circle, we never outgrow our need to be in communion with these events, rather than seeing them as unrelated or bad luck or something to pass lightly over as fate. This kind of dialogue gives us an inner look at things, as though we were able to see in the dark. In the West, we have to see in the dark if we're going to stay in the circle.

Sr. Jose Hobday tells a story that happened just after the big earth-quake in the San Francisco Bay Area in 1989. *"I was cooking a big pot of soup to take to some people, and the doorbell rang. I hoped it was the handmade sandals I had ordered from back East that I'd been waiting for. Sure enough, it was. I brought them back into the kitchen and, after opening the package, set them on the shelf over the stove and went back to stirring this big pot of soup. Just about then the phone rang, and to answer it I put my ladle down next to the package on the shelf. I went on talking on the phone for a bit. Just as I was hanging up the phone, I was also reaching for the ladle, and all of a sudden I knocked the shoes off the shelf right into the soup. You can imagine my surprise. I'm sixty years old and I've never had sandals fall into my soup before! Well, at first I rushed to take them out, but then I stopped suddenly, thinking, 'No, there must be some meaning to this.' I stood there for a moment, and then I realized what it was. I wasn't walking the earth with enough reverence. My sandals in the soup were a sign that I should try to walk as though my steps were really food for the earth."*

After she told that story, I felt inspired to go home and have a little conversation with my cowboy boots. I began to realize that they were symbolic of a way in which I walked in the world, as though I always had someplace to go. I took big strides in those boots; I had things to do. I had an air about me when I wore them; they were my persona's assurance that I was in control.

Although I didn't stop wearing them right away, I did begin to notice how I walked around in them. It was a little embarrassing; I sometimes caught myself whirling through my day, satisfied at the end of it that I had accomplished something, but exhausted and irritable. I drank coffee in the morning to rev up, wine at night to slow down. Striding along in them, I was on a roll, but I couldn't feel the divine wild through those thick soles. The Navajo say, *Walk softly the beautiful earth.* Gift the earth with your footsteps and speak to it with thanks.

The West is the direction that calls us to see whatever we've wrapped in seaweed (whatever we've tried to cover up and glorify) that needs more honest attention. Whether we wear silk unders, matching clothes, a perpetual smile or frown, a white collar or yellow robe, whether our credentials or our possessions are impressive or not, there is always a certain conflict between them and us, a hidden truth underneath. The novice looks for ways to level with the secrets in the unconscious. Facing this direction we ask, *What am I feeling? What am I hiding?* Like the woman who fell in the drink, we ponder, *How have I done this to myself?* We learn to talk to the untoward characters and the shadow in our moods and projections. We learn to talk to pride, shame, anger, remorse, regret. We talk to accidents and dreams and cowboy boots. Nothing gets left out of the conversation.

According to Ed McGaa in his book *Mother Earth Spirituality,* honoring the West may be "time to ask the Almighty for a spirit guide."[1] There are times in our inner work that we suddenly find ourselves in communion with ancestors, saints, with the Holy Ones whose work it is to look after and inspire and correct and uplift us. These figures appear often as messengers, guides, conductors to the inner world; they bring insight, warning, grace, and age-old wisdom. Their role (often impersonal and to the point) is to break through to us; to tell us where, indeed, we have gone out of sync with ourselves. They hold out their eagle feathers or their old arms to us and tell us what to do next.

One of my clients told me: *"I once saw an old Indian woman in a meditation. I had felt despairing, alone, and frightened about leaving a relationship I knew was long overdue for closure. In my mind's eye I found myself wandering in a forest of old trees. One of them held a particular fascination for me, and I approached it, wondering what was in store. Suddenly it turned into an old woman dressed in beautiful beaded buckskin. She put out her old arms to me and said, 'Come.' I buried myself in the folds of her dress, and wept. It was the first time I felt safe in a long time. Although I had no idea where I was going, no idea what to do to get out of the relationship, I just felt she would lead me. I remember the smell of her clothes, her long silver braids that smelled like pitch and campfire smoke. She was wise and quiet, and something in her eyes made me calm too. I knew everything was going to be all right."* This kind of prayerful imagination can be a doorway through which one is suddenly in touch with a helping spirit; a presence that brings strength and direction when we can't find the way on our own.

The Power of Nondoing

The most important thing to remember about the West is that its nature is the night time. It is the dark robe that draws us past the world into solitude and nondoing. The West, symbolic of feminine cyclic time, invites us to be a wanderer.

Bring the West home means we set aside time daily to reflect, sit and breathe, keep a journal, stare at the clouds. Some sort of ritual is often important here, whether that means taking time to greet the sunrise, doing a walking meditation before work, finding a small neighborhood church or temple to sit quietly in, or practicing being in a crowd, silent, but with one's inner ears and eyes open. For some people it helps to get away at least once in a while, just to minimize distractions. If a mountain or a desert or a weekend away or a patch of grass or a retreat presents itself—we should take it and sit still. It is helpful to bring along a journal, a blanket, some water, to fast (even lightly) if we can; to listen deep within; to follow the images, the signs or events that come—as though they were telling us something vital. They will. Everything around us is potentially a teaching; everything has a voice. The wilderness is alive with scripture.

When I remember to practice this, I am less fragmented, less willful, not so driven, and more in the flow of life around me. I don't run, I walk. I don't try to push the river back up to its source. I am not manipulating the world to see things my way, or reacting to things I cannot change.

It helps to remember that solitude is a practice, rather than just a condition. I don't know anyone who hasn't felt her hair stand on end from time to time. This is precisely the moment to slow down and breathe and let go of the ropes and fall inward to the dark cloister of the soul.

A woman I know who had been working faithfully on her incest issues told me once she sometimes felt overwhelmed by the immensity of her feelings. Then during a meditation she spontaneously had the following image: *"I am going into a cave. A huge mother bear is in there. She welcomes me, pulls me close to her. I can feel her strength, her protectiveness, her love. I relax into her arms. I felt like her cub. I feel secure, safe, I know I am being protected. And I know I can go back into that cave whenever I need to. There's comfort in knowing that."* This woman's intuitive ability to "see within," and her willingness to take time to meditate, brought her a powerful healing image. This kind of insight often comes when we practice the contemplative power of silence.

THE WEST AND THE DARK ROBE

In the fall, at the close of day, the winds stir in the trees; leaves begin to rustle in the cooling dusk. In the West and in the far reaches of the mind, the daytime sun fades, and light gradually gives way to night. Come then along this way of silence, and take the robe of night for a blanket.

When you walk through your dreams, through the rooms in the house of the mind, the coverings there will gently move when you speak the word. Under that blanket of stars and moon and darkening, let go of the things in your heart, and open to all that is there.

Wrapped up in the dark robe, try to name your hidden side, your shadow, your anger, your sadness. Try to open these doors long shut.

Welcome the stranger in you, the child you have long postponed. Remember the one you left behind, whom the world could not love. Sit with her on your lap and let her speak. Let him run by your side and don't be too busy to listen.

Out here under the heavens, imagine that the figures in your dreams and daydreams, the moods and tensions you experience, the events in your day, the Stoneman in your life, the seaweed coat, all have a story to tell.

Have your questions, but let go of needing to know. Just ask to feel, and try to remember that even the dark is fertile.

From time to time during the day, practice covering yourself with the West. Try to imagine that in spite of all that you have to do, you are not in a hurry, and that you and the Big Holy are not separate. If you forget, and move too quickly, speak too hastily, if you lose yourself, then pull yourself back and take refuge under the cloak; breathe and speak instead from this place under the stars. Try to find your own rhythm. Make your movements a meditation. And walk as though you have no place to go.

The North: Making the Warrior Heart

In the North one always needs two levels of strength. One is the generative masculine energy that radiates power and purpose (the outer warrior); the other is the courage to be oneself (the inner or spiritual warrior). The first level of power is about finding one's truth, taking a stand, and hanging on in the big winds; it's about learning to take up the talking stick and to live with clear intention. It's what the ego aims for in the first half of life.

People in training for level one of the warrior (whether they want to or not) sit up straight in a short saddle, learn to take risks, confront their limitations, and if there is a Pandora's box around, they look for the key. Their will for life is strong. But it is not willfulness. Rather, they are motivated by a fire within that eats limitations for breakfast. When it comes time to face the North, people who have really done the work of "sees within" are looking for a more passionate involvement with life.

A Dominican adventurer who is a friend of mine went for a two-day vision fast to a remote lake in eastern Canada. After a few days of sweats and preparation by her leaders, she packed up her gear and she and her helper rowed to a distant section of the lake. As the canoe nosed onto the shore, she stepped out onto what looked like a sturdy pile of sticks. The pile gave way and she stepped into the water. Vision fasts sometimes start this way. Not too undone by the wet welcome, she picked up one of the sticks and used it to try to navigate to drier ground. Her companion settled her in and then left just as the sun was setting. *"I wasn't hungry at all, but I was terrified. I knew there were wolves and bears out there, and I hadn't had time before the sun went down to find a place where I thought I might be safe. I wound up choosing a spot near a rock ledge. When night came I felt very afraid. I got up in the dark to go to the bathroom, and accidentally my staff banged onto one of the granite rocks in my campsite. It sounded like a drum and the sound it made was somehow comforting. Later I sat down and I started to drum on that rock, and I sang in the dark. I drummed and said prayers for everybody who came to mind; I sang until I felt calmer and less freaked out. That stick became a companion for me and I could feel a strength coming from it. When the morning came, I used the stick to dance with; so it was my singing stick and my dancing stick. I wasn't afraid after that. When I saw my helper coming in the canoe the last day to take me back to camp, I debated whether or not to bring that staff back with me. As she neared where I stood she said: 'Oh! Thy rod and thy staff shall be a comfort to you.' Here I was, the Scripture scholar, and I hadn't even thought of Scripture for the whole two days. But I had my singing staff (which I eventually gave back to the pile)."*

The inner warrior is something we begin to explore and develop in the second half of life. For some of us, it takes a long time to make a warrior's heart. We have to have walked a certain way in life, experienced over the years a rending of the veils over the personality. When the obstacles in life find us, and they inevitably will, they are not there just to be faced and endured, but to be worked through patiently and with a resolve to keep "soft" in the process. When the cold wind blows in from the North and we suddenly find ourselves in a storm of one kind or another, we have the choice to curse and rail against that wind, and to pity ourselves, or face into it. If we choose to go all the way into our pain, to allow the ego its cleansing time, then we choose to heal.

Many a warrior type, male or female, will have a great deal of fire by nature; but to develop *inner* fire, the will needs to be cleansed of fear and self-interest. When one has begun to develop the nature of the inner warrior, things like defensiveness, fear, resentment, suspicion, remorse, blame, the need to self-justify, gradually get cleansed. The strength in this archetype, when up against the test of initiation, enables us to stand up to adversity with both willpower and vulnerability. That balance of force and surrender is essential.

One of my friends recently ended not only a ten-year relationship, but a long-term profession as well. For a while, the effect of those endings (both of which were unexpected) seemed disastrous to her: *"After putting ten years of my heart and soul into a very special book-and-music store, the last two years as a co-owner, I was suddenly 'laid off.' I was stunned, as if I had heard someone had died. Someone did— me! The self I had identified with through this store. Who was I without the store? The first few days I felt washed up. I was sitting here at first thinking, 'My God, now what? I'm fifty-three and I have no job and no relationship. What am I going to do?'* " Then one morning she woke up with a different thought, a revelation of sorts: *"Wait a minute here! I'm actually starting to feel relieved, like a huge burden has just lifted. Finally it occurred to me that this was just the kick in the pants I'd needed. I'd been so involved, so busy with work, I'd lost myself. I began to see that this was a gift that the universe had given me . . . that it was time to go inward."* Her new path would be, unlike the old, one shaped by letting go, by what she expressed as a kind of "free floating" until the way was made clear. The energy of the inner warrior protects us while we yield to a process of releasing the past. That's the old buffalo in us that just stands there and patiently endures until spring comes.

The problem is that there is a thief in the unconscious; doubting voices inside that say things to us like: *You're wasting your time . . . you're not going anywhere . . . things will never change. You won't make it.*

One woman, addressing her fear of rejection, said, *"The work I'm doing is teaching me to accept myself, to love myself. But I have tremendous issues about abandonment. In the past I've always run away rather than stand up and fight for myself. When I don't want to face my issues, or somebody else, I hide."* She had been talking about a women's support group she had left. After a few months, however, she decided to return and face her fear. *"I knew I was just running away again. But the truth is, I've gotten something from everything I've worked on, whether I liked it or not."*

Both men and women who have dealt with incest have often said that the tricky part was being patient with themselves. *"I wanted to get through it; I wanted the pain to end. I wanted the shame to end. I had little patience with myself as I went through those memories. I just wanted to be done with it. Forgive, forget, move on. Now that I look back on how far I've come, I realize maybe my worst enemy was me."*

The work here is to remove counterproductive defenses. A woman I know recently quit smoking her usual two packs of cigarettes a day so that her abandoned-feeling world could come back to life. *"When I don't smoke, I can feel my feelings and not keep running from them. I've never been available to my tears like this before . . . it's hard to be this vulnerable. I've been angry, I've had wild emotions; but I've never allowed myself to cry or to feel the losses I've known in my life."* She had been in recovery work already for three years, and although the work had been difficult, she had managed to stay clean and sober. Because she had been a single parent with two young children, she not only had to work two jobs to pay their bills, she had to play the role of both parents. For a time her cigarettes had enabled her to keep going in her recovery, a little reward for keeping strong.

What began in the next stage of her work was a stripping down to a core wound of abandonment. The inner warrior here was her resolve to risk saying and feeling what was inside.

The warrior is also that strength within us that helps us to strip away projection and reclaim our own internal ground. That archetypal energy encourages us to ask: *What am I masking? Who am I? What do I stand for?* When a woman, for instance, sees that her mate is not her sole purpose in life, that he does not have to carry the decision making or the strength to manage life for her—she takes back the power she has given away. When a man sees that his mate is not his emotional container, that it is not up to her to have the feelings or carry the spirituality or the gentleness in the house, he takes back the vulnerability and the feeling world he has given away.

The North, when we can empower the healthy side of our will, reminds us to reinvest in ourselves. A woman I know who was involved in a number of worthy causes recently chose to start making some deposits in herself. *"I've given myself to so many others in my life. I'm not apologizing really, because everything I put my attention to flourished. My kids, my work, my husband, everything's had its season. I don't regret that I loved that much. But I can feel a shift coming. It's time to give to myself now. That means I honor my needs, my time, my feelings. That means I honor the dreams inside I've had on hold."*

Bringing the Warrior Home

The power in the North assists us whether we need long staying power or the strength to let go and surrender. Some of us will need the courage to turn a new corner; to leave an old situation, to break from a relationship, or to stop doing work that no longer has any wild in it. Some may need courage to give up an addiction or an old routine. Maybe we need to dress more outrageously, say outlandish things to stuffy people, or fire some of our worst friends. Maybe we need to remind ourselves every day to speak up, to say what we mean or what we need, without making excuses. Others of us need the courage to keep choosing life, to keep choosing recovery, to keep choosing to love difficult people, or to keep chasing our wildest dreams.

In the seventh direction, there is a kind of holy will at work. The inner warrior has the ability to choose to be content, even in the midst of hardships. There is a Ladakhi saying, *"The greatest courage is the courage to be happy."*[2] In a place called Casa de Luz (House of Light) I met a woman with that holy will. She had never seen me before but welcomed me like a sister. A Mexican friend of mine who had volunteered to work part-time at the Casa had taken me to meet her. In her eyes, deep blue like the sea, I felt profoundly blessed.

Her leprosy had long ago separated her from her children and family, severed her from the life she had known. In her countenance one could sense a trace of this old wound, but beyond her pain there was a presence I felt awed by. On the afternoon of our visit, I struggled to say a few sentences in Spanish, and she smiled at me good-naturedly from her wheelchair. Although I knew she was in intense pain, she held my hands in hers and wanted to know me: she asked about my children, their ages, my husband, my life in California. She gave me several intricate doilies she had painstakingly crocheted, in spite of the disease that had claimed most of her fingers. Her life, she said, was *"for God."* I didn't speak Spanish fluently, but I understood enough to hear, *"In this sea of pain, my work is to pray for others."*

Along with many third-world people, the Indian people I know have a strong faith in life. They say every road has a reason, a teaching, and that wisdom comes only when we have walked that road. *"We are born with the Spirit, and we go back to the Spirit when we die. From the time we were young we were taught that everything we do in this life should point us back to God."* (Geneva Stump).

There was an old woman on a reservation I visited in northern Montana who was an excellent beadworker. She was known throughout the village and in some of the neighboring areas. One day I went with a friend to see her and found her sitting in a small blue house in the midst of a huge stark field. My friend asked her for some special beads and some elk hide for a pair of moccasins she was making for me. The old woman gladly gave us the elk hide. As she pulled out her beads she said that someone had broken in and stolen her best beads. *"Those young people,"* she said, *"they don't have respect."* In her perception of the youth who had stolen from her there was some sadness, but no judgment. *"What can you do,"* she said, and went on with her work. She was making a brilliant red rose against a backdrop of sky-blue turquoise beads.

THE NORTH AND THE RED ROBE

In the North, there is an immense sky. The season turns from fall to winter. The cleansing snow, the big winds, and the waters that purify the land, come down on all of us. In that direction, there is a red wool cloak, a robe to warm you in the cold.

Remember that the windows of the soul must be opened again and again in order to let in healing winds. As you look to the North, let your thoughts wander toward the Cleansing White Wing. Bring all your labors and your weariness; bring all burdens, secrets, all unspoken griefs, all your losses, and come into the Great Wind.

Gather to mind the thoughts and fears that hold you back.

Gather to mind your self-doubts.

Gather to mind everything you have done or failed to do, and call your defenses by name.

Look around you and find, even in the barren cold, a place that is spacious and beautiful in its Winter coat. Walk there and stand straight and tall like the Pine Tree. Look far North to the great waters coming on the clouds. In that place when snow and rains come, in that stark immersion, open your red robe and release yourself to this wind.

Send a voice for the red robe of courage; for the heart within you that has endured, struggled, hung on, let go. Give thanks for the Voice that speaks for you in your journey; for the Hand that welcomes who you are. For the robe of protection, give thanks.

Send praise from the great prairie of your soul. For a warrior's heart, give thanks.

The East: The Daybreak Song

> *All night the gods were with us,*
> *Now night is gone;*
> *Silence the rattle,*
> *Sing the daybreak song . . .*
> —Navajo[3]

Sometimes early in the morning, I pray for far-seeing vision. I tell the Creator that I don't want to see myself anymore with the eyes of my limitations and fears, or from the dead scrolls in my past. I want instead the eyes of the heart, the visionary, so I can see myself as I really am. I tell my clients sometimes to try to see themselves as they are, or as the person they are becoming; not as the person they once were. It is a stretch to try to see ourselves from this perspective; but we should try anyway.

The sky is always breaking open its secrets to the one who gets up early. To wake up when it's still dark and wait for the sunrise, for first light, is a good way to exercise the soul. In the black before dawn, images come. Sometimes I feel acutely the sharp outlines of some mistake I have made in the days past; some oversight that I regret. People come to mind I haven't quite forgiven; I think of goals and intentions and vows I haven't kept. The undone things come to mind. The voices of dread still buried in the heart try to take me into remorse and worry. But in the streaking dawn, I know that I am free.

In the East, when we put "sees far" to work, we challenge ourselves to see through everything—conventions, enmeshments, old behaviors. Some of us need to ask, for instance, why we might be so attached to being right, to having things our way; why we chase after the approval of certain people; or why we need to be seen as so responsible, or hardworking, or kind, or tough. "Sees far" is ultimately about getting more transparent.

Often it is enlightening to ask ourselves whether our self-image empowers or inhibits us. Often the best exercise for people who are stuck with an inhibitive or perfectionistic streak is some sort of tom-foolery. Sometimes in a group, which is where our illusions are bound to be challenged, I will often ask someone to do something that might prove he or she is, beyond the shadow of a doubt, the village idiot. I don't mind modeling this erratic sort of mask-breaking myself. It is always satisfying to wreck bad conventions.

When practicing "far seeing" in relationships, one looks for old scripts that keep recycling and going nowhere. If we're up for a challenge, we ask: *What don't I like about myself in this relationship (but so far don't know how to change)?* We try to spot our own shadow in there (just in case we only passed over it lightly in the West); or we challenge ourselves to be able to see others with more compassion and less projection. A woman I was working with said once that she felt her husband was often to blame for their arguments. *"One day, after telling him for years that he was refractory and stubborn and closed off and infantile and mean, I began to discover a few of those same traits in myself. It was a terrible enlightenment."*

The old midwife who is invested in our renewal comes with every dawn. She tells us our destiny is in our own hands, and although she will listen to our pain, she doesn't go for whimpering. She insists that if we are going to give birth to a new vision, that we identify ourselves not through the failures of the past, nor through the violent or uncreative people we've survived, but through the divine wilderness in the soul. And she does that often by the power of imagination, intuition, and through prayer or meditative experiences.

In inner work, one needs an image of oneself that comes from the original blueprint of the self. We are strengthened when we can access this internal view of ourselves. A friend of mine told me of a healing image that seemed clearly a metaphor of her inner work: *"I had taken a hot bath and was just lying stretched out on my bed when an image came to mind. I saw a woman (maybe it was me) talking to a little girl that had found a small torn butterfly. The little girl was feeling sad that the butterfly was so disheveled. The woman in my image said, 'It's okay. Even though the butterfly is torn, it is beautiful. Even though it is fragile, it's strong.' "* She wrote in her journal, *"And so it is with me. In less-than-perfection, I am perfect, and I walk towards an unfolding grace."*

A young man in seminary had a spontaneous experience of his divine side that further illustrates what emergence is about. He had been trying to sort through a painful childhood, the impact of which had made him alternately sad and enraged. On one occasion I asked if we could bypass some of these negative memories to see if something else within him wanted a voice.

Gradually a feeling of quiet settled over us. After a long time we opened our eyes and started to check in with one another. He told me that it seemed as though the figure of Jesus had come and stood by his side. *"I don't know why he would, but he handed me a baby. It seemed so odd. Here I am feeling all of this, and I get a tiny baby girl. What shall I do with it?"* As he pondered this, it seemed to him that he had been given the child to name. We settled in again and waited in the silence.

My mind was beginning to drift when inside a voice clearly said a word that sounded like "Ruah." I knew it was Hebrew for breath or spirit. But it didn't seem to fit for a name, so I pushed it aside. When he came back from his meditation, he had a very puzzled look on his face. The name he had heard was "Joy."

"*Oh*," I said.

"*I can't imagine why in the midst of all this that's going on, that I would ever be given the name 'Joy.' It's totally opposite from what I'm experiencing.*" Nonetheless, he decided to keep it for this tiny girl. He asked me if I had heard or sensed anything. I told him I only got something that sounded like the Hebrew word "Ruah," which didn't seem to fit. We were both in a slightly altered state when we left my office.

As I drove home, the sound "Ruah" came over and over again, making a little nuisance of itself. I tried to put it out of my mind, but it persisted. The following day I was thumbing through a catalog that had just come in the mail from a nearby retreat center. My eyes fell on a photo of a rabbi who was scheduled for a seminar there. I read the caption under his photo: "Join us again this year for a special time of songs, dances, storytelling. A time filled with as much 'Ruach' as last year." Behind the word "Ruach" was the word "Joy" in parentheses! I called this man on the phone and told him what I had found. It was just like the Spirit, gypsy that she is. She had spoken English to one of us, and Hebrew to the other.

Each of us has a name that comes from within, from the "sees far." Chances are it's not the name we have, and it may be the opposite of what we feel or what our circumstances are. But when turning East, it's good to imagine, to pray for an image of our essential Self, for a name that fits. *Who am I beyond the things that have happened (or not happened) to me? Who do You say that I am?*

THE EAST AND THE YELLOW ROBE

In the East, the dawn star shines down from an indigo sky. Take a moment, wherever you are, and watch its passing into a day; a sign that the long fast of night and winter is over. One by one the stars fade and the first light begins to come. The yellow robe you pull around you is the garment of spring; the daybreak that spills into the world.

Notice the power of the sun; how it anoints the tops of the trees, ignites with gold the high peaks and rolling hills, spills warm light down the cliffs and stones, the grasses on the plains; how it streaks silver across the dark waters of the sea, spreads its fire on lakes and streams, touches even the dew underfoot. Ask what in yourself needs the bright downpour of daybreak. What labor is yours to do?

From the eye of the heart, see what situation or person in your life calls for more far-seeing. Let the things or people come to mind that may need some detachment. As you draw the dawn robe around you, what possessions and securities, what old self-image, what habits and relationships do you hold on to that do not honor life?

Imagine the generations that have gone on before you. Gather up all your relations and try to imagine all of them in the Morning Light. Those who passed on what they could of their wisdom, and those who never gave birth to life; gather them up and ask for their healing, for their blessing. Ask yourself what wisdom comes to you from the path you have walked.

Think about the story you want to tell about your life, when the time comes to leave it.

The South: The Inner Lover

This quadrant in the circle is about exploring the heart and "the power to make grow." The corn maiden myth is, I believe, based on healthy love. All the great lovers of humanity, known and unknown, have given themselves away to life. When we can forgive and honor and give heart to ourselves, and to the Spirit of life within, there will always be enough to go around.

When it comes to loving, it feels as though one must pass through this circle many times in order to get to the inner lover. Our first pass at love on the planet is always mixed. We love because we have to; we don't do it right at first (or someone else in our early childhood doesn't). It takes years of hard work, practice, wrong turns, and immense patience. I tell my clients that love is an experiment nobody gets right until forty years in the desert, forty lifetimes, forty millenniums. The important thing is to take heart again and again, and not give up. I may not do it right, but my inner lover says: *Feel free to make plenty of mistakes, but don't stop this practice.*

The second pass at loving always has to be inward. We have to love ourselves past our mistakes and failures, and see where self-compassion takes us. A greening heart, after all, is not conservative. It affirms and reaches out to itself time after time, and it takes risks. When we are practicing self-acceptance, we accept credit for the work that we've done, the things and the people we've struggled with. Self-acceptance does not mean that we won't be tempted by fear, perfectionism, or self-doubt. It means we don't judge ourselves when up against those things.

Being in the South is about turning inward and seeking the inner lover. If we're going to be in relationship to the green, we begin to wake up to our heartache (or the lack of it) and we ask ourselves: *If I could love myself perfectly without blame or fear or self-doubt, what would I have to let go of?* Love and fear don't make good companions; but in most lives, they have to share the same psyche. And the inner lover cannot thrive in such a contradiction. I want to relate the following story of a friend and colleague of mine, because it poignantly illustrates the need for self-compassion and forgiveness.

"In the early summer of 1974 I heard a talk on self-hatred and self-forgiveness. The person speaking explained that forgiving others is important, but forgiving yourself is even more important. 'Each time you put yourself down, it is as if you plant little seeds of self-hatred in your flesh, under the skin, that later must be drawn out—that is, spiritually purified.'" My colleague was thirty-two at the time of this talk, and just beginning to feel his own repressed anger surface.

"About two weeks later I had the following dream. I saw myself at about seventeen (a teenager), tight-lipped, wearing a crew cut. I was in the control room at the center of a large disc-shaped spaceship, like a flying saucer. The ship, deep in space, was speeding out of control; its engines were going powerfully but its steering mechanism was damaged. A circular corridor surrounded the control room. Opposite this door was a panel with the damaged steering mechanism behind it. People kept coming along the corridor to the panel, to try and fix it and bring the ship under control. I had a ray gun, and as each person came in view I shot him or her dead. I was enraged at all of them. I didn't care what their reason was, I wanted to be left completely alone. Finally I had my wish: I had killed everybody on the ship. Then a sort of ghost appeared in the control room: my ghost. It was not exactly like a ghost, but a spirit self. We began to wrestle, each trying to kill the other. But it was as if we existed in separate dimensions: we could grapple, but we could not really hurt each other. Each self was in a rage, or at least my physical self was in a rage at my spirit self. I

seemed to be doomed to struggle hopelessly forever, trying in my rage to destroy myself.

"As soon as I awoke I knew this dream was trying to show me my inner state. I felt grateful to God . . . but it was years before the balance of my emotional life shifted from rage to the grief that lay beneath it."

A fertile heart takes time to develop. It is a heart that has had holes poked in it. Nothing, after all, grows in hard soil. The heart that will allow itself to be pierced can in time be generative. Sharp defenses, anger, old hurts, wounded love, or relationship struggles cause us pain, and they are the very thing that pierces our hardness. The man who dreamed of wrestling with his spirit was indeed struggling with his own soul. Luckily, the spirit in him (which could not be killed) was fighting back. This man's compassion for others (which is strong today) was seeded when he had that dream; when he could let himself feel the self-compassion (not the self-pity) that was "under his skin."

By the time one has circled through the directions at least once, the hardest, most obdurate places in the heart have gradually been tilled. When one has endured the penetration of one's deepest wounds, then compassion is felt with much more intensity. When one turns through the seasons and moves again southward, there is tenderness, softness, a kind of humility that comes from brokenness. Like summer rising in the soul.

People working to love themselves unconditionally (in order to love others without so many conditions) have to practice softening. So many of us have dissociated from pain as young children that later in life we have to feel our way back. Right in the midst of a relationship's most stubborn impasses—that's where we have to let go; to try not to react or lash out, or run. If we can stay in the thick of some emotional storm and not do what we've always done, then we have begun to practice self-acceptance in relationships.

One of my clients told me she had been abandoned not only by an alcoholic and raging father, but also by a passive mother who wasn't available enough. She had worked on her fear of intimacy, aware that she kept at an emotional distance from others. She also knew that she didn't want to continue to recycle those issues in every relationship.

"I woke up yesterday morning . . . it was still early. My partner and I woke up about the same time, having had a fight the night before. (I had wanted to be close, he had pulled away, and I felt totally rejected.) We started to talk, and all of a sudden I felt a million miles away. I couldn't

feel anything inside, nothing . . . I just felt far away. Then I was aware of a really heavy feeling, like a two-by-four over my chest. But I knew that this wasn't really about him, it was about me. These were old feelings for me. They went way back to old abandonment stuff. I lay there and just held the feeling inside, an emptiness, a sadness. I didn't push it away or try to change it because I also knew that it was all right. I tried to let go. Then I felt a vibration over my chest, a fluttering that went all the way down into my stomach. Then I saw that the two-by-four was dissolving into a shimmering light. I could actually feel it in my chest . . . it was an incredible feeling. The old wound was melting before my eyes. I felt such a compassion for myself. It was like I could hold myself in total acceptance, and for the first time I felt real love for myself."

Some days before, she had done a drawing of a large tree with slender roots going down deep into the earth, after an image that had come up for her in meditation. All week the drawing had sat on her mantel and each time she'd looked at it, it had spoken in some way to her. *"As I lay there, I felt like I became the roots of the tree that I had been drawing; and I became the life that was coming out of the base of the tree. I became a new seed coming out."*

The flowering stick—the symbol of transformation and the "power to make grow"—does not develop into a great tree overnight. It grows from a seed. This woman had experienced a deep depression for several months before finally giving in to what she was feeling. The inner lover is not afraid to feel pain; she is not afraid to submit to its intensity.

A woman who had been working hard to heal some long-standing trust wounds recently told me a flowering stick story. She had taken the day off and had gone on a long walk on the prairie near her house. Finding a patch of ground to sit on, she decided to ask the question all of us ask at one time or another: *"Okay, God, where are you?"* Then she started to meditate, and after a bit she had another image. *"From every corner of the sky I saw these hands. They were hands of all different colors, of all different peoples, gently pulling to lift a huge quilt. Each pair of hands worked slowly with purpose; each pulling and lifting was deliberate and filled with attention and love. Then it was as though a voice said, 'This quilt is for you. It will envelop you and anyone else who asks, or is in need. . . .'"*

Then when she opened her eyes and looked up, she saw a light in the clouds. *"The clouds looked as though they were a fetus, and there was a brilliant white light inside. The fetus grew and stretched in the sky, and then eventually phased into the rest of the clouds."* For her these images meant welcome, self-acceptance, help and support from Above; the fetus in the clouds was herself being enveloped by the Spirit of life.

One of the tasks of the inner lover is to help us reclaim the self we have asked others in our lives to carry for us. Most of the women, and some men I have worked with, have experienced the negative side of the corn maiden story (grinding oneself away to the point of invisibility) in relationship to others. Many of us give birth to everything but ourselves.

A young woman at an impasse in her life recounted a dream that had been a powerful awakening for her. The background of the dream was that she had been in a long relationship with a young man, but had begun to see her need to break free. They had tried living together and living apart; they had tried breaking up and reuniting; they had been engaged. Whatever they tried seemed unworkable, yet they couldn't release each other. Gradually the young woman began to realize that she had projected something of the hero onto this young man. She also knew he had projected his emotional life onto her.

Then she had the following dream: *"I am in a castle and I am a lady-in-waiting to the queen. I'm about to have a baby with this man who is a prince [her boyfriend]. I go to take a shower and all of a sudden my labor starts. I call and call for him, but he doesn't come. Then I realize I will have to have this baby all on my own. I feel something dropping from my loins but at first I don't look at it. When I finally look down, the baby is there, lying in the dust. It was abnormally tiny and bluish gray, but it seemed as though it might still be healthy. I picked it up off the ground and held it in my arms. I realize that no one is responsible for this baby but me. I am amazed because the look in its eyes is deeply loving. I sense no one has loved me like this baby, and I am deeply moved by the intensity of its love. The baby has dust on it and I wipe it clean and carry it close to me, feeling proud."*

The baby in this dream has come on its own; once labor began the young woman found that she was able to manage on her own. It was clear to her that she was responsible for her own inner child, her own soul; no one else could really help her in this birth. The baby at first was undernourished and hadn't had enough air to breathe. But once she claimed it, picked it up, and began to hold the infant, she knew it would thrive. Although it was premature and tiny, in its eyes she saw a love strong enough to lead her into a new kind of self-regard.

This poignant dream, it seems to me, belongs to all of us struggling with our autonomy. Such a dream is really a collective dream, in that any one of us might have had it. Most likely the infant here belongs to all of us. It is the abandoned child asking us to pick it up out of the dust and wrap it up and take it home. That baby is everything about ourselves we may have judged, rejected, neglected, been slow to claim, not known about—but it's ours. In dreams of this nature, the message seems consistently aimed at a whole world that has forgotten to be in relationship to the infant (the soul). In looking deeply at this quadrant in the psyche, the need to love and relate to ourselves in a healthy way is crucial.

The Tree in the Granite

In the South, it helps to remember that all but the gods are here for the first time. None of us knows much about loving; it's an experiment. Sometimes I ask myself what I know about things of the heart, and the answers I get are not so impressive. But one thing I do know about love is that it always begins small. Once I sat pondering the South and the flowering tree, and, still in my novice stage (maybe I'll always be there), I asked the soul side of my unconscious to give me an image for loving. As I sat there in the dark of early morning, in the back of my mind I saw a small green branch with tender shoots beginning to bud out. In that tiny branch are the fragile shoots of compassion, tenderness, forgiveness; and even a need perhaps to humble ourselves before the power of the heart.

My husband and I have spent many vacations hiking in the high country of the Sierra Nevada, and if there is one sight that always impresses me, it's the power of the green. Sometimes in the highest places, in the biggest outcrop of granite, there is a tiny fissure. And in that narrow crevice is almost invariably something green poking through: a tiny cluster of flowers, a small pine or juniper tree, a cedar as old as the hills. Authentic love is like this shoot, it presses up underneath the most inhospitable forces, until one day there it is.

In terms of what it means to integrate this quadrant in the psyche, this is a time for fertile growth in relationship to oneself and others.

The metaphor of summer growth implies we actively use every relational event as an opportunity to push through to the sun. We ask: *What do I need to forgive and stop judging in myself (and others)? What part of me needs a hand of welcome? How can I love without so many conditions?*

Bringing the South home means we take out our journal, paints, and clay, the unfinished poems buried under the bills on the desk. It means we write love letters to people we need to forgive and be forgiven by; or call someone we've been thinking of. It means we find excuses to go outside and take long walks and sniff the air; that we shun company and don't take on too many thinking projects. It's a time when the inner world unfolds its Flowering Tree to us, and we open all our senses to receive it.

THE SOUTH AND THE WHITE ROBE

In the white robe you stand before a great and luminous sun. Summer gathers its blanket of warmth around you and everything turns gradually full of day. When you walk or sit outdoors, try to feel the light in growing things; become the movement of creation rolling in waves; be the pollen that fertilizes the summer months; and the breeze stirring through long grasses.

Imagine the seeds of self-acceptance that have been planted in you coming into bloom. Press down inside the soil of the heart, and let all self-doubt and condemnation go. Remorse, regret, and self-judgment, all evaporate in the warmth of day. Clothe yourself in trust and innocence, and take back the live heart you owned as a child.

Look around you at the life in created things, and know that the life inside you is like that. You are constantly changing, growing, sprouting from seed, pushing through the soil. In that cloak of summer, you are constantly in the process of awakening; you are powerful and resolute in your loving, strong in your compassion, humble in your forgiving, alive and fertile in your being.

On some days in your wandering through meadows and forests, the trees will be talking to you. When you stand under the branches of a great tree, ponder its years and the life it holds; the roots that go deep underground, the sheltering in its great mantle. Reach out and touch its trunk, and let it talk to you from the life it holds. Lean or climb into it and let it hold

*you. Somewhere within you, try to feel the flowering stick whose roots
are deep and whose branches reach into the sky.*

The Earth: Honoring and Celebrating the Ground

Whether we are old backpackers, Native Americans, or adult children
who have never outgrown the love of mud between our toes, Mother
Earth is a healing force that is vital to each of us. It makes great sense
that we pause to honor her as we complete the circle of our meditations
on the self. She is, after all, our ground, our beginning. In the earlier
chapter on the Earth as the fifth direction, I told many yarns and
stories about her life-giving powers, both in metaphor (as a restorative
presence in the mind's eye) and as the actual ground we are nourished
and refueled by. The earth (even in her most broken state) is a healer.
Our primary task in this direction may be to ask ourselves how we
can celebrate her more consciously.

Earthiness is always a part of ceremony with the Indians; one never
goes too far away from Mother Earth. In all ceremony people stay in
constant touch with the ground; we sit on her, dance on her, honor
her with our prayers. Soil, stones, fire, water, wood, smoke, sage, the
greening bough pressing up through the granite, she is everywhere
we are.

In one sacred ceremony I was invited to participate in, I sat with
a large circle of people on the ground. Indians often sit on the ground
in a circle; a reminder to humble ourselves, to remember our beginnings. All creation-centered worship is likewise inclusive of the
ground; it honors the soil of the earth and reveres the natural humus
(rather than the lofty hubris) in our nature. When used as an altar,
the ground is an offering place.

Before the dancing began, we sat in a huge lodge made from five
tipis, open at the top. The opening was to leave room for the smoke
that rose from the fires, and to leave a window open for the Spirit.
When I listened to the songs, when I danced for my ancestors, I
constantly felt that opening. In that dance there was no separation
between me and the ones who had gone before me. Just as I danced
for them and gave thanks for their seed, I knew they were looking
down upon me, nodding, laughing, making prayers for me from the
heavens that whirled out there in the dark. Ceilings in holy dwellings
should always have openings. St. Francis knew that. And my mother,

who had just died some weeks before, must have also known that, because in that dancing I lost all sense of grief. Her presence, just above me in the stars, was palpable.

There is a lot of blessing in the earth, and over the years my contact with it has always been renewing to me. My husband and I have camped and fished many of the lakes and streams of northern California, British Columbia, and central and southeast Alaska. In the outdoors the colors in the landscape were always vivid. When I wasn't hiking or fishing or boiling up cowboy coffee, I used to sketch and photograph everything. The light, sweeping across the horizon or splitting through dark clouds before a thunder storm, was always more dramatic in the wilderness. I thought I recognized, with wonderful intimacy, places I seemed always to have been before. The sounds in the wilderness seemed more acute, clearer than in the city. The voices of coyote, owl, loon, dragon flies, they all said something.

In the wilderness, a shift occurs between our conscious and unconscious mind. The load one endures in the city, the crazed spinning of a dog chasing its tail, vanishes out there in the big sunsets. One's thoughts and feelings, the insights and perceptions that come, are more expansive, and more sharply detailed. People say their dreams and images take on a life of their own, and that the wind out there has a song.

What I'm most aware of as I meditate on this direction is a sense of gratitude. The earth has given me a much clearer sense of a connection to the tremendous life force inside even the smallest stone or shell. She has often told me, *This is who you are. This is where you came from. This is where you are coming back to. Do you see the stones, the green boughs on the trees, the rolling hills, the waves of wind in the wheat; do you hear the droning bee, the mockingbird, the rumbling in the waters, the thundering? Do you feel the wind, the sun, do you feel the waters and the pollen swirling in your flesh? Can you fly with the wingeds, can you follow the shining salmon in the gyre? This is who you are.* She tells me in the gentlest ways, as any good mother might, that one day that flesh of mine will come back to her. She tells me, *Don't waste one moment of this life. Be glad. Be filled with laughter and celebration and tears and dance and let the rivers run in your veins. When it comes time for you to lose yourself again in me, to come home, we'll all be waiting with open arms. We'll all be singing. In the meantime, leave your cowboy boots behind and remember to walk in beauty.*

This isn't something one easily puts into words. Better just to get out and feel the wisdom in nature. All of us are meant to have earth stories and earth songs.

GRANDMOTHER EARTH AND THE GREEN ROBE

This Earth is your grandmother, your mother. She is the womb you came from and the womb you will return to. She is a greening thing, a Flowering Tree that sends up her shoots to shade and delight, to nurture and rest you. She is a stream of running water, a cup to drink, a cleansing bath to restore the body, a benediction to renew each moment.

Let her winds wrap you in gentle, powerful blankets. Let her voice soothe your thoughts and fears, the things of long ago that wound you still. Let her words and sounds comfort you until you hear only the voice of her prayer; the wind, the stream, the flowing rivers, the pounding sea, the rains and thunders, the songs of birds, the cry of wolves and doves, the shrill whistle of the hawk and eagle, the flutter of tiny moths, the droning ones, the silence.

When you walk her meadows and fields, forests and plains, her generous carpets of mulch and leaf, stone and clay, her beds of cedar and sage, her long beaches, remember to walk there in soft, in reverent, in mindful dance.

Let yourself wander until you find a place where you can sit or stretch out. Greet everything around you and speak to the earth you touch. Let your thoughts sink into your flesh.

Imagine that there's always room for you in the Great Lap. Let the warmth and the life in the earth rise up and touch you; let all her elements begin to fill you. Breathe deeply and slowly, letting everything else go. Let her into your feet and calves; your legs and lower back and coccyx. Welcome her into your hips, your pelvis, and genitals. Let her warmth and fire gently spread through your whole body; your belly and solar plexus and chest, your upper back and neck, your shoulders, arms, and hands. Let her healing touch into your throat, your jaws and face. Let her move like a river of warm light, caressing your whole being.

Receive into yourself all her gifts, all the elements of water, sand, soil, clay; all the green things of the earth, the grasses and flowers in the field, the holy fire from the center of Mother Earth. Let it all come up and bless your body. Breathe deeply and slowly. When you are ready, allow yourself to image what part of you most needs her healing touch. What area is the most symptomatic? What part is most wounded? What holds the most tension? When you focus your attention on this part of the body, what images or feelings come up for you? Try to stay with whatever memories or thoughts or physical symptoms come. Take your time and breathe.

> *I honor life, I give thanks for life*
> *I honor the womb of creation*
> *May the heart in my sexual center be restored*
> *May it be cleansed and renewed*
> *May the heart of the earth, my mother, be full in me*
> *May she be compassion in me*
> *May she be light in my mind*
> *I honor her power and her green*
> *I honor her sacred heart in my body*
> *I give thanks for the life in all creation.*

In the House of the Blue Robe

Just after my studies began with Native peoples, I had been hiking up a trail in the mountains of northern New Mexico, not far from some cliff dwellings. It was a warm afternoon in late fall and I had been walking up a steep bank that had begun to open out over a canyon. I had just finished writing *The Road By the River,* and I was taking a few days to hike in some of my favorite holy places. The song of a canyon wren filled the air and I slowed my pace to take it in. When the song died, I thought I heard voices. I stopped and listened, then all I heard was the wind. But as I continued up the trail, a song spontaneously began to come. I sang it as it came, but the words were not mine.

> *Open your heart and hear us,*
> *open your mind and praise us,*
> *open your body and celebrate us,*
> *and Grandfather and I,*
> *we will always look over you.*

Other words poured through me which seemed, now that I think of them, a benediction song for the land; a thanksgiving for rain, for sun, for corn, for blessing, for lovemaking, for times gone by. I walked and sang, feeling grateful that Someone Up There had called me Granddaughter. I had heard that I was a child of the Creator when I was a small child. But I had never heard it on the wind before.

One of the greatest gifts I got from my mother as a child was her sense of humor, her wild playfulness, and her mother, Anne Pool. My grandmother was an exceptionally holy woman, a healer of sorts. I say "holy" because she knew about the earth and how things grew; she knew that God was, in spite of what the pastor said, not in the church, but in the dark soil of her garden. She read the Bible daily, turned everything she touched into some kind of magic, and sang like a bird. Things came to her, little animals, birds, and butterflies swarmed around her as she worked in her garden, as though she were one of them. She was one of them. It was she who first gave me the distinct impression that God was a relative of mine. It was that simple.

The God my Grandmother told me about did not live in a church or mosque or temple, but in the heart. The God I heard about on warm sunny afternoons on the porch swing was loving, seldom moody, and had a poor memory for our faults. Moreover, this God, I was told, was not the exclusive type, but lived in everything (moving or not). Hiking along the trail in New Mexico through dark redrock and sandstone, I remembered that.

By the time we get to the sixth direction, wholeness depends on being able to practice dialogue with the Spirit. Even for the many people I meet who are out of sorts with God, or with the religious institutions as we have known them, the task is still the same: to come as a beginner; to humble oneself and start again. In the sixth direction we table all our hurts, and we confront the false side of religion as we have learned it—the dogma that has not honored Spirit, the condemnation that has not honored love, and the gatekeepers who have not spoken words of wisdom or held the flowering stick.

The only salvation I know of is our ability to temporarily let go of all our past associations and impressions of God; to sit with the blue robe and ask for help. We bring everything, and we let go until we hear someone call us by name. People have been incessantly hurt by religion, but I've never known the Spirit to do anyone a bad turn.

I believe, like my Grandmother, that people don't need more religion. People need more relationship with God that's honest and real. Furthermore, most people need an earthy spirituality that doesn't take them outside themselves, but challenges them to come back in.

One of the most cherished gifts I received from my Native American teachers is their ability to be genuinely transparent before the Creator. In the sweat lodge I have often heard people crying out to God. Many of the people I sat with as teachers or friends, including my Hidatsa teacher, knew how to humble themselves in that sweat, and they didn't care who was listening. They modeled in wonderful ways how to trust that in the house of the Grandfathers, there was room for everyone.

Prayer, when we can celebrate it holistically, is an art. We don't need too many forms to make art happen, just a willingness to experience life moving inside of us, and an agreement to move where the Spirit says to move. The best relationships are always open to that sudden and immense kind of incarnation.

Years ago at a seminar in the Swiss Alps, I sat with a gathering of women around an old table in a big stone chalet. We had broken into small groups to create a ritual that was supposed to fit who we were. Being five totally different personalities, we spent the first half hour debating what our collective identity should be. We debated about whether to have an identity. We argued and joked about everything, we laughed at our absurdities. We shared a cigarette and then fell silent, gazing out the window at the huge snowcapped mountain over the little village.

Someone slowly started drumming on the table. The hubbub quieted and one woman spoke. *"I think I'll be that mountain."* Another said she wanted to be a shaman; another, Mother Earth. Someone else said, *"I don't want to be anything, I think you're all crazy."*

The drumming got more rhythmic and others joined in. I started to sing about the earth; her streams and trees and mountains, her seas and lakes and skies. All of us went inward. Soon one of the women stood up on the table and began to dance and move, her body gracefully given to the crude music we were making. Someone else slid off the wooden bench we shared and lay under the table, sprawling under the sound of the drumming we made on the table. I took off my turquoise necklace made from hundreds of tiny stones and laid it in the middle of the table. Hands reached for it and it became a rattle. There was a current of the Spirit moving powerfully through us and all of us were deeply stirred. One Jew, two Christians, one atheist, and one slightly Zen Buddhist. After a while we became still.

One of the women said, *"I felt my center in that ritual. I became the mountain and felt such an incredible deep peace inside. As long as I can have this center to return to inside myself, I can go anywhere."* Another said, *"I was under the table the whole time because I felt I had to get as close to the earth as possible. Something was coming to birth in me. I realized, among a lot of other things, that I've always been afraid to be myself."*

The woman who had done the dance said that something alive and beautiful had come to life in her. Another said she was itching to get up and dance too, but she felt like she wanted to be a wild animal and that somehow it wouldn't fit. *"You all looked so holy, I was afraid to bring in this wild creature."*

One of the women said, *"I got up and left and just stood across the room looking at this whole thing. I thought, 'I don't belong in this group. I can't relate to this drumming thing at all.' I just felt critical, and so in my mind I stood there with my arms crossed and I criticized you guys, all drumming and chanting like a bunch of Tibetan monks. But then the sound just drew me in again. I think I felt like it didn't matter what I thought anymore. It just didn't matter. I reached for the table and started to drum again, but this time with more of my own rhythm. I didn't feel separate anymore."*

We all finished saying what had happened for us and then fell silent. In that ritual we had expressed what we were feeling, what we were sensing. Never mind the different personas or the different religious beliefs we had come from. In the drumming and chanting there was communion. In spite of our differences, we were one body.

Prayer and ritual that arise from the deep well of the Spirit come often from the most ancient place inside. It is prayer that makes itself up as it goes along, a litany of spontaneous body movements, joyful dance, voice sounds, tears—a kinesthetic and emotive experience one simply follows.

In one women's group recently, there was a woman working in the center of the circle who was certain that God had overlooked her. She saw things happening to others, but she didn't see anything happening for her. At one point I asked her if she wanted to go inside (to a meditative imagery process). She would then follow the images, the feelings or body symptoms as they came. As she agreed, the group, a creative and spirited handful of Colorado mountain women, settled in and began to chant and pray in a spontaneous way. One of the women, who had a headache, left the room to go outside and lie down, and the rest of us went on with our song.

We had only been into this chanting and prayer about five minutes when all of a sudden a wind swept through that place. We began to sing our previously cacophonous song completely in unison, as though we had a script in front of us. The power that came from our voices nearly knocked everybody over. The person in the center laughed and wept, the woman who had gone outside with the headache came in laughing, her headache gone. The message that had come to the woman who had taken the inner journey was not to doubt herself. *Trust yourself. Know that you are my beloved* was what she heard.

Songs from the Mountain

In our ordinary religious training, most of us don't have too many genuinely mystical experiences. In terms of my own religious practice, I am a vagrant of sorts. I try to keep company with the children and the mystics I know, hoping their presence will rub off on me. I give myself to the Great Lap from time to time; I pray out under the stars, in my backyard, or on the mountain. I go to church and I still sweat sometimes. The spirit world is a big place, and there is no place God is not.

In the sixth direction, the work is simply to reconstitute our dialogue with the Creator. Whenever we stand to pray, the place we stand is the center of the circle; that is our kabir, the ground we need to keep coming back to. As the Lakota people say, the crossing at the center of the Hoop and Four Winds, when we stand there in supplication, is holy. This simple but profound idea is woven throughout all mystical traditions; the divine ground is wherever we stop to pray.

Meister Eckhart tells us that every one of us comes from the "intimate depths" of the divine wilderness. When we pray from our feelings, our most intimate depths, when we are utterly ourselves, we are automatically in that wilderness. Whatever our thoughts, feelings, reservations, conflicts, and hurts, that is our prayer. Wilderness (or wild) means untamed, unexplored, unkempt, stormy, uncivilized, unrestrained, eager. What better way to be in dialogue?

GRANDFATHER SKY AND THE BLUE ROBE

When the wind moves in great waves across the land of the Sky, take the path that leads you home. Walk now in this blue robe. It is made for you, hand sewn of indigo and lapis and turquoise.

Whatever you have lost, let go of, whatever you have suffered, release; whatever vow you have forgotten, remember again. Now comes the surrendering, the yes to emptiness, the yes to unknowing. The praise for the unknown path.

Everything comes to life in this prayer, nothing is left unspoken, all is revealed. All is known. From the day you were born and lifted up for your first breath, to this moment—all is known. From the day you were brought from your mother's womb, all is seen.

All is forgiven.

All is well.

When you wear this blue robe, you are no longer who you think you are. You are no orphan. You have walked in a vast land, and though you have lost your bearings from time to time, you have not lost your way.

Come here, beloved. You are a deep heart shining, bathed by the sun and moon and stars. You belong to us.

You there, streaming in the Light; you are Something to behold.

Epilogue: A Flowering Tree for the World

This year when I go out for my fourth fast (four completes the series one commits to), I will abandon my rough-out boots and wear moccasins. In terms of feeling the wonder of the ground underneath me, elk hide is infinitely softer than thick-soled boots. The beads reflect the colors of the directions, and picking up the light of the sun, they make a little light on my path. Made for me by a friend of mine in northern Montana (the woman who prepared me for my second vision fast), they symbolize the journey I have made over the last several years. In their own modest way they mark the gradual transition from a subtle cowboy mentality I carried for years (are we not all children of the patriarchy of this culture?) to a softer, yet clearly bolder, feminine way of being on the earth.

The Flowering Tree in Black Elk's vision (which forms the outline of the six directions) showed him a message relevant not only to his time and to his people, but to the world's people. That message, still profoundly powerful today, shows us the way to "keep soft," to bless the world with our footsteps, our prayers, and our work for peace, rather than destroy it with a materialism that, by its very nature, kills life.

When I first read *Black Elk Speaks,* I wept. When I read it a second time the vision stood out with more clarity. When I began to sweat and to spend time on the mountain, the gifts of the directions as profound spiritual truths began to offer themselves; they became food. They called me to walk more purposefully and gave me a wider vision of life. In his last days Black Elk addressed the six Grandfathers in a final prayer on Harney Peak in the Dakotas. He wept that the Flowering Tree he had seen in his vision had withered; he cried out to them that his vision had not been able to save his people from the *Waisichus* (the encroaching white world); he wept that the hoop of the nation was broken. But he also prayed that there might be a root of the tree that still had life.

The root of that tree is the life in the soul. No matter what our religion, the heart inside each of us holds the potential for flowering and life. The Holy One I love (a little wilder than the one they portray in the churches) always went out on the mountain with me, burned sweet grass by my side, sat under the starry heavens weeping with me over the broken hoop among the nations of the world, spoke words of challenge and consolation to me out there. Laughed when I nearly fell off the mountain. Came singing on every dawn breeze, every sunrise, came like a warrior to breathe over the withered tree and to reclaim love.

Whether we sit on a wood bench in a stupa or temple or church, or perch on hard ground in the wild, when we admit we don't know much about vision or courage, about wisdom or loving, about the seeds within our own soul, one thing is certain: God comes into that kind of unknowing. To long for the mountain, to open to the winds there, and to move the way love calls us to move, is bound to heal and to nurture the life in the heart of the Tree.

Notes

INTRODUCTION

1. Rainer Maria Rilke, *On Love and Other Difficulties*. Translated by John Mood. New York: Norton and Co., 1975, 25.

1. ON THE EDGE OF BREAKTHROUGH

1. Shiela Moon, *Dreams of a Woman*. Boston, MA: Siego Press, 1983, xii.
2. *Meditations with Meister Eckhart*. Translated by Matthew Fox. Santa Fe, NM: Bear & Co., 1983, 126.
3. Ibid., 68.
4. Otto Rank as cited in Matthew Fox, *Original Blessing*. Santa Fe, NM: Bear & Co., 1983, 250.
5. C. G. Jung and Richard Wilhelm, *The Secret of the Golden Flower*. New York & London: Harvest Books, 1962, 104. (Jung quoting Goethe.)
6. C. G. Jung, *Symbols of Transformation*. New Jersey: Princeton University Press, 1956, 125.
7. C. G. Jung commentary in *The Secret of the Golden Flower,* New York & London: Harvest Books, 1962, 106.
8. C. G. Jung, *Aion*. New Jersey: Princeton University Press, 1978, 32.
9. *The Secret of the Golden Flower,* commentary by C. G. Jung. New York & London: Harvest Books, 1962, 93.

2. DREAMS AND SACRED GROUND

1. William Stolzman, S.J., *The Pipe and Christ*. Pine Ridge, SD: Red Cloud Indian School, 1986, 196.
2. Gandhi quoted in *Original Blessing,* Santa Fe, NM: M. Fox, Bear and Co., 1983, 68.
3. Richard Wilhelm, *The Secret of the Golden Flower*, commentary by C. G. Jung, New York & London: Harvest Books, 1962, 102–104.

4. J. C. Cooper, *An Illustrated Encyclopedia of Symbols.* London: Thames and Hudson, 1978, 55.
5. *Meditations with Meister Eckhart.* Translated by Matthew Fox. Santa Fe, NM: Bear & Co., 1983, 76.
6. C. G. Jung, *Mysterium Coniunctionis.* New Jersey: Princeton University Press, 1973, 487.

3. TIME ON THE MOUNTAIN: THE VISION FAST

1. William Stolzman, S.J., *The Pipe and Christ.* Pine Ridge, SD: Red Cloud Indian School, 1986, 191.
2. Ibid, 191.
3. Evelyn Eaton, *Snowy Earth Comes Gliding.* Independence, CA: Draco Press, 1973, 33.
4. Ed McGaa, *Mother Earth Spirituality.* San Francisco, CA: HarperCollins, 1990, 62.
5. William Stolzman, S. J., *The Pipe and Christ.* Pine Ridge, SD: Red Cloud Indian School, 1986, 74.

4. THE WEST AND SEES WITHIN

1. Wallace Black Elk, *Black Elk, the Sacred Ways of a Lakota.* San Francisco, CA: Harper and Row, 1990, 39.
2. John Redtail Freesoul, *Breath of the Invisible.* Wheaton, IL: Quest Books, 1986, 66.
3. John Neihardt, *Black Elk Speaks.* New York: Pocket Books, 1932, 22.
4. Wallace Black Elk, *Black Elk, the Sacred Ways of a Lakota.* San Francisco, CA: Harper and Row, 1991, 62.
5. James Finley, *Merton's Palace to Nowhere.* Notre Dame, IN: Ave Maria Press, 1978, 32.
6. Evelyn Eaton, *Snowy Earth Comes Gliding.* Independence, CA: Draco Press, 1973, 29.
7. Ibid., 25.
8. *The Kabir Book.* Translated by Robert Bly. Boston, MA: Beacon Press, 1977, 55.
9. Matthew Fox, *Original Blessing.* Santa Fe, NM: Bear & Co., 1983, 94.
10. Yves Troendle, *Raven's Children.* British Columbia: Oolichan Books, 1979, 195.

5. THE NORTH AND THE WAY OF COURAGE

1. William Stolzman, S. J., *The Pipe and Christ*. Pine Ridge, SD: Red Cloud Indian School, 1986, 196.
2. John Neihardt, *Black Elk Speaks*. New York: Pocket Books, 1959, 23.
3. *Meditations with Meister Eckhart*. Translated by Matthew Fox. Santa Fe, NM: Bear & Co., 1983, 83.

6. THE EAST AND BIRTHING WISDOM

1. John Neihardt, *Black Elk Speaks*. New York: Pocket Books, 1959, 23.
2. Evelyn Eaton, *Snowy Earth Comes Gliding*. Independence, CA: Draco Press, 1974, 45.
3. Jean-Pierre de Caussade, *Abandonment to Divine Providence*. Garden City, NY: Doubleday Image Book, 1975, foreword.
4. *Julian of Norwich: Showings*. Translated by Edmund Colledge, O.S.A., & James Walsh, S. J. Paulist Press, 1978, 117.
5. Ibid., 88.

7. THE SOUTH AND THE HEART

1. Hyemeyohsts Storm, *Seven Arrows*. New York: Ballantine Books, 1972, 6.
2. John Niehardt, *Black Elk Speaks*. New York: Pocket Books, 1959, 24.
3. Ibid., 24.
4. *Hildegard of Bingen, Book of Divine Works*. Translated by Matthew Fox. Santa Fe, NM: Bear & Co., 1987, 225.
5. *Mother Meera Answers*. Ithaca, NY: Meeramma, 1991, 110.
6. Self-Acceptance Training, originated by Dick Olney and Cherie McCoy.
7. Adrienne Rich as cited in Matthew Fox, *Original Blessing*. Santa Fe, NM: Bear & Col., 1983, 140.
8. *The Francis Book*. Edited by Roy Gasnick, article by P. Pourrat. New York & London: Collier Books, 1980, 84.

8. OUR MOTHER, SACRED EARTH

1. Fredric Lehrman, *The Sacred Landscape.* Berkeley, CA: Celestial Arts, 1988, preface.
2. *Touch the Earth.* Compiled by T. C. McLuhan. New York: Promontory Press, 1971, 6.
3. Ibid., 6.
4. Quote from a 1987 newsletter for the *Big Mountain Defense Fund,* for the Arizona Navajo.
5. *Touch the Earth.* Compiled by T. C. McLuhan. New York: Promontory Press, 1971, 5.
6. Ibid., 23.
7. Fredric Lehrman, *The Sacred Landscape.* Berkeley, CA: Celestial Arts, 1988, 68.
8. *The Francis Book.* Edited by Roy Gasnick, O.F.M. New York & London: Collier Books, 1980, 108.
9. *John Muir: the Eight Wilderness Discovery Books.* London, Seattle, WA: Diadem Books, 1992, 237.
10. J. E. Cirlot, *A Dictionary of Symbols.* New York: Philosophical Library, 1972, 243.
11. J. C. Cooper, *An Illustrated Encyclopaedia of Symbols.* London: Thames and Hudson, Ltd., 1978, 160–1.
12. Matthew Fox. *Original Blessing.* Santa Fe, NM: Bear & Co., 1983, 64.
13. Ibid., 91.
14. Ibid., 57.

9. IN THE HOUSE OF THE GRANDFATHERS

1. Anelia Jaffe, *Memories, Dreams, Reflections,* an autobiography of C. G. Jung. New York: Pantheon Books, 1973, 251.
2. Robert Bly, *Mirabai Versions,* New York: Red Ozier Press, 1984, 2.
3. Fredric Lehrman, *The Sacred Landscape.* Berkeley, CA: Celestial Arts, 1988, 34.
4. Geronimo (cited in a lecture at Mesa Verde).
5. John Dourley, *The Psyche as Sacrament.* Toronto: Inner City Books, 1981, 8.
6. Ibid., 44.

7. *Rumi, Fragments and Ecstasies.* Translated by Daniel Liebert. Santa Fe, NM: Source Books, 1981, 41.
8. Robert Bly, *Mirabai Versions.* New York: Red Ozier Press, 1984.
9. *Meditations with Meister Eckhart.* Translated by Matthew Fox. Santa Fe, NM: Bear & Co., 1986, 46.
10. *Book of Divine Works.* Translated by R. Cunningham. Santa Fe, NM: Bear & Co., 1986, 348.
11. *Rumi, Daylight.* Translations by Camille and Kabir Helminski. Putnam, VT: Threshold Books, 1990, 159.

10. COMING HOME: THE SEVENTH DIRECTION

1. Ed McGaa, *Mother Earth Spirituality.* San Francisco, CA: Harper-Collins, 1990, 65.
2. Andrew Harney, *A Journey in Ladakh.* Boston, MA: Houghton Mifflin Co., 1983, 104.
3. Daybreak Song as quoted in *Walk Quietly the Beautiful Trail.* Kansas City, MO: Hallmark, 1973, 14.

About the Author

Djohariah Toor is a licensed family therapist and founder of Creative Process Training, and of Arbor House, an ecumenical counseling center. Her previous book is *The Road By the River*. She lives in Livermore, California.